D1134166

FOOD FOR THOUGHT

Extraordinary Little Chronicles of the World

Ed Pearce

Author's Note

I'd like to thank Les and Lynn Gosden, Penny and Angus Maddison, Mark and Amanda Adams, Jon and Amanda Scroggs, Paul and Paula Verlinden, my godparents, Janet and Victor Cole, and Iris Pearce for their advice, encouragement, suggestions, and cooking. It's been a long process getting this into print and I'm grateful for all the help you've given me.

Copyright © 2004 O Books
46A West Street, Alresford, Hants SO24 9AU, U.K.
Tel: +44 (0) 1962 736880 Fax: +44 (0) 1962 736881
E-mail: office@johnhunt-publishing.com
www.0-books.net

E-mail: U.S.A. and Canada
Books available from:
NBN,
15200 NBN Way
Blue Ridge Summit, PA 17214, U.S.A.
Email: custserv@nbnbooks.com
Tel: 1 800 462 6420
Fax: 1 800 338 4550

Text: © Ed Pearce 2004

Design: Text set in Sabon by Andrew Milne Design
Cover design: Krave Ltd

ISBN 1 903816 86 6

A CIP catalogue record for this book is available
from the British Library.

Printed by Tien Wah Press (Pte) Ltd, Singapore

INTRODUCTION

People are interested in food. Bookstores teem with volumes containing numerous recipes for anything from a simple student meal to a grand gourmet feast. However, not so numerous are books on how different foods came about and what people ate through the ages, which is surprising as it's a fascinating subject. When researching this in my local library I barely found anything on the history of food. The books I did track down on this topic generally told the story in a fairly scholarly manner.

With *Food for Thought* I have attempted to keep things lighthearted and interesting by including snippets of what famous people down the ages ate and incorporating many anecdotes and trivia about how the food we consume today came into being. I guess there are two main ways you can approach this book. Either you can start from the first humans (the Paleolithic peoples) and zip all the way through to AD 2000. Or you can simply poke around and randomly pick out fascinating facts like how the phrase "to eat humble pie" came into being, or the unusual way Alexander Graham Bell consumed his soup.

A CULINARY CHRONOLOGY

A long time ago whilst still in the Garden of Eden and living on a vegetarian diet, the first man, Adam, is informed by God that he can freely eat of the fruit of every tree – except one; "for on the day you eat of it, you will surely die." The first regulation issued to man is a dietary law.

1,000,000 BC. The first humans (the Paleolithic peoples) find their food by hunting wild animals and gathering plant materials. Their chief foods are raw meat, fruit, and grains. They do not have good ways of preserving food so they usually eat it as they find it. The men do the hunting while the women collect anything that grows near the camp and seems fit to eat. Berries, eggs, fruit, leaves, and roots are all gathered.

500,000 BC. The first humans have discovered how to make fire by rubbing two sticks together. The control of fire marks the first major change: food, in particular meat, can now be eaten cooked. This is a development that has a crucial effect on the anatomy of the eaters. Cooked meat is easier to chew, a factor that is contributing to the decrease in the size of the jaw and the consequent increase in cranial capacity. Cooked meat is also easier to digest. It would appear, therefore, that cooking is enabling humans to evolve; food consumption is becoming a community feature as families gather around the fire to share the foods they have baked or boiled.

———————

100,000 BC. Man is learning to use fire in a variety of different ways apart from cooking. For instance, forests can be cleared of underbrush so that game can be better seen and hunted. Meat is now the main source of food for humans. Reindeer meat is a widespread food. Hunters stalk and kill the reindeer which they find crossing their territory and their lives follow the rhythm of the herds' migrations. Other widespread meats are wild ox and mammoth, the latter being in America the principle source of meat.

———————

10,000 BC. The climate is warming up after the last Ice Age. However, in North America the mammoth is beginning to die out and the buffalo is taking its place as the principal source of meat. When there is a shortage of meat, plants, berries, and seeds are gathered.

In Europe the warmer weather means that sources of meat are widespread so animals are still an important part of the European diet.

———————

8000 BC. Rather than moving from camp to camp in search of food, the people who dwell in the Tigris and Euphrates river valleys (the Fertile Crescent) have began to plant seeds themselves and grow their own barley and wheat. They are also rearing their own goats and sheep. These people now have a permanent source of food and they no longer have to depend on hunting for their meat. They are less subject to variations of the weather and the dangers of hunting.

7500 BC. Independently a type of agriculture centered upon maize in Peru and rice in South Eastern Asia is emerging.

7000 BC. Fish and game acquired from hunting is not disappearing entirely, but is eaten as a supplement to these new sources of nourishment. Now the supply of food is more regular, humans are beginning to cook stews, wheat and barley cakes, and soups of lentils and meat. As diets improve and people no longer rely on hunting for their meals, the human population is increasing.

6500 BC. Tribes who live at the edge of Swiss lakes, builders of the earliest civilized communities of Europe, have domesticated walnuts and apples. Apples are pale green, red, or yellow and consist principally of the core. These Swiss lake dwellers along with other cultures around the world are baking unleavened bread.

6000 BC. Man is used to obtaining the salt he needs from eating animal meat. As he turns more to agriculture and his diet changes he finds that sea-salt from sea water, inland springs, or saltwater lakes gives his vegetables the same salty flavor he is accustomed to with meat. Also, rock salt is being extracted from mines in various locations such as Austria. It is the only rock that can be used as food.

EARLY BREAD-MAKING TECHNIQUES

PREPARATIONS of baked grain products were being used as food in many cultures as far back as 10,000 BC. The first bread was made from acorns or beechnuts, or crushed seeds of wild grains; they were ground between stones, mixed with water, and cooked on flat hot stones heated directly in a fire. Later in Europe bread was made from spelt, a type of primitive, tough grain with a tight-fitting husk that protected against pests and diseases but was hard to grind. Pounding stones were used to crush the grain, which was then moistened, compacted, and cooked on a hot stone.

By 5000 BC hot stones were being covered with an inverted pot to contain the heat. Bread was being baked by this method in several areas including Bulgaria, Egypt, and Mesopotamia.

Around Lake Yuncheng in China each year, when the lake's waters evaporate in the summer sun, people gather the valuable salt square crystals on the surface of the water. As a consequence there are numerous battles fought over control of the lake.

Soup is being consumed in the Mediterranean area with the main ingredient being hippopotamus bones.

At first soups were cooked by dropping hot stones into the liquid. Now pots have been developed that can withstand the direct heat of a fire.

5500 BC. In many villages in the Middle East and Europe a kitchen is appearing as a separate room in the house. It is associated with not only cooking but also religious practices. The hearth where meat and vegetables are cooked is also the altar for worshipping the household gods.

4000 BC. Honey in now being used in most Egyptian households as a sweetening agent. Honey is valued highly; it is used to feed sacred animals and as a tribute or payment. Meanwhile, confectioners use honey as a sweetener and mix it with various fruits, herbs, nuts, and spices. The candy is then used as an offering to the Egyptian gods.

Bitter types of citrus can be found southeast Asia and India. As a species, some varieties of citrus come from China, but the orange is found in northwest India as well as southwest China. The oranges are used primarily for the fragrance of their rind. They are held in the hand so that the warmth releases the scent.

Someone in the Mediterranean area has had the bright idea of cooking a cereal paste on a stone in the sun to make pancakes.

3300 BC. A warrior has died in the Tyrolean Alps in Central Europe. His last meal was unleavened wheat bread, goat meat, and a herb or other green plant.

3200 BC. The Sumerians and Egyptians are making cheese from cow's and goat's milk and storing it in tall jars. It is made wherever animals produce more milk than people can use in fluid form. The method used is letting the milk curdle, then beating it with branches, pressing it on stones, drying it in the sun, and sprinkling it with salt. Its discovery was probably accidental; probably a herdsman pouring milk into a pouch made from an unweaned animal's stomach would have noticed that milk-curdling enzymes, which are found in the stomachs of unweaned animals, had separated the milk into a watery greenish-yellow liquid (whey), and solids (curds).

3000 BC. Mangoes are being cultivated in northeast India. At present they are small, fibrous fruits, somewhat like plums, with a taste like turpentine.

In Egypt, aided by advances in irrigation techniques, the River Nile's floodwaters are ensuring that the land along its banks is very fertile. Amongst the range of crops the Egyptians are harvesting are pomegranates. A special magic power is attributed to the pomegranate, as it is the only fruit immune from destruction by worms. Also, it is regarded as a symbol of love and fertility because of its numerous seeds.

2838 BC. Soya beans are being eaten in China and the Far East. The bean itself is yellow or black, small and round and is derived from a wild plant of East Asia. As well as a food, the soya bean is also used as a component of medicine.

2700 BC. The Chinese *Png-tzao-kan-mu (The Classic Herbal)*, the first ever treatise on pharmacology, records more than 40 types of salt. It describes two methods of extracting and processing salt.

Png-tzao-kan-mu also records rhubarb being cultivated for medicinal purposes, primarily for its internal cleansing qualities.

2600 BC. In Egypt broad beans, which originated in Persia, North Africa, and Europe, are mostly eaten by the common people. The upper classes consider them to be unclean and unworthy.

The delicious flavor of mushrooms has intrigued the pharaoh of Egypt so much that he has decreed that they are food for royalty and that no commoner can ever touch them. This assures for himself the entire supply of mushrooms.

The earliest form of leavening is a type of yeast, or breadmash, discovered accidentally by an Egyptian when a piece of dough had become sour. With dough made by mixing a type of flour made from ground nuts, salt, water, and leaven the Egyptians are now producing over 50 types of a raised and coarse bread.

They vary the shape and use such flavoring materials as poppyseed and sesame.

The Egyptians are using sesame oil, the first oil to be used for cooking purposes.

2500 BC. At Giza workers building the Great Pyramid are eating garlic, radishes, and onions for strength.

Garlic and watermelons, along with other food, are often placed in the burial tombs of Egyptian kings to nourish them in the afterlife.

2347 BC. In the Near East after the great flood it is said that Noah is making a pudding with all the food remaining on board: beans, chickpeas, dried fruits, nuts, rice, and wheat.

2200 BC. The Andean Mountains of South America is the birthplace of the white potato. The Aymara Indians have developed over two hundred varieties on the Titicaca Plateau at elevations above 10,000 feet.

2100 BC. In the Middle East butter is being made by beating milk in a bowl. Also, churns have been developed made of hollow logs or leather bags that are swung from trees to create a churning action.

2000 BC. Ice cream is invented in China wh
packs a soft milk-and-rice mixture in snow.

In Egypt marshmallows are being made from the sticky
root sap of the marsh mallow plant, a genus of herb that is
native to parts of Europe, North Africa, and Asia, growing in
marshes and other damp areas.

They are made by boiling pieces of the marsh mallow root
pulp with honey until it is thickened. The mixture is then strained
and cooled. The resulting candy is reserved for gods and royalty.

———

1900 BC. Carrots with yellow flesh and a purple exterior
are being cultivated in Afghanistan, its native land. They are
also being cultivated in the Mediterranean area, but aren't
considered to be an important food. Instead they are being
grown for their leaves, which have a pleasant fragrance.

———

1800 BC. In Israel Esau, a Hebrew grandson of Abraham,
sells his birthright as Isaac's eldest son to his younger brother
Jacob for bread and a "mess of pottage" which is a hearty
red lentil soup.

———

1490 BC. The Hebrews under Moses' leadership flee Egypt
and head for the Promised Land. However, they are walking
in circles in the Sinai desert. To feed them God has provided
manna, which is a type of lichen, called *Lecanora esculenta*.
It curls into balls when dry and blows in the wind. The
people gather it, grind it like grain, and make it into honey-
tasting pancakes. The Hebrews are lamenting their meager

EARLY CUTLERY

Early flints were used to cut meat and dig for vegetables. The flint-maker used a rock to chip off the pieces of flint, or it was prepared by hitting it against a large stone set on the ground. Tree bark, seashells, or tortoise shells were used as containers to collect, transport, preserve, cook, and eat food. Spoons cut in a simple fashion out of wood, bone, or shells were used both to prepare and eat the meal. By 4000 BC the first two-pronged forks were being used in Turkey.

Around 1700 BC chopsticks made of ivory, bone, or wood, were being made in China. With tables virtually unknown, one hand had to be free to hold the bowl and they proved to be a practical solution. The replacement of chopsticks over knives for eating at the table indicated the increased respect for the scholar over the warrior in Chinese society.

desert diet: "We remember the fish, which we did eat in Egypt freely, the cucumbers and the melons and the leeks and the onions and the garlic," they complain. They did not bring any leaven with them from Egypt for their bread so have to exist on matzo, an unleavened bread.

The Torah, given from God to Moses on Mount Sinai, imposes dietary restrictions that form the basis for kosher food requirements. Among these restrictions is a ban upon mixing meat and dairy products ("You shall not boil a kid in its mother's milk"). Kosher animals are those that chew their own cud and have split hooves. Fish must have fins and scales. Fowl have a very detailed list of requirements before they can be eaten.

———

1300 BC. The first recorded fish recipe (a fish salad based on marinated and spiced carp) comes from China. The Chinese have been trading live fish for over 3,000 years.

The Egyptians have developed the process of pickling (preserving foods in salt/brine or vinegar). They pickle both fish and melons. Food preservation techniques, such as storing in oil, using salt, and smoking, have been in use for many years throughout the eastern Mediterranean area. They are ensuring that the old cycle of plenty followed by shortage is finally broken.

———

1160 BC. In Egypt, King Rameses IV has died and is entombed with onions in his eye sockets. Onions have become an object of worship by the Egyptians, who regard the spherical onion bulb as a symbol of the universe. The onion symbolizes

THE DIET OF EGYPTIANS

THE Egyptians usually only had one main meal every day, at lunchtime, with light snacks for breakfast and supper. Rich Egyptians feasted on game from the hunt such as antelope or geese and ducks, which were hunted among the reeds of the Nile. They never ate fish as they regarded them as evil creatures. Many different condiments, such as garlic, salt, and juniper berries were used to flavor their foods, and honey cakes were eaten as a dessert. The common people were lucky to eat meat once a year; they had to make do with fish and vegetables such as beans, cucumbers, onions and leeks. Everybody ate bread, for which the Egyptians had 15 different words; it was the most important part of most people's diet.

eternity to the Egyptians, who for over a thousand years have buried onions along with their pharaohs and used them as funeral offerings. They see eternal life in its anatomy because of its circle-within-a-circle structure. Both large, peeled and slender, immature onions are consumed by the common people, however priests are forbidden from eating them.

———————

1063 BC. A Hebrew shepherd boy called David is sent by his father to present 10 cheeses to the captain of the army drawn up to do battle with the Philistines. Skills have been developed to preserve milk either as an acid, curd-based cheese or as a sort of unsweetened natural yogurt.

———————

1056 BC. Having graduated to being armor bearer to King Saul, then falling out with him, David is forced to flee to the desert and become leader of an outlaw band. In the desert and having not eaten for three days he devours a cake of pressed figs and two raisin cakes possibly flavored with a feathery herb which tastes like lemon peel, called coriander.

———————

1035 BC. David is now king of Israel. He places great importance on the cultivation of olive trees. He even has guards watching over the olive groves and warehouses, ensuring the safety of the trees and their precious oil.

———————

992 BC. An account of the daily provisions of King Solomon of Israel reveals they consist of 30 kors (6,700 liters) of fine flour and 60 kors (13,500 liters) of meal, 10 fatted oxen, 20

pasture-fed oxen, and 100 sheep and goats, besides deer and gazelles, roebucks and fatted geese. Cattle are imported from east of the Jordan River, and fatted geese from Egypt.

The Queen of Sheba makes a journey to King Solomon in Jerusalem to develop and maintain trade relations. When she arrives in Jerusalem she is overwhelmed by the fare of his table, and the service of his attendants.

---

850 BC. Homer travels around Greece singing his epic tales the *Odyssey* and the *Iliad*. Here the gods eat ambrosia and drink nectar, thus preserving their immortality.

Obviously not a lover of seafood, Homer describes fish as "A wretched food, the last resource of shipwrecked sailors." He describes his countrymen as "flour eaters" as they eat a lot of bread. They learnt the secret of leavened bread from the Egyptians. They cook loaves made of rye, wheat, or oats on a grid or a sort of oven.

In the *Iliad* he mentions Achilles washing cabbages. The Greeks are cultivating a headless cabbage, which has loose, narrow leaves, a thin stem, and whitish-yellow flowers. They ascribe its origin to Zeus who worked himself into a sweat trying to explain two conflicting prophecies. From this sweat sprang cabbage.

Pears have captured the praise of Homer, who refers to them as a "gift of the gods."

THE DIET OF OLD TESTAMENT JEWS

URING Old Testament times it was customary to eat in the late morning then take the main meal before dark. The rich could afford to eat meat such as venison, goose, or ox and kosher fish was a favorite. Accompaniments included eggs of wild fowl, cheeses, and butter made of sheep's milk. A selection of fruits such as figs and dates were gathered from trees.

Olives were eaten raw or pickled or oiled. Goat was the main meat of the poor and anyway the common people generally only ate meat at the Passover sacrifice or on rare festive occasions. The most basic food, which was the staple of the poor, was barley bread baked on hot stones covered with cinders accompanied by lentils and beans.

800 BC. In Sparta Lycurgus, a member of the royal house, has given the Spartans their constitution and system of education. Black brouet is the national dish of Sparta, a liquid stew made of blood, fat, meat, and vinegar, it is served at communal civic meals which all citizens aged from seven to sixty are required to attend.

---

715 BC. Babylonia is being ruled by King Merodach-Baladan II. The peaceful hobby of this brutal soldier is horticulture, and in his royal gardens he is cultivating 64 different species of plants. He has created the world's first written dissertation on vegetable gardens, with explicit instructions concerning the cultivation of a long list of spices and herbs including coriander, garlic, saffron, and thyme.

---

607 BC. Daniel, a Jewish exile in Babylon and a member of the royal household, is refusing to eat meat.

The food being offered to him is "non-kosher" and may have been slaughtered as part of pagan religious rites. As a consequence Daniel, along with three others, is opting for a vegetarian diet and is amazing the chief official by appearing healthier and better nourished than any of the young men who eat the royal food.

---

600 BC. The fig is one of the principal articles of sustenance among the Greeks. The Greek district of Attica, which includes Athens, is particularly famous for its luscious figs, and they have become an obsession for its citizens, rich or poor. Solon, the ruler of Attica, has made it illegal to export figs out of

Greece, making sure there are plenty for his subjects.

The Greeks chew garlic before going into battle, their breath being a deterrent to invading forces.

Lentils are well known in Greece as a poor man's food. A popular saying that applies to the upwardly mobile Greeks is "he doesn't like lentils any more."

Phoenician traders have arrived in Cornwall in search of tin. They have introduced there a technique for making clotted cream.

---

560 BC. The Greeks are eating raspberries. They attribute their origin to the nymph Ida. When she was picking berries for the young Jupiter she pricked her finger and so raspberries, which had been white until then, turned red.

---

550 BC. Aphtonite, a Greek cook, has invented black pudding, a savory sausage consisting mainly of seasoned pig's blood and fat contained in a length of intestine. Homer's *Odyssey* mentioned a forerunner, a stomach filled with blood and fat roasted over a fire.

---

540 BC. A Chinese child called Confucius has an insatiable thirst for knowledge and a tremendous intellect. He is being brought up in poverty and is living on a diet of rice and cabbage with possibly a little pork and bean broth.

---

530 BC. The Greeks are using onions to fortify their athletes for the Olympic Games. Before competition, athletes consume many pounds of onions and drink onion juice. Furthermore, they rub onions on their bodies in preparation.

---

529 BC. The Samian philosopher Pythagoras has founded a sort of educational society, which is half-religious and half-philosophical. He is preaching abstention from meat, beans, and mallows and he desires a return to the golden age. He believes that a vegetarian diet helps with his clarity of thought. He forbids the eating of broad (fava) beans as it is thought they contain the souls of the dead. He even refuses to walk through fields of broad beans. It is probable that he is prone to favism, which is almost entirely confined to genetically susceptible people of Mediterranean origin. Favism occurs when such individuals consume broad beans or inhale the pollen and it leads to the destruction of red blood cells resulting in severe anemia.

---

528 BC. Six years earlier the Indian prince, Buddha, renounced the world and became a wandering ascetic.

He has now become enlightened under a Bo tree. After six years of fasting in the desert he is little more than skin and bone. Now he is eating one fairly substantial meal a day but nothing else. So the depictions of a plump Buddha appear to be somewhat unrealistic.

EARLY VEGETARIANS

Vegetarianism probably first featured in connection with religious purification rituals, for instance a vegetarian ideology was practiced among religious groups in Egypt around 3200 BC, with abstinence from flesh based upon their reincarnation beliefs. Another example was Daniel's refusal to eat the tainted Babylonian meat (607 BC). Advocacy of a regular fleshless diet began around 500 BC in India through the teachings of Buddhism and Hinduism. These religions condemned the taking of animal life to obtain food because of their belief in the rebirth of the soul in animal bodies. Meanwhile in the eastern Mediterranean the teachings of the philosopher Pythagoras included advocating a diet which precluded meat (it is not known if he ate fish) in relation to the gluttonous excesses of his fellow Greeks. In ancient times non-meat eaters were generally known as Pythagoreans or adhering to the "Pythagorean System." The word "vegetarian" to describe non-meat eaters wasn't coined until the nineteenth century.

501 BC. Pythagoras has met his death at the hands of the people of Crotonia in Italy. Pursued by them, he came to the edge of a bean field and, rather than set foot in it, is caught and killed.

Confucius accepts the governorship of a small town and distinguishes himself in the suppression of crime and promotion of morality. He is unhappy with his wife, as she hasn't fulfilled his expectations as a cook.

The fastidious governor demands that meat should always be served in its proper sauce, be cut perfectly square, and have exactly the right color. For him, even the choicest of rice is generally not white enough, and minced meat rarely fine enough.

500 BC. The Egyptians, Greeks, and Romans all consider honey to be a gift of the gods. They hope for magic, healing, and life-enhancing properties from honey cake.

The Greeks, Egyptians, and Romans use celery as a flavoring and in funerals where it is made into garlands. Meanwhile the Chinese are using it as a medicine.

Soy sauce has been developed in China and Japan. It is becoming particularly integral to Japanese cooking as Japan has no rock salt, and it has been discovered salt can be obtained through the fermentation of soybeans.

490 BC. There is a tremendous famine in the Roman Empire and the Roman Senate has decided to introduce the first official price lists, purchasing a large quantity of wheat from Italy to distribute for free to the poor or sold to those

who can afford it. The Romans are both toasting the grains and boiling wheat in water. These *pastilli* (pasta) can then be eaten as such, or used as flour, once they are boiled.

---

475 BC. The peach has become a symbol of immortality to the Chinese. They place bowls of peaches in the tombs of close family members to prevent the bodies from decaying. Giving the fruit as a gift is a sign of friendship.

---

430 BC. The Greek physician Hippocrates is possibly the first ever advocate of a fiber diet. He is pressing his fellow countrymen to bake their bread with bran for its "salutary effect on the bowels."

---

429 BC. The Greek philosopher Socrates lives a very frugal lifestyle and eats as little as possible, with no seasonings at all. "Other men live to eat, whilst I eat to live" he has quipped. He advocates a diet that does not involve animal cruelty.

---

400 BC. Ship biscuits are being introduced for Roman and Greek sailors. The word "biscuit" comes from *bis coctus*, twice baked. The Romans call these biscuits *panis nauticus* or nautical bread. The dough of seasoned wheat flour and water is baked in moulds twice or even more times for long voyages. They are very crunchy, indeed the sailors are recommended to soak the biscuits in soup or water in order to avoid losing their teeth.

---

392 BC. The longest word to occur in a literary work has to do with a meat dish cut into pieces served in sauce, with 17 sweet and sour ingredients, including brains, fish, honey vinegar, ouzo, and pickles. The word appears in *Women at the Ecclesia*, a satirical comedy by Aristophanes, an Athenian playwright. In Greek, the word is 170 letters; transliterated into English it is 182 letters:

Lopadotemachoselachogaleokranioleipsanodrimhypotri mmatosilphioparaomelitokatakechymenokichlepikossyph ophattoperisteralektryonoptekephalliokigklopeleiolagoio siraiobaphetraganopterygon.

---

385 BC. The Greek philosopher Plato has founded his Academy in order to train a new ruling class after Socrates' death. Plato enjoys nibbling olives, indeed his Academy contains a grove of olive trees.

---

370 BC. Cheese is a popular food item in Greece, but fresh milk and butter aren't. This is due to the way the climate spoils milk and butter quickly. The Greeks are so fond of goats' or ewes' cheese that they reward their children with it as others might give them candy. "Little cheese" is a special term of endearment.

Every market in Greece sells cheeses to those who cannot make their own, and the popular fresh white Greek cheeses are being flavored with herbs and spices and baked into all manner of cakes and pies.

GREEK BANQUETS

FOOD and drink had a special importance for the ancient Greeks. Hospitality was a much-valued virtue; when the head of the house was entertaining, female slaves ground the corn and prepared the food. The host then cooked the meal, sometimes with the help of friends. Any visiting stranger was seated in the best place and it was customary to offer him, before the meal, a bath or foot wash.

Greek men liked to attend banquets called symposia, a continuation of dinner in which cheeses, fresh and dried fruit, salted cakes, and yogurt in honey were served.

The Greeks believed that mealtimes offered an opportunity to nourish the spirit as well as the body. They reclined on couches while eating with poetry, lyre playing, and dancing in the background.

Butter was introduced to the Greeks by the Scythians, but they use it mainly as an ointment, medicine, or illuminating oil.

---

360 BC. In his book about a utopia, *Republic*, Plato has pictured the ideal state where men live to a healthy old age on a vegetarian diet of bread (wholemeal bread ground from local wheat), cheese, fruit, vegetables, and, unsurprisingly, olives.

---

355 BC. Archestratus, a Sicilian Greek, has traveled extensively. He has gathered the culinary knowledge of the middle Mediterranean he has obtained into a poem, *Hedypatheia*. Thus he has become the world's first food writer. He has attracted controversy, however, as his work is becoming a byword among moralists for encouraging gluttony.

---

350 BC. In Sparta, men over 20 are required by law to eat at least 2lb of meat a day. This is supposed to make them brave.

---

336 BC. The Macedonian king Philip is murdered and his son Alexander succeeds to the throne. At his court fruit salads and purees are served, mixed with honey and snow.

---

327 BC. Alexander has reported on the cultivation of sugar cane in India. From this reed a raw, dark brown sugar is extracted from the cane by chewing and sucking. He is bringing this "sweet reed" back to Athens.

Also he has discovered bananas in India. Back in Athens this new fruit is called "pala". Another discovery is rice.

His troops habitually chew licorice root on the march due to its thirst quenching qualities.

---

323 BC. On an expedition seeking a potion guaranteeing immortal life Alexander the Great came across some apples, which supposedly prolonged the lives of priests who fed on them and nothing else up to 400 years. It hasn't worked for him. The Macedonian conqueror has died of typhoid fever aged 33.

---

300 BC. The Chinese are dining on rich stews of meat and vegetables accompanied by fluffy grains of millet that they have steamed over the stew. They have little use for the foreign cereal, wheat, which many centuries earlier had been brought to China by travelers from the West. For them, it is food for the miserably poor or as a last resort when stores are running low.

---

275 BC. The Greeks are importing rhubarb from a barbarian area called Rha in Russia. There it grows in grows in abundance around the Volga river. The Greeks, because of its source, call it "rha-barbaros".

---

250 BC. Chinese courtiers are required to carry cloves in their mouths to sweeten their breath when addressing the emperor.

For the first time, the Chinese have begun grinding wheat into flour with a grindstone, instead of cooking it whole. They are mixing the flour with water to make a dough, which they steam and boil. From the cooked mixture they are

EARLY FISHING

AROUND 400,000 BC *humans began catching and eating fish for food. They obtained fish from the shallow water of lakes and along the seashore, from small ponds remaining in previously flooded areas, from tidal areas, and from small streams. However, fishing became easier around 200,000 BC when man developed the gorge, a piece of wood, bone, or stone covered with some kind of bait. When a fish swallowed the gorge, a pull on the line wedged it across the fish's throat, and the fish could then be pulled in.*

By 4000 BC fish was a very important source of food. Developments in sailing were facilitating fishing in deeper water as well as in lakes. The Egyptians were catching fish in the Nile with nets or metal hooks or a short rod with line.

People either ate the fish or sold their catches to buy other foods. By 350 BC the Romans were using a longer, jointed fishing rod and the Chinese were catching fish with a silk line, a hook made from a needle, and a bamboo rod, with cooked rice as bait. By this time the Chinese had developed fish farming and the first treatise on carp culture had been written by Fan Li with useful advice on the construction, harvesting, and economic management of fishponds.

Later in Africa and South America fish was caught in basket traps or by drugging them with poison, which was poured into the water.

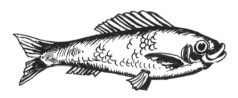

making buns, dumplings, noodles, thin pancakes, and steamed breads, calling them all "ping." Ping tastes delicious compared with the more traditional but bland boiled wheat. Consequently wheat has usurped millet in the social scale and is becoming the grain of the emperor and his court.

---

200 BC. Butchers, who are responsible for buying the beasts required to feed both their own troops and the occupied countries, are accompanying the Roman soldiers. Sometimes the troops eat their meat in pies. The pastry made from flour, oil, and water is wrapped round the meat keeping it warm on long marches.

When not eating meat their diet is gruel made from wheat together with cheese, onions, and salted fish.

---

130 BC. Tofu, which is derived from soya beans, has been developed by prince Liu An in China while searching for a substance to help him achieve immortality. Liu An is the grandson of Liu Bang, the founding emperor of the Han Dynasty.

---

120 BC. The Romans are passionate about fish and the best quality eels, lampreys, etc are kept, transported, and sold live. The highest recorded price ever paid for an auctioned fish (two live red mullets) is 20,000 sestertii, (about $20,000). The wealthy aristocrats use ice mixed with seaweed to keep fresh fish (they transport ice from the mountains near Rome) along with salt. They then stage lavish banquets where as many as a hundred types of fish may be served. The Romans regard sole as their favorite

THE DIET OF
THE GREEKS

BREAKFAST *for most Greeks was a hot porridge made from cereal. Lunch was bread baked in clay ovens from wheat or barley and goat cheese. The main meal was at dinner; the poor would make do with fruit, vegetables, and mushrooms gathered from the wild. The more wealthy had a two-course meal, the first being vegetables with mutton, beef, or pork. Those who lived near the coast would eat fish such as squid and octopus, turbot and salted or marinated tuna. The meat or fish would either be fried in olive oil or roasted. A favorite recipe was dormice roasted in a vinegar and honey sauce. This would be followed by items such as goat cheese, grapes, figs, honey cakes, and almonds.*

Food also had a religious significance and the Greeks often make food offerings at temples.

cooked fish; in Rome it is known as *Solea Jovi* (Jupiter's sandal) and it is cooked in a variety of ways including frying, roasting, stewing, or steaming. Sometimes it is made into pate or soup or marinated in salt and thus preserved.

***

73 BC. The wild sweet cherry tree has been grown for centuries by the Egyptians and Greeks. Now the Roman general Lucullus has brought sour cherry trees to Rome from Turkey after his victory over Mithridates VI, King of Pontus in northeast Asia Minor. Lucullus has adopted the lifestyle of the Greek influenced Middle East. His army returning from Asia is bringing many other new luxury foods to Rome, such as pheasant and peaches.

***

58 BC. The ruby-red color and tangy taste of cherries have ensured their popularity amongst the Greeks, Romans, and Chinese. Indeed, General Lucullus commits suicide when he realizes he is running out of cherries. The increased influence of the more luxurious Middle Eastern lifestyle in Rome is resulting in meal preparation becoming a lengthy and costly business. Cooks are demanding high wages.

***

55 BC. Julius Caesar lands on the shores of Britain. In a gluttonous age Caesar is moderate in his food intake and when on a campaign he eats the same food as his men do. According to Caesar the Britons live on milk and flesh.

6 BC. After defeating Pompey and his sons, Julius Caesar is awarded a 10-year dictatorship. He hosts a banquet for 200,000 guests to celebrate his victory over Pompey.

---

40 BC. The Roman general Mark Antony has moved to Egypt to be closer to his lover, Cleopatra, the Egyptian queen. Cleopatra is giving a lavish banquet for Antony at Alexandria. The Roman expresses his surprise at the outlay involved. Cleopatra, to impress him further, takes a pearl eardrop and dissolves it in vinegar to prove she can consume a fortune in a single meal. Antelope is a favorite meat of the Egyptian queen. She is also fond of figs.

---

31 BC. Augustus defeats Antony at Actium, thus becoming sole leader and master of the Roman world. He doesn't have a large appetite but is very fond of asparagus. He has originated a saying, "Quicker than you can cook asparagus." In the Roman Empire asparagus is not only eaten in season but is dried for later use. Apart from asparagus the emperor prefers the food of the common people and his diet consists of coarse bread, a little fish, cheese, and green figs.

---

25 BC. The chickpea is regarded by the Romans as a food for peasants and poor people. At festivals chickpeas are frequently thrown over the heads of people and are caught with much hilarity. In Gaul it is a common ingredient in vegetable soup.

The Roman poet Horace writes his four books of *Odes*. Horace prefers straightforward country pleasures to busy

ROMAN BANQUETS

AT a Roman aristocrat's banquet, before eating the guests changed their clothes, putting on a woolen tunic provided for this purpose. The dishes were presented first to the master of the house, accompanied by music and with a servant executing a dance step. Meanwhile the guests, both men and women, ate reclining with a crown of flowers over their head. If a diner became too full to eat any more, a servant was called over to tickle his throat. He then vomited into a special bowl kept for that purpose, and proceeded with the rest of the meal. Belching at the table was a sign of politeness. The banquets were livened up by performances by acrobats, dancers, flute players, and theatrical performers. Knives and spoons were only occasionally used; most people ate with their fingers despite the prevalence of sticky sauces.

town life. He is going against the current Roman fashion for pretentious and complicated dishes. Instead he longs for a simple dish of chickpeas and pasta. He is also promoting wild boar as a noble, highly flavored dish.

---

0. Pineapples originally evolved in the high plateaus of central South America and are now widely transplanted and cultivated. Highly regarded for their intense sweetness, the fruit is a staple of Indian feasts and rites related to tribal affirmation.

AD 8. Ovid, a Roman writer, completes his epic poem *Metamorphosis*. He writes "And so in the midst of the wealth of food which Earth, the best of mothers has produced. It is your pleasure to chew the piteous flesh of slaughtered animals." Unsurprisingly Ovid is a vegetarian.

AD 14. Emperor Tiberius succeeds Augustus. Tiberius is a lover of pickles and grows cucumbers in carts; he gets his slaves to wheel them around to catch the sun. He has cucumbers at his table throughout the year.

AD 25. Toasting bread began as a method of prolonging the life of bread. It has become a very common activity for the Romans. *Tostum* is the Latin word for scorching or burning.

AD 27. John the Baptist is living in the Palestinian desert preaching a message of the imminence of God's judgment. He is baptizing those who repent in self-preparation for it. He survives on locusts and honey.

———

AD 29. Jesus Christ, John the Baptist's cousin, is traveling throughout the Galilee area preaching a message of repentance and forgiveness of sins and performing miracles. Amongst his miracles is feeding a crowd of 5000 with five loaves and two fishes.

———

AD 30. An extraordinary event, Jesus Christ's crucifixion and resurrection has occurred, when Christ died on the cross as a sacrifice for all our sins then rose from the dead thus creating a way out of the consequences of sin for all those who follow him. Just before his crucifixion, Christ and his 12 disciples participated in the most famous meal ever, The Last Supper, a Passover meal, when he predicted his imminent betrayal and death as a sacrifice for the sins of humanity. The meal was roast lamb eaten in its entirety, served with bitter herbs and unleavened bread. The house where they were eating was daubed with the blood from the freshly slaughtered lamb. In referring to the bread as his body and the wine as his blood and bidding the disciples to participate of each, he has instigated the Eucharist/Holy Communion/Mass.

———

AD 35. A well-known Roman gourmet and epicure called Apicius has spent vast sums to satisfy his craving for exotic foods and has written 10 books on the art of cooking which are summarized in *De Re Coquinaria (On Cookery)*. His recipes include numerous spices including pepper intended to preserve food, aid the digestion, and improve the flavor of the dull Roman fare. "Sprinkle with pepper and serve" is the last step in a recipe for diced pork and apples from one cookbook. He even recommends the use of pepper in sweet desserts.

Apicius' colossal banquets have driven him to bankruptcy. Calculating how little money he has left, he has decided to poison himself rather than turning to a more modest way of living.

———

AD 41. Caligula is assassinated by one of his own guards. The unstable Roman emperor thought it fun to behead people during a meal. Banquets for the Roman gentry can be bloody affairs. A cook who dishes up underdone meat will be stripped and beaten.

———

AD 43. The Roman emperor Claudius invades Britain. He likes to feast on stuffed kidneys and guinea fowl in a hazelnut crust and fish sauce.

———

AD 50. The Romans are using rice pottage as a medicine to settle upset stomachs. They regard rice as an expensive import to be used mainly for medical purposes.

AD 60. The Roman emperor Nero has leek soup served to him every day, as he believes the leek makes his speech honeyed and thus gives him a clear and sonorous voice for delivering his orations. Due to his inordinate appetite for leeks some people have nicknamed him "Porrophagus" (*porrum* being leek in Latin.)

———

AD 64. Nero sets fire to Rome, blaming the new followers of the Christian sect for it. The emperor sends slaves to the tops of the Apennines Mountains to bring fresh snow down to the royal kitchens where the snow is then flavored with fruit pulp and honey or nectar.

———

AD 65. In a show of honor the Romans burned a year's supply of cinnamon at the funeral for Nero's wife. The spice is supplied to the Romans by Arab traders, who are protecting their business interests by deliberately shrouding its source in mystery. They are spreading fantastic tales that cinnamon is grown in deep valleys swarming with poisonous snakes.

———

AD 68. Roman baths are much more than public places to bathe. They are also social centers where families and friends come to gather together and eat snack food and drink. The Roman philosopher Seneca writes of the noisy "cake sellers, the sausage man, and confectioner" who each peddle food to hungry bath patrons.

———

CUTLERY DURING THE GREEK AND ROMAN ERA

B Y 1500 BC bronze cutting implements were being used from the British Isles to China. The ancient Greeks and Romans used two-pronged kitchen forks to assist in the carving and serving of meat. The teeth prevented meat from moving during carving and allowed food to slide off more easily than it would with a knife. However, they did not use forks whilst eating; instead they washed their fingers between every course. The Romans used two different types of spoons made of bronze or silver. One with a pointed oval bowl and a handle ending in a decorative design was used for soups and pottages. The second was a small spoon with a round bowl and a pointed, narrow handle for eating shellfish and eggs. Knives of all sizes were used, made of iron, with bone, wood, or bronze handles. The poor would use spoons made of bone. When the food was ready it was served on a discus, a large circular silver, bronze, or pewter plate. The Romans also molded them from glass paste. The poor would use wood plates.

By the end of the first century porcelain had been perfected in China and some culinary utensils were being made with it.

AD 77. Pliny, the Roman scientist and historian, has completed his epic *Naturalist Historiae*, a 37-book encyclopedia of geography, science, zoology, and medicine. He writes of the artichoke as being "one of the earth's monstrosities." However, artichokes are enjoyed by his fellow Romans, who prepare them in honey and vinegar, seasoned with cumin, so that the treat will be available year round.

The author has given broad beans the highest place of honor among vegetables and speaks of bean meal being mixed with wheat or millet flour in the baking of bread to make the loaves heavier. The Latin word for bread, *panis*, comes from the Greek word for broad bean, *puanos*. The Greeks and Romans both like their bread white: color is one of the main tests for quality. Pliny has written: "The wheat of Cyprus is swarthy and produces a dark bread, for which reason it is generally mixed with the white wheat of Alexandria." The Romans often flavor their bread with cumin, parsley, or poppy. There are certain miserly bakers who knead the meal with sea-water to save the price of salt. Pliny does not approve of this.

AD 80. Taverns called *stabularia* are used for food and accommodation by travelers in the Roman Empire, but no upwardly mobile Roman or his beast will be seen in them. However, at night time on the quiet side streets of Rome, men of all ranks can be spotted sneaking into alternative taverns called *lupanar* to dine, drink, and gamble.

AD 90. For centuries the Greeks have believed that lettuce induced sleep, so they serve it at the end of the meal. The Romans have continued the custom. However, the dictatorial Emperor Domitian serves it at the beginning of his feasts, so he can torture his guests by forcing them to stay awake in the presence of the Emperor. The leaf vegetable is popular with both the Greeks and the Romans because of the milky sap it exudes when cut.

AD 100. Members of the new Christian sect gather together to celebrate Communion, where they share bread and wine in remembrance of Christ. At Communion time the rich and poor all share a meal known as *agape* from the Greek word for love. Its aim is to recall the ideals they preach of sharing and charity.

AD 180. In the mountainous areas of the Mediterranean, where cereals do not grow well if at all, the chestnut is a staple food. Galen, a Roman physician to various emperors, has written of the flatulence produced by a diet that centers too closely on chestnuts and has commented on the nuts' medicinal properties, which supposedly protect against such health hazards as dysentery, poisons, or the bite of a mad dog.

AD 220. The Roman emperor Varius Avitus Bassianus, who is known as Heliogabalus, is becoming notorious for his culinary extravagances. A different colored dinner service appears at every feast he gives; the feasts are composed of such meats as chicken, pork, or pheasant. He has devised a

DIET OF THE ROMANS

MEAT was an expensive food, as herds of domestic animals were rare so the majority of the population in the Roman Empire, especially in its early days, lived on pulmentum, a porridge of barley, chickpeas, or emmer wheat flour. It was made by roasting and pounding the grain, then cooking it in a large cauldron. Sometimes it was diluted with milk and it was accompanied by bread, fish, or ground pine nuts.

Meanwhile, in a Roman villa in Britain, the day began with a light breakfast of bread and fruit, whilst wealthy citizens in Rome started the day with such items as bean meal mash and unleavened bread-cakes.

Lunch, or prandium, at noon consisted of a cold meal of eggs, fish, and vegetables or in Rome fruit, a sweetmeat, and cheese. Dinner, the convium, would commence at 4.00pm and last several hours. It would start with a small course of something like cheese with herbs, seasoned eggs, nuts, and shellfish, followed by two main courses of enormous quantities of meat or fish.

Fish sauces were often used to disguise the poor taste of the food, a popular one was liquamen made from the gills, blood, and the inside of the fish, left with salt to stew in the sun. The exceptionally wealthy Romans ate elaborate dishes such as dormice and songbirds garnished with rich sauces, herbs, and spices. Other choice dishes were grilled feet of a camel or pink flamingo tongue. The diners would then finish off with elaborate pastries sweetened with honey and finally fruits with wine.

The native lower class Briton saw little change in his diet after the Roman occupation. The normal insubstantial, dull meals were bean or pea pottage cooked on an open-hearth fire, in confined conditions, with flat bread made from course grain flour. Dental damage began early in life largely as a result of a coarse and insufficient diet.

moveable day-long feast around the city of Rome, eating the starter at one house, the main course at another, and the dessert at a third.

AD 225 . Athenaeus, a Greek gourmet, is the author of *The Deipnosophists (The professors of dining)*.

This composition on food and food preparation is in the form of an aristocratic dinner party in which a number of both fictional and real-life learned men, including the famous physician Galen, meet at a banquet and discuss for days topics such as cooking utensils, culinary discoveries and well-known chefs. They relate recipes for dishes such as stuffed vine leaves and cheesecakes.

AD 350. Sausages have been banned in the newly Christianized Rome because of their association with sinful pagan festivities. A black market has been set up.

AD 375. The scholarly Jerome has began a search for inner peace as a hermit in the desert. A gourmet with a weak stomach, he is eating the sparse desert food as a penance.

AD 404. Jerome has finished his translation of the Bible into Latin. He has written "Many years ago I had for the sake of the kingdom of Heaven cut myself off from home, parents, sister, relations, and (hardest of all) from the dainty food to which I had become accustomed."

AD 408. The Visigoths have attacked Rome and their leader Alaric I is demanding a ransom, part of which is 3,000 lbs of the much-prized spice, pepper. This pay-off is his price for sparing the population from death.

AD 426. The Christian theologian and bishop, Augustine, has completed his book *City of God*. He once denounced the vegetarianism and teetotalism of the Christian Manichean sect: "who would think they sinned if they took a little bacon and cabbage with a few mouthfuls of pure wine, but will be served at three in the afternoon with every kind of vegetable; the most exquisite of mushrooms and truffles flavored with a wealth of spices." Contrarily in a letter to his sister's nunnery he recommends abstinence from meat and drink.

AD 450. According to the Romans the Huns drink blood. This allegation may or may not be true. It is a fact that the Huns live on the roots of such herbs as they can get. With the herbs they devour the half-raw flesh of any animal which they merely warm by rapidly placing it between their own thighs and the backs of their horses. Their chief, Attila, eats off a wooden plate unlike many of his chieftains who eat off silver plates.

AD 495. The 15-year-old Benedict has fled from Rome to a cave in the mountains of Subiaco. He is disgusted at the vices of the city and is living in a cave on the face of a cliff. He has bread lowered to him in a basket attached to a rope by Romanus, a monk living at one of the numerous monasteries nearby. Benedict has forsworn the consumption of meat in order to suppress his own carnal desires.

AD 542. After founding the Benedictine Order about 10 years earlier, Benedict compiles a series of rules by which the Benedictine monks should live. In his Rule he allocates each monk a pound of bread and two cooked dishes each day, though meat is forbidden.

Benedict writes practically in his Rule, "For the daily meal let there be two cooked dishes so that he who happens not to be able to eat of one may take his meal of the other. Avoid excess – above all things, that no monk shall be overtaken by indigestion."

AD 550. The Welsh have won a victory over the Saxons and they are attributing their success to the leeks they wore to distinguish themselves in battle.

AD 595. The 25-year-old Mohammed of Arabia is an experienced spice merchant. As a youth he worked with Meccan tradesmen who dealt in spices with Syria and South Arabia. Subsequently he became a camel driver and caravan leader for a widow of means named Khadija, 15 years his senior, whom he has just married.

AD 597. Augustine of Canterbury lands at Ebbsfleet, Thanet in order to introduce Catholic Christianity to England. He is encouraging the Britons to slaughter animals for their own food rather than sacrificing them to the devil.

AD 610. Monks at a monastery on the border between France and Italy are making bread, folding scraps of dough to look like a child's arms in prayer. The three holes represent the Holy Trinity. The monks are offering the warm dough as a reward to children who memorize their Bible verses and prayer. The fame of these new pretzel-like snacks is spreading into Austria and Germany.

AD 622. Twelve years ago Mohammed had two visions from the Archangel Gabriel, warning of impending judgment of the world with reward and punishment for actions. Also revealed were the teachings of Allah. His proclamation is not being received well in Mecca so he emigrates to Medina. The Muslim era is dated from here. Mohammed refuses garlic as "I am a man who has close contact with others."

He lives mainly on barley bread, dates, and water. His favorite dish is rice cooked in butter.

AD 732. Boniface, the Archbishop of Mainz, has lobbied the Pope for several years to place horseflesh into the forbidden category as many northern European pagans eat it as a religious ritual. His campaign is successful and Pope Gregory III has banned horseflesh from Christian dining tables, the only food the church has ever outlawed.

AD 745. Due to the decline of the Roman Empire, the use of oriental spices has been drastically curtailed in the normal diet of Europeans north of the Alps. Ecclesiastical groups and a few merchants can obtain only small amounts. For instance, Gemmulus, a Roman deacon, has sent a gift of pepper and cinnamon to Archbishop Boniface.

––––––––––

AD 791. Macaroon cakes are being made in a western European monastery at Cormery in the shape of monks' navels.

––––––––––

AD 800. Charlemagne is crowned Holy Roman Emperor by a grateful Pope Leo III, who has been restored to the papacy by Charlemagne. The Holy Roman Emperor likes to invite everyone, whatever their rank, to dinner. Whilst eating he prefers to listen to a public reading instead of having jesters perform. He decorates the walls of his banquet halls with ivy, floors are strewn with flowers, and the tables are laid with silver and gold utensils. On special occasions, ladies are admitted to the royal table.

––––––––––

AD 810. Fish is an important part of the diet for people around the world who live by the coast or near rivers and lakes. Fish consumption in Europe is being promoted by the Catholic Church, which has ordered 166 days of fasting a year (including 40 days of strict fasting for Lent), during which fish but not meat can be eaten. Rulers usually reinforce this situation; for instance, Charlemagne has ordered that all his farms have fishponds.

––––––––––

AD 812. Charlemagne is partial to chickpeas and cheese, especially Brie, "one of the most marvelous of foods." He insists on having two mule loads of his favorite blue cheeses sent to his palace every Christmas. The emperor discovered

DIET OF THE VIKINGS

THE Vikings had a varied diet. The first meal of the day, called dagveror, was a porridge consisting of a mixture of barley and rye cereals. With it the wealthy might have rye or wheat bread, which was considered superior to barley as it rose better. However, barley was cheaper and barley bread was still the chief bread of the poor. The second meal, nattveror, eaten at the end of the day, often was fish such as cod or herring, which was either eaten fresh or preserved by salting or drying in the wind. Seaweed, vegetables, and fruit accompanied this. Most of the vegetables and fruit were home grown and products such as cabbage, horse beans, onions, parsnips, peas, swedes and apples, berries, cherries, and pears were found in their gardens.

The poor, apart from occasionally in soups or stews, rarely ate meat, though eggs, cheese, and fat for everyday food preparation were obtained from the livestock. Sometimes puffins' and gulls' nests were raided for their eggs. The rich would dine on beef, deer, duck, goose, ham, and pigeon. Most families had a table of some sort, and wealthy families used a linen tablecloth.

blue cheese while on a tour of his territory, when at a stop at the priory of Rueil-en-Brie he was given some Brie as a tithe.

The Holy Roman Emperor hates physicians, as for health reasons they want him to give up his favorite roast beef and eat boiled meat instead.

AD 850. Goulash, a beef stew, has been developed in Hungary. Before setting out with their flocks, Hungarian Magyar shepherds (*gulyas*, after whom it is named) prepare a portable stock of food by slowly cooking chunks of meat and onions, until all the liquid is boiled away. The meat is then dried in the sun and packed into bags made of sheeps' stomachs. The resulting meat is used to prepare a stew or soup by boiling it in water.

AD 877. A story is doing the rounds about the king of Wessex, King Alfred. He was seeking refuge, incognito, from the Vikings who had conquered the kingdoms of East Anglia and Northumbria and reduced Mercia to a fragment of its former size. The King stayed in a hut on the Isle of Athelney in Somerset, belonging to a poor Anglo Saxon swineherd and his family and the wife asked the unrecognized monarch to keep an eye on the baking cakes. Alfred was deep in thought and the cakes were burnt. As a result, the royal refugee was verbally roasted by the woman of the house. English cakes are at present well spiced and sometimes enriched with butter, cream, eggs, honey, and preserved fruits.

AD 990. Moslems living in the Holy Land are growing sugar cane, which they are then milling and boiling in large open vats. Leaving the pulp to cool and to harden, the resulting products are flat cakes. Breaking off bits, they describe them in their Arab tongue as *sukkar qandi*, meaning "sugar pieces" which they either chew like candy or use to sweeten their meals. In Europe, having been introduced to Sicily, the sugar trade is now established in the Mediterranean area centered on Venice.

AD 997. In Naples in Italy the first pizzas are being made. They are herb and spice covered circles of dough that are cooked in a hot oven. They are served up as a snack or appetizer. A dish that resembled pizza was common in Roman times and called *focaccia*.

AD 1000. Because wild pecans are readily available, many Indian tribes in North America and Mexico use the wild pecan as a major food source during autumn. A milky fluid is extracted that is used in making corn cakes. The pecan tree is the only major tree nut that grows naturally in North America and the North American Indians were the first to cultivate it. The name "pecan" is a Native American word of Algonquin origin that is used to describe "all nuts requiring a stone to crack."

1005. The first documented recipe for pasta is in the Italian book *De arte Coquinaria per vermicelli e macaroni siciliani*, (The Art of Cooking Sicilian Macaroni and Vermicelli) written by Martino Corno, chef to the powerful Patriarch of Aquileia.

1050. Corned beef (preserving beef with "corns" or large grains of salt) has been developed in Europe. In the Irish text *Aislinge meic Con Glinne* there is a reference to "perpetual joints of corned beef."

———

1066. William the Conqueror's Normans defeat the Saxons at the Battle of Hastings. Britain was rabbit free but William has brought with him a colony of bunnies. In France the Normans are fond of rabbit pie and stew and rabbit is a favorite of French monks, because they consider them fish and can eat them when abstinence from meat is called for.

———

1086. The Domesday Book, a summary of William the Conqueror's survey of England, is completed. It lists over 5,500 watermills used to grind grain to produce flour for the population south of the River Severn and Trent. It also mentions Britain's first named cheese, Cheshire cheese. In his early days William was disciplined in eating and drinking. He abhorred drunkenness. But now he has developed a large belly.

———

1111. The Dunmow Flitch starts. This is a long-standing tradition established at Dunmow, Essex, England whereby married couples who stay together for a year and a day without arguing or regretting their marriage and can prove this are able to claim a gammon of bacon. The saying "bring home the bacon" originates from this.

———

DIET OF THE AZTECS

MAIZE *was the staple food of the poor Aztecs, so much so it was inter-linked with their religion in which they worshipped Cinteotl, a maize god and Chicomecoatl, a maize goddess. They made popcorn by roasting dried maize kernels of a particular variety, which they not only ate but also used for ornaments on statues of their gods.*

Tortilla pancakes made with maize were eaten with every meal. The kernels were boiled to remove the husks, crushed to form a paste, then cooked on a pottery plate over an open fire. Then they were filled with beans or spicy turkey or dog meat and eaten with a hot sauce made from chilli peppers and tomatoes. Chilli was available in many guises. Also included in their diet were avocados, onions, peanuts, papaya, pineapple, sweet potatoes, and tomatoes. They used avocados, onions, and chopped tomatoes to make a sauce called ahuaca-mulli, *a sort of guacamole.*

1140. The Aztecs have established their empire in Mexico. The wild tomato originated in the Andes Mountains of Peru, but the Aztecs are now cultivating them. The word tomato comes from the Aztec *tomatl*.

———

1150. Spinach has been introduced into Europe from eastern Asia by Arabs. It is proving to be popular in religious communities, particularly during Lent.

Another popular Lenten vegetable, particularly in England, is the pea. There were no known "green peas" until after the Norman Conquest of England. Among foods currently stored at the Barking Nunnery, near London, are "green peas for Lent." Dried peas are one of the principal foods for the poor as they are cheap and filling.

———

1158. The English Chancellor Thomas a Becket eats little despite all the lavish hospitality on offer. An exception is a meal in Paris where he paid 100 shillings (around $7) for a plate of eels.

Henry II is allowing an expedition of barons from South Wales to establish Anglo-Norman supremacy in Ireland. Henry has simple tastes in food and is a moderate drinker. On one occasion the monks at St Swithe's, Winchester, groveled in the mud before Henry, as their bishop had suppressed all but three of their customary courses. Henry replied that in his court he was content with three and so should the monks be. He has popularized Cheddar cheese, a hard cow's-milk cheese, by declaring it the best in England.

———

1180. Apricot trees have spread by means of silk dealers from China to Italy. Now they have arrived in England. However, the Europeans are suspicious of the apricot fruits as they are thought to cause fever.

1191. At the Siege of Acre, which the Moslem leader Saladin is defending against the Crusaders, he sends presents of the most luscious peaches and pears and fruit flavored snow to the kings of England and France when they are confined to bed with fever. England's King Richard refuses to respond in an equally chivalrous manner.

1192. Knights returning from the Crusades in the Holy Land are introducing to Europe many Middle Eastern ways of cooking, which mix sweet tastes with savory. Recipes of meat cooked with fruit and sweet spices are especially popular. The Crusaders have also brought the first samples to Europe of gingerbread, and are introducing fritters and puff pastry. They are reporting on various types of sugar being sold by apothecaries.

1195. In western Europe a slice of lemon is being served with fish. It is believed that if a person accidentally swallows a fish bone, the lemon juice will dissolve it.

1201. In France the Normans, using knowledge acquired from the Danes, have established the widespread local production of butter. However, butter is not supposed to be eaten during Lent. Meanwhile, in Rouen the southern tower is now called the "Butter Tower" because the people who have contributed the money for its building are in return given dispensation to eat butter during Lent.

1202. King John of England proclaims the first English food law, the Assize of Bread, which prohibits adulteration of bread with such ingredients as ground peas or bean.

1203. The first Inca emperor is Manco Capac. The influence of potatoes is permeating the Incan culture.

For instance, Incan units of time correlate to how long it takes for a potato to cook to various consistencies. Potatoes are even used to divine the truth and predict weather.

The Incas are storing their potatoes and other food crops on the Andean mountain heights. The cold mountain temperature freezes the food and the water inside slowly vaporizes under the low air pressure of the high altitudes. This is the first instance of freeze-drying food.

1205. In western Europe each citizen eats over 600 grams (just over 20 ounces) of bread each day, but the type of bread eaten by individuals depends on their income. The upper and middle classes prefer white wheaten bread. The poor, for whom bread represents three-quarters of their budget, have to be content with black or brown bread, made from bran, oats, rye, or barley.

1209. England's King John, finding insufficient game for his personal falconry, has issued a proclamation forbidding the taking of wild fowl by any means.

———————

1219. After his father died, the Mongol Genghis Khan and his small family led a life of extreme poverty, eating roots and fish instead of the normal nomad diet of mutton and mare's milk. Now, as he and his fellow hordes sweep westwards, one of their dishes is *kyrgyz*, which tastes like the smell of a cow and carries quite a kick. They don't eat fruit or vegetables as they are unwilling to be tied to the land. Everything they eat comes from animals. As a sweet treat he and his horsemen eat *mikong*, a honey bread.

———————

1220. Frederick II is crowned Holy Roman Emperor. Frederick only eats one meal a day, in the evening. His favorite meal is "scapace," which is a sort of fried fish and vegetables marinated in a white wine and saffron sauce.

He lives in a variety of castles, which he moves amongst in the course of a year. Each castle has a large dovecote built within and sharing some of the castle walls. The court relies on this source of pigeon meat for a significant proportion of its fresh meat.

———————

1228. Francis of Assisi, the founder of the Franciscans, dies. Despite his refusal to kill any animals he was not a vegetarian. Francis was particularly partial to pig's knuckles and chicken legs and marzipan.

———————

VEGETARIANS IN THE MONASTERIES

FOR many centuries Christian monks, hermits, and ascetics forsook flesh eating as cruel, gluttonous, and expensive. In addition to Benedict of Nursia (see entries for 495 and 542) other medieval vegetarians included:

❖ *Pope Gregory I (c.540-604), who introduced the Gregorian chant into Christian church services. From his mid thirties, as befitting his ascetic life style, he ate only raw fruit and vegetables.*

❖ *Bruno of Cologne (1030-1101), who along with six companions founded the Carthusian Order in the isolated valley of Chartreuse, near Grenoble. There they lived as hermits, eating only vegetables and coarse bread.*

❖ *Bernard of Clairvaux (1090-1153), a son of a French baron, entered Citeaux monastery along with 27 of his relations, including four of his brothers. He had elected to withdraw from riches to live a life of extreme austerity and a diet of cooked beech and herbs.*

*By the thirteenth century though many monks
still lived in austere circumstances, not so many
were vegetarians. For instance, Dominic, the
founder of the Order of the Dominicans ate
sparingly, sometimes just a couple of egg yolks,
but his diet did often include a small piece of
fish. In 1339 the pope conceded that the monks
might continue to eat meat provided that only
half their number did so at a time, the other half
maintaining a vegetarian rule.*

Occasionally he enjoyed a fancy pastry and on his deathbed asked a dear friend, Lady Jacob, to bring him some almond cakes.

1230. Umble pie is a dish made from the "umbles" (liver, heart, brains, feet, etc.) of a deer, or other animal killed in a hunt. After being topped with a layer of dried fruit the mixture is put into a pastry case and baked. This pie, however, is not for the aristocracy, who eat only the superior fleshy part of the deer; it is only considered suitable for the huntsmen and the servants. That is why the phrase "to eat humble pie" means that someone of lower rank is forced to give way to those in higher positions, and be made humble.

1234. Rice is being imported into North Europe. In Britain it is included in King Henry III's current household accounts where it is used to make milk puddings.

1235. There is a major famine in England resulting in 20,000 deaths in London alone. The starving are resorting to eating tree bark and grass.

1242. Louis IX, the saintly French king, forces Henry III of England to renounce his claims to Normandy, Anjou, Maine, and Poitou. He once invited to dinner 20 poor people, whose smell so revolted the soldiers of the guard that they voiced their objections to the king.

1250. In Europe Catholic monks have begun to bake gingerbread for saints' days and festivals, constructing it into specially designed theme cakes. Often depicting celebrated saints and religious motifs, they depend on large and beautifully carved wooden molds that impress an all-over surface pattern onto a fairly stiff rolled dough.

1266. English bakers have been ordered to mark each loaf of bread so that if a faulty one turns up, "it will be knowne in whom the faulte lies." The bakers' marks are among the first trademarks.

1274. The newly crowned King Edward I of England has a kingly appetite and eats large quantities of meat such as beef, game, and poultry as well as some fish such as carp, eels, lamprey, and pike.

For his coronation feast he has ordered his sheriffs to provide 278 bacon hogs, 450 porkers, 440 fat oxen, 430 sheep, and 22,600 hens and capons.

1275. Ground beef has been developed by Mongolian and Turkic tribes known as Tartars, who shred low-quality beef from Asian cattle to make it more edible and digestible. These Tartars have introduced the delicacy to their German trading partners from the port of Hamburg. The Germans flavor it with regional spices such as onions and either eat it raw or fry the meat. It is becoming a standard meal for poorer classes and in Hamburg has acquired the name "Hamburg steak."

DIET IN MEDIEVAL WESTERN EUROPE

*I*N Britain and western Europe the daily diet of *peasants and the poor urban people was tediously banal. They contented themselves with oatmeal gruel and the basic dish was pottage, a porridge-like stew of peas or beans. Vegetables such as broad beans, cabbage, onions, and dried peas improved the daily diets. Meat was expensive (a leg of roast mutton at a London market cost a day's wages) and was only eaten on special occasions, when it had to be dried or preserved in fat or salt.*

While broth was a basic foodstuff for many Europeans of all classes, the wealthy considered the solids in a prepared dish to be the important ingredient, the liquid was there to keep the solids warm. It was also intended to be a sauce, imparting its own particular flavor, often peppery due to the incorporated mustard and horseradish.

The affluent ate meat on a much more regular basis and if possible it was slaughtered just before being cooked. In addition to beef, mutton, and pork (often made into sausages), a wide variety of highly spiced game such as bear (often stewed), boar, crane, deer, peacock, pheasant, and wild ox were served. The meat was roasted over fires on spits or boiled in pots of boiling water positioned close by the tables and huge quantities were served up whole before the guests. Leeks, and later garlic and onions, were often used as seasonings but vegetables were seldom eaten separately. Other popular dishes consumed by the wealthy in western Europe included freshwater fish, pies, shellfish, and spiced sauces and they would finish with fruit, custards tarts sweetened with honey, nuts, cheese, and wafers.

1282. The Sicilian Vespers have started a rebellion against the rule of Charles I of Anjou and all identifiable Frenchmen have been massacred. The unfortunate French were betrayed by their inability to pronounce the local word "ceci", meaning chickpeas.

1295. The traveler Marco Polo has returned to Venice after spending 17 years in China. He has brought back with him a recipe for making sorbets (fruit-flavored water ice) by running a mixture of water and potassium nitrate over containers filled with the substance to be cooled.

He observed in Cathay that whilst the poor have to be content with meat steeped in garlic juice, the wealthier people eat meat that has been preserved in several of their spices.

In Java and Nicobar he became the first European to have encountered the coconut. He calls it "the Pharaoh's nut," describing it as a fruit full of flavor, sweet as sugar, and white as milk.

1298. In Europe many believe barnacle geese hatch from goose-necked barnacles. They are thus considered fish, not birds, and are eaten on Fridays when only fish is permitted.

1300. Herring are being caught in huge numbers in northern Europe where its economic importance rivals that of spice. The Dutch have introduced salting herring onboard. This is allowing longer fishing trips and reduced post-harvest losses, thus improving the production and economics of salted herring.

1316. In England the Guild of Pepperers has issued a decree banning the moistening of cloves, ginger, and saffron to make them heavier, as they are sold by weight.

———

1319. Sugar is available in London at the exorbitant price of "two shillings a pound."

———

1320. Pope John XXII is engaged in a long conflict with the emperor, Louis of Bavaria and the Franciscans who are preaching the absolute poverty of the clergy. The pontiff is a great mustard enthusiast and has created the post of great mustard-maker to the pope for his nephew.

———

1340. Many monks are forbidden to speak at meals. So an elaborate sign language is evolving. When the monks are forbidden to communicate with their hands they talk with their feet.

———

1350. In Europe butter is being colored with marigold flowers and is thus yellow; without coloring it is more of a creamy white. However, in France this has been prohibited, as has selling butter on a fish stall.

———

1368. In Europe since the Crusades, garlic has become increasingly popular. Its strong smell is believed to be a devil repellent, as the evil one is allergic to it. King Alfonso of Castile has been forced to decree that no noble should enter his presence within 30 days of eating garlic.

———

1375. *Le Viandier* is written by Guillaume Tirel, more familiarly known as Taillevent (literally "cut the smell") because of the length of his nose. The first important French cookbook, it is a collection of his recipes commissioned by King Charles V, whom he serves as his master cook. His menus consist mostly of soups, meats, poultry, fish, and soups, which are so heavily seasoned by spices that the taste of the food is largely obscured. As cookery often has to conform to Church rules, Taillevent has given considerable attention to meal preparation during Lent and other days of abstinence.

1379. The monks of western Europe are using the round-fruited, wild strawberry in their "illuminated" manuscripts. The alchemists consider the fruit to be an elixir for a long life. King Charles V (The Wise) of France has 12,000 strawberry plants set out in his Royal Gardens.

1380. The strawberry has not enabled King Charles V to live an extended life. He has died aged 43.

1385. In England game or mutton pie is popular. These pies topped with rich aspic jelly and other sweet spices are cooked for hours in a slow oven. The eating of "hote pies" is mentioned in William Longland's poem, *Piers Plowman*.

1387. In England, Richard II has invited 2,000 of the country's rich barons to dine with him. 200 cooks have prepared a menu, which includes 11,000 eggs, 720 hens, 1,400 oxen lying in salt, 200 rabbits and 120 sheep's heads. Pudding is a three-foot high marzipan castle.

1390. Possibly the first cookbook written in English, *The Forme of Cury*, (the word "cury" is a term for cooked food) has been compiled by Richard II's chefs; it consists of 196 recipes, many of which are of French origin. Several of the recipes are for soups and pottages, which are poured over bread that has either been toasted or dipped in liquid.

1395. Scottish soldiers carry bags of oatmeal and are making themselves fresh oatcakes wherever they camp. The dough is rolled out then one side is baked on a flat iron plate and the other side toasted by the fire.

1399. European royal salad chefs are often combining as many as 35 ingredients in one enormous salad bowl, including items such as rose petals, marigolds, and violets.

1400. A European baker fell asleep and left his pretzels in the oven. He now finds his customers prefer the hard baked biscuits, toasted to a golden crispness, to the original doughy snack.

CUTLERY IN THE MIDDLE AGES

A MEAT-BASED *Viking dish was served on wooden plates and eaten with a personal knife. Soups and pottages were served in wooden bowls and eaten with wooden or horn spoons.*

Meanwhile the Normans were developing the saucer. The small plate contained sauce, each diner having an individual saucer in which they dipped their food to enhance the flavor.

In the late eleventh century small two-pronged eating forks began to appear in mainland Europe. Forks had been introduced into Venice by a Byzantine princess and then spread throughout Italy. Thomas Beckett was one of the few Englishmen to use a fork when eating. He introduced a two-pronged fork to England after his exile in Italy but when he tried to explain that one of the advantages of the fork was that it could be washed Henry II replied "But, so can your hands."

Broth was usually served in bowls made of a thick slice of stale bread that soaked up the juice. When they become too impregnated with broth or sauce they were changed or sometimes at the end of the meal they were given to the poor. These trenchers were shared by two people, the lesser helping the more important, the younger the older, the man the woman. The former in each case broke the bread, cut the meat, and passed the cup. The liquid was sipped directly from the bowl. Diners used their right hands to pull out chunks of meat or vegetables from shared bowls. The more finicky used knives to spear the solids and convey them to the mouth.

By the beginning of the thirteenth century cutlery manufacture had began to settle in London and Sheffield in England and in places on the continent where craft guilds existed. Craftsmen produced elaborately ornamented blades and fashioned handles of such fine materials as amber, ebony, gold, ivory, marble, and silver. England's King Edward I's 1307 royal inventory showed 7 forks – 6 silver and 1 gold – and thousands of knives.

By the end of the thirteenth century in the homes of wealthy western Europeans it was becoming usual to provide knives for guests, though most men carried their own. These knives were narrow and their sharply pointed ends were used to spear food and then lift it to one's mouth.

Dinner hosts also usually supplied spoons, generally made of wood or horn. Forks were still rarely used apart from in Italy as clergymen condemned their use, arguing that only human fingers, created by God, should touch God's provisions. Also the use of the fork by men was considered effeminate.

1402. Portuguese explorers have discovered bananas in western Africa and are taking them to the Canary Islands. The word "banana" is the native word for the fruit in Guinea.

1425. Italian shops are producing pasta commercially through a process involving treading barefoot on the dough.

1429. Joan of Arc helps relieve Orleans. The young French peasant girl eats bread, made from barley, rye, or bean flour, soaked in inferior wine. She is a highly competent cook.

1444. Any merchant caught selling adulterated saffron in Bavaria is burned alive.

1445. Throughout Europe pancakes have a place among Easter foods, especially on Shrove Tuesday (or Mardi Gras), the last day before Lent. Customs vary from country to country. In England a potentially new popular custom, a pancake race, is being held at Olney in Buckinghamshire.

1450. With the ascendancy of the western European nations in the Oriental spice trade spices such as cinnamon, ginger, and pepper are being used to camouflage bad flavors and odors and are making food increasingly delectable for the richer classes. In addition, such spices are believed to have a beneficial preservative action in meat and it is also thought that their consumption will prevent illness.

DIET OF TUDOR ENGLAND

I N Tudor England cereals were still the staple foodstuffs for the poor, occasionally accompanied by a few vegetables such as beans, peas, and turnips and very exceptionally meat. Bread flours milled from barley, rye, or wheat were baked into loaves. At the main midday meal, pottage might be flavored with bacon and thickened with eggs. The pottage, often made with peas, might contain cabbage or spinach to give it extra nutritive value and bread would often be used as a thickener and as an accompaniment. A smaller supper was taken around 5.00 in the afternoon.

The average Englishman was better fed than his fellow European citizens were. Standard food for the middle classes included beef, mutton, pigeon, and oysters, sometimes cooked in pastries and puddings. English beef and mutton was believed to be the best in Europe. Due to the warmer climate after the several centuries of colder weather a greater volume of food was being produced. To eat well meant to eat a lot. Greater body weight was a sign of wealth and good health during a time when famine was always a threat.

1475. A humanist Italian called Bartolomeo Platina has produced the first printed cookbook. In *De Honesta Voluptate (On Right Pleasure and Good Health)* he has recorded recipes for all kinds of food. The success of his treatise is helping to revive the Roman love for good cooking. Amongst his many recipes are some for making marzipan and other candy. Confectionery is still regarded mainly to be an apothecary's product, but they are also regarded as a luxury food, packaged in decorative boxes and offered as a gift to royals.

———

1477. The first single-subject food book has been printed. *Summa Lacticiniorum* has been written on the subject of cheese.

———

1492. Christopher Columbus discovers America. Two of Columbus' scouts in Cuba have come back with wild tales of a sort of grain, which is "well tasted baked, dried, and made into flour." The natives in their language call it mahiz; Columbus is calling it "maize." Columbus' crews have survived on salted meat or fish stews cooked on wood burning stoves, hard biscuits, and watered wine.

———

1498. Portuguese explorer Vasco De Gama has sailed round Africa's Cape of Good Hope to reach Calcutta, India. Now he is returning to his home country with cinnamon, ginger, pepper, and deals for the Portuguese to continue trade with Indian princes. By finding a sea route round Africa to India the Portuguese explorer Vasco Da Gama is opening up the Oceanic spice route from Asia to Europe.

1502. Following the death of his uncle, Montezuma has become the Aztec chief speaker. Montezuma eats plenty of spicy food made from hot chillies and sweet peppers, especially tortillas made from corn. For meat he eats deer, rabbit, turkey, even dog with beans, and as a snack roasted ground seeds.

1503. Three years after Vasco Da Gama's journey to India 100 tons of spice arrived in Portugal. Now pepper sold in Lisbon is five times cheaper than in Venice.

1504. During his fourth voyage westwards Columbus is anchored off Jamaica and rations are low (the natives won't trade him any). His crew waits until nightfall before tucking into another meal of crumbled biscuit pottage so they don't see the worms. The explorer learns from his Zacuto almanac that on 29 February 1504 there is to be an eclipse of the moon. Columbus summons the Jamaican chiefs and tells them if they don't give him food he has the power to blot out the moon. They laugh but then the eclipse begins. The terrified natives beg him to bring the moon back and they will give him what he wants.

The Italian sculptor Michelangelo has executed a 13ft high stone carving of David, which is astounding the public with its realism. The workaholic artist tends to have just a little bread when working with a proper meal in the evening when finished.

Another Italian, Leonardo Da Vinci, has commenced his painting, which he is calling *Mona Lisa*. Previously the inventive artist and engineer has drawn a partially automated spit for roasting meat that turns over a fire as hot gases flow up a chimney, driven by a fan-like structure in the chimney. Da Vinci is unlikely to develop the contraption for himself as he doesn't eat meat. Indeed, he is such a fervent vegetarian that he is known to buy caged birds from poultry vendors and set them free.

―――――――

1508. The beautiful Lucrezia Borgia, the illegitimate daughter of Pope Alexander VI, is married to the son and heir of the Duke of Ferrara. She is making the court a center of culture. A new Italian egg pasta in the form of flat ribbons called tagliatelle has supposedly been inspired by a nobleman's love for Lucrezia's hair.

―――――――

1509. In England a spicy pottage has been developed whereby wheat is boiled in water until it turns into a gruel, milk, currants and other dried fruit are stirred in, then egg yolks and spices such as cinnamon and nutmeg are added. Finally, the mixture is cooked into a stiff pudding. When eaten at Christmas some people are beginning to refer to it as Christmas pudding.

―――――――

1517. Martin Luther nails a list of 95 theses on the door of the Wittenburg church. The monk kills his own pigs to make sausages. He is known to fast for four days in succession from both food and drink. At other times he relies for several days in a row on a small allowance of bread and herring.

———

1519. The Spanish conquistador Cortez embarks on his first expedition to Mexico. When Cortez and his fellow Spaniards arrive, the Aztec emperor Montezuma wants to find out if the newcomers are gods or mortals. So he tests the matter with gifts of food. His first offerings make the Spaniards sick as they are splattered with blood (Montezuma thought this would be suitable for gods). Now they are delighting on such novelties as maize, turkeys, tortillas, and many different types of fruit including avocados and cacti.

Cortez has sent back to Spain a consignment of the ground vanilla beans, which the Aztecs regard as sacred and of divine making. Vanilla beans are so valued that they are one of the ways in which common people pay tribute to the Aztec emperors. According to their legend, their origin goes back to the early days of the world when the gods still walked the earth. One god, Xanat, was in love with a human youth and she transformed herself to look like a vanilla vine so she could remain on earth with him and his people.

———

1521. Ferdinand Magellan is attempting to be the first man to reach the East Indies by sailing west. He has run out of food half way across the Pacific, having discovered dishonest

ITALIAN RENAISSANCE COOKING

*O*NE *aspect of the Italian Renaissance, the revival of classical culture, was that during the first half of the sixteenth century the Italians led the way in culinary arts. The upper and middle classes dined in elegant style on recipes such as thick slices of beef fillets with garlic and mushrooms and pasta dishes such as lasagne or ravioli. Truffles had returned to popularity after centuries of little use as it had been felt they were a manifestation of the devil. Such delicacies were being served in a manner befitting the affluence of the household, the dining table being decorated with fine tablecloths, earthenware, and silverware.*

For the poor, cereals, in the form of bread, cakes, or pottage, were the mainstays of most diets with the addition of a few vegetables, such as beans and cabbage. Meat was only eaten on feast days or on special occasions. The peasants usually sold the dairy products they made; they couldn't afford to eat them themselves.

traders had only supplied half the food he'd paid for. Consequently the men are surviving on a diet of stewed rat, sawdust, and the leather fittings of the ship with an occasional banquet of fresh fish. (His men are selling rats to each other at one ducat each.)

1529. The first European colonists in America have found plenty of wild turkeys; indeed they have saved many of these early settlers from famine. Because they are easy to raise and quickly put on weight, the birds are proving very popular. Bernardino de Sahagun has recommended their meat as fat and savory. The turkey is the only new edible animal species to be introduced to Europe from the New World and is now creating a great stir in Spain.

1532. Richard Posse, the Bishop of Rochester's cook, has an idea for a joke. He puts a laxative herb into a stew. Unfortunately he poisons 17 of the bishop's guests, killing two of them. For this he is boiled alive in his own stockpot.

1533. The 14-year-old Florentine great-granddaughter of Lorenzo the Magnificent, Catherine de Médici, has married Henry, duc d'Orléans, the son of the French king, Francis I. She has brought with her a group of Florentine cooks from her native Italy. With their help, she is introducing many new Italian dishes such as artichoke hearts, asparagus, macaroons, pasta, raspberry, lemon and orange sorbets, sweetbreads, and truffles. As a wedding present, her uncle,

Pope Clement VII has presented to her a new bean, the haricot bean, which has been imported from the New World.

1533. Anne Boleyn has become the queen of England having married Henry VIII. Anne has a rather off-putting habit, first observed during her coronation banquet, of vomiting during meals. So one of her ladies in waiting has to hold up a sheet to shield her from other diners at appropriate moments. In her younger days whilst lady-in-waiting to Catherine of Aragon, she created a recipe for a small tart with an almond, curd cheese and lemon filling. Henry VIII was so enchanted he named the creator of the cake maid of honor.

1534. Henry VIII proclaims himself head of the Church in England, transferring ecclesiastical jurisdiction and revenues from the Pope to himself. The abbot of Glastonbury is trying to bribe the King with the gift of some lands, as he is concerned that Henry VIII is going to pull down the abbey. The abbot orders a massive plum pie to be baked and in it he puts the deeds to 12 of the manors of Glastonbury. He sends off to the King with the pie his chief steward, Jack Horner, but the King can only find 11 deeds inside.

Jack Horner has picked out for himself a nice "plum."

1536. Jane Seymour marries Henry VIII. She is known to have enjoyed a Cornish pasty on several occasions. The pasty originally evolved to meet the needs of tin mining, in Cornwall. These pasties contain meat and vegetables wrapped in pastry, sometimes one end contains jam or fruit as well, thus giving the hard-working men a very practical lunch (or "croust", as they call it) down in the dark and damp tunnels of the mine. Cornish housewives also mark their husband's initials on the left-hand side of the pastry casing, in order to avoid confusion at lunchtime.

1537. Spanish invaders in South America are finding all kinds of new things to eat, including tomatoes, peanuts, and potatoes. Spanish forces discovered the latter when entering a Colombian village from which the inhabitants had fled; they discovered what they thought were truffles. They turned out to be potatoes.

1540. The French king, Francis I is a great lover of poultry and veal and with the arrival several years earlier of the Florentine cooks who are schooled in the subtleties of Renaissance cooking, he has revived the days of opulent eating and drinking.

1542. A Jewish doctor from Constantinople is treating King Francis I of France for intestinal trouble with yogurt, a semi-fluid fermented milk food. Though new to western European tastes, it has been made for centuries in the Balkans, Turkey, the Middle East, and India where it was once called the food of the gods.

Andrew Borde has made the first mention of bacon and eggs in literature in England. In *A Compendyous Regyment, or a Dyetary of Health* he writes "Bacon is good for carters and plowmen I do say that collopes (slices of bacon) and egges is holsome for them."

———————

1543. Henry VIII marries his sixth wife, Catherine Parr. The King gives his ladies in waiting a daily allowance of two loaves, and a joint of beef each day for breakfast. At his court peacocks are cooked then put back into their feathers so guests can see they aren't being hoodwinked with chicken. The portly king himself eats two huge meals a day, dinner at 10.00 with 600 courtiers and supper at 4.00. Henry is so large now that he has had a cage installed in his palace with a pulley to carry him upstairs.

———————

1544. After the Spanish explorers brought the tomato to Spain from Mexico, a Moor brought it to Tangiers. From there, an Italian brought it to Italy where it is called "pomo dei mori" (Moor's apple). Although there is culinary use of tomatoes by the Italians, it is not widespread, as most Europeans are convinced that tomatoes are both a lethal poison and an aphrodisiac, rendering them a danger both to spiritual and physical health. Their acceptance by Europeans as food is very slow.

———————

1548. In King Edward VI's England, a law ordering abstention from meat on Fridays has been passed by Parliament.

———————

1550. In Lorraine, France, an open tart filled with beaten eggs and cream, called a quiche has been developed. Its popularity has been enhanced as it can be eaten on meatless days.

___

1551. In England recipes for pastry have begun to appear. Previously a coarse, tough pastry was used principally to seal in the juice and flavor of the meat during cooking and protect it against contamination. It wasn't meant to be eaten but people have began to snack on the tasty meat juice flavored pastry fragments.

___

1555. Queen Mary Tudor of England uses a marmalade made of almonds, cinnamon, cloves, ginger, musk, orange peel, quinces, rosewater, and sugar in an unsuccessful attempt to help her get pregnant.

In France Nostradamus, who recently published a book of prophecies *Centuries Asrtologiques*, has also published a recipe book, *Excellent er Moult Utile Opuscule a tous necessaire qui desirent avoir connaissance de plusieurs exq uises recettes (An excellent and most useful little work essential to all who wish to become acquainted with some exquisite recipes)*. Included are recipes for various fruit jams such as cherry, lime, or oranges made with ginger, honey, cooked wine, and sugar.

___

1558. The 16-year-old Mary Queen of Scots has married the sickly Francis, heir to the French throne, having been betrothed to him since the age of seven. Mary is partial to an orange marmalade, which is made by her Turkish chefs. For salad the teenage Scottish queen likes boiled celery root diced and tossed with lettuce, creamy mustard dressing, truffles, and hard-cooked egg slices.

1563. The English tavern has for centuries provided food and drink for travelers. Now, due to the development of providing a daily meal at a fixed time, townsmen of all but the lowest classes are utilizing their facilities for dining out. Most taverns offer a good dinner for one shilling (about 7 cents) or less, with wine and ales as extras.

1565. King Charles IX of France has issued a decree that fixes the beginning of the year at 1 January instead of 1 April. This innovation is not very popular and on 1 April both as a protest and as a joke people are sending sweetmeats in the shape of fish to one another as mock New Year's gifts. These April fool fish are being sent as the sun happens to be in the constellation of Pisces.

1571. The City of Paris celebrates the arrival of Elizabeth of Austria in the capital with a lavish banquet, which includes whale on the menu. In Europe, particularly around the Bay of Biscay area, whale blubber is a common food for the poor, especially around Lent when it is the main diet for many, often accompanied by peas.

THE DIET OF THE RUSSIANS

IN Russia, soldiers' and peasants' meals were monotonous, usually consisting of a handful of millet flour, a little pork or salted fish, accompanied with beetroot, cabbage, swede, and turnip.

The diet of Russian sovereigns and nobles was much more varied. Roasted swan and crane, bear's paws, haunch of reindeer, and salted cucumbers were amongst the food served at Russian banquets. Much food had a sour flavor; for instance, dark brown rye breads were made with sour yeast doughs and pickles were often used.

1573. Potatoes are being planted in European soil. Many are suspicious of them, in part because people realize that it is a member of the nightshade family, all of which are very poisonous. However, they are becoming a standard supply item on the Spanish ships as it is noticed that the sailors who eat potatoes do not suffer from scurvy.

1574. Henry III becomes king of France. He enjoys Italian sorbet delicacies and consumes them daily. He is reintroducing a strict etiquette at his table with a series of bows not only to himself but also to his personal belongings.

1576. At the wedding of Marquis de Lomenie and Mlle de Martigues, Catherine de Médici has eaten too many of her favorite cockerel kidneys and artichoke bottoms and for a time became so ill with diarrhea she thought she would die. Artichokes are enjoying a vogue in European courts and are gaining a reputation as an aphrodisiac.

Catherine has introduced a new elegance and refinement to the French table and for the first time ladies are being admitted to the royal table.

1583. English fruit salads are served hot or cold. They can be as simple as lemons sliced and sprinkled with sugar, or they can be a mixture of many fruits, herbs, nuts, spice, and sugar. Flowers such as cowslips, marigold, primrose, or violets are often used; these can be pickled, sweetened, or eaten raw.

1585. After making raids against Spanish settlements in the West Indies Francis Drake has introduced potatoes to England from Colombia. However, Englishmen are shunning the strange tuber. It has been decried as a dangerously unwholesome vegetable.

—————

1586. Pepper is being sold by the individual grain and guards on the London docks are having their pockets sewn up so they can't steal any spices.

—————

1588. Francis Drake has given some potato seeds to Raleigh. He plants them at his Irish estates but is unimpressed. It is generally agreed that Raleigh's potatoes are a health hazard leading to consumption, flatulence, and unnatural carnal lust. Meanwhile the arrogant Raleigh only eats white bread as brown bread is only fit for lower orders.

—————

1589. France has a new king, Henry IV. The King has a preference for sweet things and so sugared almonds, marzipan, and jam are becoming fashionable in France. Almond is presently the most common flavoring in candy, followed by cinnamon and clove. He also has a great fondness for melons, which grow in his gardens in glasshouses.

—————

1590. The English writer Robert Greene, in his book *Arcadia*, makes the first written mention of an apple pie: "Thy breath is like the steame of apple-pyes."

Queen Elizabeth of England has issued a law ordering her

people on certain days to eat fish in order to encourage the fish industry.

———————

1591. Pilchards are being caught, salted, and pressed in Cornwall as a preserved fish and exported to the continent. However, Sir Francis Drake is urging Queen Elizabeth I to block the trade, to stop supplying England's enemies abroad with nutritious food.

———————

1595. At Christmas the English are eating "minced" or "shred" pies, which are at present a huge covered tart filled with sueted chicken and ox tongue, eggs, lemon peel, dried fruits, and sugar. Cinnamon, cloves, and nutmeg are traditionally added, representing the three gifts given to Jesus by the Wise Men. The mixture is baked in an oblong pastry case to represent Jesus' crib and a little pastry baby often decorates the lid. Over the 12 days of Christmas a pie is eaten in a different house in order to bring good fortune to the household and the eater for the next year.

———————

1597. Queen Elizabeth I dislikes gluttony and still has a reasonably slim figure. Her regular breakfast is a biscuit and undercooked boiled beefsteaks. Her teeth have turned black in her old age through eating too many sweet things. In fact, black teeth is a status symbol as sugar is very expensive; sugar costs nine times as much as milk.

———————

1600. King Henry IV of France is attempting to encourage agricultural expansion. Feeding the bulk of their peoples is important to rulers of this time, as a well-fed population is unlikely to revolt against a monarch.

The King often dines on boiled chicken with an appetizing seasoning of pepper and cloves. He wants to make this chicken dish the Sunday meal of the French as a symbol of modest comfort and an improvement in the condition of the commoners.

The King is described by a contemporary as "chewing garlic and having breath that would fell an ox at twenty paces."

———————

1602. William Shakespeare writes his comic play *Twelfth Night*. A favorite Twelfth Night joke is a surprise pie. A very large amount of pastry is prepared and baked as an empty pie case. Holes are cut in the bottom and live birds and frogs are put inside the pie. Then, as the nursery rhyme goes, "When the pie was opened, the birds began to sing."

———————

1605. An English visitor to Scotland has described a "pottage" made of oatmeal flour, boiled in water and eaten with butter, milk, or ale. This meal, which is becoming known as porridge, has many regional variations in Scotland and is either served at breakfast or as the main course at lunch or dinner.

———————

1606. Rhubarb roots are being exported from China to Europe. It is believed that eating rhubarb improves one's state of health, as it results in pouring excess humors from

DIET OF NATIVE AMERICANS

THE buffalo, which numbered around 50 million in North America at the turn of the 17th century formed the mainstay of the Native American's diet. After a successful buffalo hunt an adult might consume as much as 4lb of buffalo meat a day. They ate thin slices of raw meat from the buffalo's hump or feasted on the perishable parts such as the brains, blood, kidney, and liver. The meat was roasted or broiled over a campfire with the addition of just a little salt and sometimes flavorful herbs. The meat that wasn't eaten immediately was cut into thin strips and hung up to dry. Tougher cuts were mixed with berries, melted bone fat, and herbs and packed into a solid block called a "pemmican"; these were kept in pouches and used by hunters and gatherers when they were away from home.

Rabbit, squirrel, and deer meat was also eaten. Sometimes they made stews to which they added a highly pungent wild onion.

Many tribes also grew crops, especially maize. Many Native Americans believed maize has a spiritual origin and it lay at the center of tribal and personal religious beliefs. They held a fresh corn feast when the maize was ripe and boiled then ladled it into wooden bowls so that everyone could eat their fill. The rest of the harvest was dried and stored away. Sometimes maize, acorns, nuts, and seeds were ground, mixed with some water, and salted to form a dough, then cooked like cakes in the fire. Villagers also enjoyed meals of beans, pumpkins, and squash or berries mixed with fresh blood. As a treat strawberries were eaten fresh.

the body. William Shakespeare has mentioned rhubarb in this very sense in his new play, *Macbeth*.

At English theaters in this period, the food the audience eats is mainly apples and pears (often used as ammunition at the players), also nuts (principally hazelnuts) and gingerbread.

1609. In North America the settlers in Jamestown, reduced almost to starvation, are kept alive by gifts from Indians of wild game.

1610. The first printed mention of bagels has been recorded in the Community Regulations of Krakow, Poland. It states that bagels will be given as a gift to any woman in childbirth. The word is derived from the German word "beugel," meaning a round loaf of bread.

1611. Around 50 scholars under the authorization of King James I of England have produced the *King James Version* of the Bible. The King himself has uncouth table manners caused by his tongue being too large for his mouth so he slobbers his food all over the table.

Rice pudding is growing in popularity in Britain. Shakespeare has referred to its making at a celebratory feast in *The Winter's Tale* Act IV Scene iii Lines 36-49, where the clown plans this menu: "Let me see: what am I to buy for our sheep-shearing feast? Three pound of sugar, five pound of currants, rice ... I must have saffron to color the warden (winter pear) pies; mace; dates, none – that's out of my note;

nutmegs, seven; a race or two of ginger, but that I may beg; four pounds of pruins, and as many of raisins o'th' sun."

1621. The first ever Thanksgiving Day is celebrated. It is an acknowledgment of God's provisions for the Pilgrim Fathers after they arrived the previous year in New England. They had faced starvation but were rescued by friendly Native Americans who showed them how to grow corn and squash and how to catch the local birds, fish, and shellfish. Now the Pilgrims have invited the Indians to a Thanksgiving feast celebrating their first successful harvest. Included on the menu are deer meat and wild turkey. Despite being plentiful the Pilgrim Fathers refuse to eat lobster because they think it is a big insect.

1622. Native Americans flavor their beans with maple syrup and bear fat, and bake them in earthenware pots placed in a pit and covered with hot rocks. The Pilgrims are learning the slow cooking technique for making baked beans from the Indians. They are substituting molasses and pork fat for the maple syrup and bear fat.

The Native Americans pop popcorn in a pottery vessel with heated sand and use it to make popcorn soup, among other things. Meanwhile in Massachusetts the Native Americans are bringing popcorn snack to meetings with the English colonists as a token of goodwill during peace negotiations.

St Teresa of Avila, the reforming Carmelite nun, is canonized. The Carmelites are manufacturing macaroons,

FOOD-RELATED DEATHS

F*ROM the dawn of man there have been many food-related deaths. The early Palaeolithic peoples had to quickly learn to be excellent botanists lest they mistook a poisonous root for a nutritious one. Their botanical knowledge was handed down from one generation to the next:*

❖ **AD 54.** *The Roman emperor Claudius was poisoned with amanita mushrooms by his wife Agrippina, after her son, Nero, was named as his heir.*

❖ **1135.** *King Henry I of England died from indigestion caused by eating moray eel.*

❖ **1159.** *Pope Adrian IV, the only English pope, choked to death when he accidentally swallowed a fly.*

❖ **1216.** *In England, King John died of an intestinal illness at an East Anglian abbey having hastened his death by eating an excess of peaches and drinking too much cider.*

following Teresa's principle that "almonds are good for girls who do not eat meat."

———————

1625. Galilei Galileo publishes his controversial *Dialogue Concerning Two Chief World Systems*. This updates Copernicus' theories about the Earth going around the Sun and ridicules the position taken by the Church. The scientist and mathematician is fond of good food; for treats his nun daughter Sister Marie makes him marzipan shaped like little fish.

Various Native American tribes have different names for the pink small berries they are fond of. However, it is the Pilgrims' name that is sticking. They call the fruit "crane berry" because the cranberry plant's tiny stem and pink blossoms resemble the neck, head, and beak of cranes. They eat cranberries fresh, ground, or mashed with cornmeal and baked into bread. Maple sugar or honey is used to sweeten the berry's tangy flavor. The European settlers are learning to appreciate these tiny berries. Early French voyagers exploring Wisconsin waterways are bartering for cranberries with the Native Americans and American sailors are beginning to take barrels of cranberries to sea with them for the prevention of survey.

———————

1626. The statesman and philosopher Francis Bacon is driving in his carriage one wintry day in Highgate, North London, when he decides on impulse to observe the effect of cold on the preservation of meat. He stops his carriage, purchases a chicken and stuffs it with snow. Soon after he is seized by a chill, which develops into bronchitis. Feeling ill and beginning to shiver violently, he makes his way to the nearby house of his friend the Earl of Arundel. He is given a damp bed – so damp that Bacon's condition worsens and he dies of pneumonia.

1630. Dutch settlers are arriving on American soil seeking freedom from the strictly enforced Writs of Pastry. These laws were created after a freak accident in which a cow kicked over a giant fryer causing much of Strudeldorf to be drenched in hot hog's fat and fried to a golden brown. The new arrivals, careful not to mention the Strudeldorf incident back in Holland, are allowed to resume the making of their fried cakes, which are known as doughnuts. These American doughnuts do not have holes at all; they are quite literally little "nuts" of dough.

1633. The first time bananas are seen in Britain is when a bunch is sold in the fruiterer, Thomas Johnson's London shop window.

1638. The English colonists arriving in North America are finding only one type of apple, the crab apple, which they call "winter banana" or "melt-in-the-mouth. These are the only apples native to the United States. Settlers are bringing with them European apple seeds and attempting to grow them but the early orchards are producing very few apples because there are no honeybees to pollinate them. Now the first colony of honeybees has landed in the colony of Virginia from England. The Native Americans call these honeybees the "white man's flies."

1640. The potato is still being damned as an evil food in Europe. The Scots refuse to eat it because it isn't mentioned in the Bible. In other European countries they are being blamed for starting outbreaks of leprosy and syphilis.

1641. At a state banquet hosted by Charles I of England, his French chef, Gerald Tirsain, has developed a delicious new variation of flavored snow. Milk, cream, and eggs have been added to make it much creamier and sweeter than any other iced dessert. The guests are delighted, as is Charles who summons the cook, and has him promise to keep the recipe for his frozen cream secret. The King wants the delicacy only at the royal table and offers him £500 a year to keep it that way.

1645. The MP Oliver Cromwell's Parliamentarian troops have defeated the king's soldiers at the bleak moorland of Marston Moor near York. Cromwell's family eats for breakfast toast topped with a variety of toppings such as hot honey, ginger, and cinnamon.

The Puritan Cromwell comments on food: "Some people have food but no appetite; others have an appetite but no food. I have both, the Lord's name be praised."

1648. Having defeated Charles I, Parliament has abolished Christmas and declared it to be an ordinary working day. Cromwell, the leader of Parliament, refers to Christmas pudding as "an abominable idolatrous thing."

———

1649. England's Charles I is executed. Before his execution Charles has a condemned man's breakfast of claret and swan pie.

———

1650. Nougat goes back many centuries to ancient Greece where honey, together with walnuts or other nuts, was beaten into egg whites and then sun dried. The Greeks imported the confection via Marseilles, to Provence, France where it is proving very popular using almonds instead of walnuts.

———

1651. 35-year old François de la Varenne originally learnt to cook in the kitchen of Catherine de Médici's cousin, Marie de Médici. Now he has written *Cuisinier Français*, which is the first book to establish cooking rules, to present recipes in alphabetical order, and to include instructions for vegetable cooking. It is the foundation stone of French classical cooking.

———

1655. The Lord Protector Oliver Cromwell has dissolved Parliament and England is divided into 11 military districts, a major general responsible for each one. Cromwell has banned the eating of pie, declaring it a pagan form of pleasure.

———

FRENCH COOKING IN THE SEVENTEENTH CENTURY

PARTLY because of the influence of La Varenne, cookery was changing in France; seasonings and spices began to be used to improve rather than hide the flavors of meat and fish. Truffles and mushrooms were added to meat dishes giving them delicate qualities and roasted meat was served in its own juices to help it to maintain its flavor. French cooking, after being heavily influenced by Italian cooking for the last century and a half, was creating its own style, where the emphasis was increasingly placed on enhancing the quality of food rather than the old medieval approach of disguising its deficiencies. In the homes of the wealthy a wide variety of different elaborate dishes were being served each meal. From now on France would be at the vanguard of the culinary arts.

Meanwhile the French peasant continued to exist on his dull diet of bread, bean pottage with perhaps a little meat, fruit, herbs, berries, and nuts.

1658. Paris police have raided a monastery and sent 12 monks to jail for eating meat and drinking wine during Lent.

1659. In France the Sicilian chef Francesco Procopia dei Coltelli has perfected the making of ice cream.

1666. Some clergy are claiming that the Great Fire of London, which started at the house of the king's baker, is God's judgment on the gluttony of the people.

The Cambridge graduate Isaac Newton has fled into the country to escape the plague. Seeing an apple fall from a tree (probably a Flower of Kent, a large green variety), he enters into a profound train of thought as to the causes that could lead to such a drawing together, or attraction. Newton cares little for meals and often forsakes eating for hours when he is caught up in his work.

1667. Louis XIV of France attempts to annex Spanish Netherlands but is frustrated by an alliance of Holland, England, and Sweden. The King has a passion for vegetables and fruit and he is developing gardening. His magnificent royal feasts always end with marmalades and jellies served in silver dishes and made from fruit grown in the king's own gardens and glasshouses. The fruit dish he favors is strawberries in wine. He has a great liking for asparagus and he regularly receives supplies of his favorite vegetable. Also the Sun King is hooked on aniseed lozenges to "sweeten his breath."

The writer John Milton has completed *Paradise Lost*.

Milton has coined the phrase "Fine words butter no parsnips." For supper the blind writer habitually has "olives or some light thing" and a glass of wine.

1670. The first English cookbook written by a woman is Hannah Wooley's *The Queen-like Closet; or Rich Cabinet.*

In Europe the pineapple remains so uncommon and coveted a commodity that King Charles II of England has posed for an official portrait receiving a pineapple as a gift, an act symbolic of royal privilege.

1674. King Louis XIV has established a new dining etiquette. Instead of dishes being placed on the table all at once without any thought to complementary dishes they are served in a defined sequence.

1675. In North America colonial housewives are serving popcorn with sugar and cream for breakfast. The corn is popped by means of a cylinder of thin sheet-iron that revolves on an axle in front of the fireplace.

1677. In Britain barley sugar sweets are being made. They are being sold in the form of twisted sticks and are thought to be helpful for getting rid of a winter cold.

The word "hash" for a fried leftovers dish has come into English from the old French word *hacher*, meaning to chop. Corned beef hash has its origins in being a particularly delicious combination of odds and ends.

CUTLERY IN THE FIFTEENTH AND SIXTEENTH CENTURIES

I N the second half of the fifteenth century a
change in the design of spoons was required
once men and women started wearing large,
stiff-laced collars called ruffs. Originally those
wearing ruffs around their necks couldn't easily
drink soup from bowls, as the early spoons with
their short stems were not able to transport the
soup past the ruffs without spilling. So spoon
handles lengthened and the spoon's bowl became
larger, permitting more liquid to be transported
to the mouth with less chance of dribbling the
contents on the ruffs.

In the 1570s Henry III of France, during a visit
to the court at Venice, noted that two-pronged
table forks were being used. He brought some
back to France and some of the French nobility
started using them. Meanwhile in England very
little cutlery was used; even Queen Elizabeth I
would pick up her chicken bone deftly in her
long fingers rather than use cutlery. The few
plates there were would be made of wood or
pewter and the spoons of wood, silver, or tin.
In 1608 an Englishman named Thomas Coryate

brought some forks back to England after seeing them in Italy during his travels there. But by the 1650s forks were still rarely used, apart from in the kitchen or at the serving table to hold meat when it was being cut. Indeed, at European banquets hands were still being used to serve much of the food, even though the servants were only using their fingertips. It wasn't until the 1670s that the fork began to achieve general popularity as an eating implement. Once their efficiency for spearing food was noted there was no longer any need for a pointed tip at the end of daggers that were used as toothpicks and to cut meat.

Consequently in France King Louis XIV ordered rounded knives, which Cardinal Richelieu had introduced 35 years earlier so that the diners couldn't stab each other. Further, he decreed all pointed daggers on the street or the dinner table illegal, and all knife points were ground down in order to reduce violence.

1682. King Louis XIV has abandoned his old home, the Louvre, and moved his court to establish his independence from the Paris nobility. At his new home at Versailles he is dining in magnificent pomp and ceremony on food prepared by nearly 500 kitchen staff. His meal is carried to the royal quarters by a procession of high-ranking personnel crying "the King's meat". Behind them are a parade of servants carrying baskets of cutlery, seasonings, spices, and toothpicks.

1685. By now every region in Europe had its own version of a sausage, but in Frankfurt-am-Main, Germany a butcher, Johann Georghehner, has created a particularly popular long smoked one, which is becoming known as a frankfurter sausage.

1686. Francesco Procopia dei Coltelli opens Le Procope, the first café in Paris. Here after being considered a dessert for royalty alone, water ices, cream ices and sorbets are being made available to the general public for the first time.

1686. The Moslem Ottoman (Turkish) army has been victoriously advancing from the East and has succeeded in conquering a vast expanse of territory in South East Europe. Now it has reached the outskirts of Budapest. To reach the center of the city, the Turks are digging underground passages. Bakers, working during the night, hear the noise made by the Turks and give the alarm. The assailants are repulsed and to highlight its defeat, the bakers produce, as a totally novel line, a roll of flaky pastry made of pounded almonds and sugar shaped in the form of a crescent, which is the emblem of Islam. It enables the rejoicing Budapest citizens literally to devour with relish the very symbol of their enemy.

———————

1688. Though the Turks were forced to retreat, the edible croissant-like crescent is advancing further west, and has reached France.

———————

1689. Le Procope is proving very popular. Customers are gathering in his establishment, which is elegantly decorated with chandeliers, mirrors, and wood paneling, to sample the choice of around 90 flavors of different ices and sorbets. It has also become a meeting place for Parisians to discuss politics and read news-sheets.

1691. Ireland is recognizing the food value of potatoes and has become the first country in Europe to plant them as a staple food crop.

For years members of the court and other dignitaries have considered it a privilege merely to stand by and watch Louis XIV devour his food. Entire families of Parisians crowd round every Sunday to admire the dexterity of their king, who can knock the small end off an egg in a single stroke. Despite being forbidden during Lent for centuries due to their richness, boiled eggs are becoming a favorite breakfast meal in France.

———————

1695. In London chophouses are selling slices of meat the size of individual portions to busy city dwellers. These are the first ready to be cooked meals.

1696. King Louis XIV is growing in his gardens a new type of green pea introduced from Italy and is creating a fashion for them. However, his second wife, the puritanical Madame de Maintenon, does not approve. She writes: "Some ladies, even after having supped at the royal table, and well supped too, returning to their own homes, at the risk of suffering from indigestion, will again eat peas before going to bed. It is both a fashion and madness."

1697. Previously in England, when making such dishes as toasted cheese, the toast was generally moistened in wine. Now the fashion is to butter it. Hot buttered toast is now being eaten at breakfast.

1703. In North America the word "cookie" has appeared in print for the first time. The word comes from Dutch settlers who are introducing their recipes for various types of "koekje," which means "little cake."

1706. Due to the popularity of Le Procope in Paris, many imitators are setting up similar establishments. There are now around 250 icemakers in the capital.

1709. In the country districts of Sweden, it has been customary for a number of centuries for guests to contribute to the fare at large gatherings. All the donations are placed together on long tables from which the diners help themselves. These meals are known as a smorgasbord.

1713. The Peace of Utrecht ends the War of Spanish Succession and the French supremacy in Europe. Still a gourmand even in his late 80s, Louis XIV's diet continues to astound onlookers and frighten his doctors.

1718. Mrs Mary Eales publishes the first English recipe for ice cream. Whilst the continentals favor water ices, the British have a preference for their iced desserts being made with cream.

1719. The first permanent potato patches in North America are established near Londonderry, New Hampshire. As in Europe, potatoes are slow to gain popularity and they are still used primarily as animal fodder.

1720. England's King George I takes his meals in private attended by two Turkish servants. He particularly likes oysters and oily salads.

Mustard was formerly made up into balls with honey or vinegar and a little cinnamon, to keep until needed, when they were mixed with more vinegar. It was sold in these balls but now a Mrs. Clements, of Tewkesbury, Gloucestershire, has invented a method of drying the seeds sufficiently well

NUTRITION

THE laws given to Moses included possibly the first ever guidelines on nutrition. God wanted the Hebrews to eat only "kosher" food for health reasons. Indeed, the Hebrew word "kasher" literally means "proper."

The father of medicine, Hippocrates, often referred to the importance of a nutritious diet in his writings. He claimed to have discovered a principle for prescribing diets that were suited to individual's constitutions. It wasn't until the fourteenth century that there was any advance in understanding nutrition when in China philosophers began to find links between diet and diseases. They regarded all foods as having an influence on health so they claimed there was no distinction between foods and medicines.

By the fifteenth century some enlightened European physicians were emphasizing the importance of a healthy diet. One physician from St. Bartholomew's hospital in London suggested his patients should be encouraged to eat honey, river-crab, and dried figs for their health. With the discovery of other lands new fruits and vegetables were introduced into Europe. The beneficial effects they had on health were noted, helping to prevent such things as skin diseases.

In the sixteenth century Andrew Borde, the physician and author of a Dyetary of Health was using Hippocrates' humoral theory to explain and to treat illness. Sickness, he taught, resulted from unbalanced humors. Therefore it was important for the sick to maintain a balanced diet and they should eat food suited to their temperaments. The choleric man should avoid hot spices; the melancholic, fried meat; the phlegmatic man should avoid white meat and fruit; and the sanguine, garlic.

Another problem that was occurring was scurvy, a potentially fatal disease that made the gums bleed, teeth fall out, and legs swell up. It particularly affected seamen on long voyages. By the year 1593, Sir John Hawkins and his men were aware that citrus fruit was a good remedy against scurvy and by the turn of the century the East India Company was supplying its crews with lemon water and oranges to counteract the disease.

for them to be made into a powder.

Gasparini, a Swiss pastry cook from the small town of Meiringen, has developed a mixture of beaten egg whites and sugar, called a meringue.

———

1721. Peter the Great becomes Emperor of all Russia. The energetic Czar generally eats simple food and has lousy table manners; he regularly tramples across the banquet table, treading on dishes and cutlery with his unwashed feet. However, he lays on lavish banquets, modeled on the splendor of Versailles. The embroidered cloths, caviar from the Caspian Sea, and oysters from the Baltic all match the sumptuous feasts Louis XIV used to host. He prefers at banquets to be seated near the door so he can slip away early.

———

1725. The American Benjamin Franklin, at the age of 16 years, has come across a book recommending a vegetarian diet. His devotion to study and refusal to eat flesh means he often has no more than a biscuit or a slice of bread, a pastry tart or a few raisins, and a glass of water. His new diet is saving him money.

———

1732. Benjamin Franklin publishes his first *Poor Richard Almanac*. "Fish and visitors smell in three days" he writes. After a few years of vegetarianism, despite his dislike of their aroma, Benjamin Franklin's liking for fish has tempted him back to eating flesh.

———

1733. The word "barbecue," which first appeared in print 80 years ago, has now taken on in America the meaning of meat cooked on an apparatus in the open air over a fire and the social gathering incorporating such cooking. It comes from a word Arawak Indians in Haiti use – they smoke strips of meat over an open fire on a grating of wood called a "berbekot."

1735. George II gives Britain's first Prime Minister, Robert Walpole, 10 Downing Street for his official London residence. The Prime Minister often sits munching Norfolk apples in the House of Commons.

1739. The word "cracker" is first used in North America, for a plain, unsweetened, dry, hard, bread product. When crackers are broken into pieces they make a cracking noise, which accounts for the name.

1742. George Handel's *Messiah* premieres in Dublin. The composer loves his food, especially generous helpings of sausages. Once he ordered dinner for two in the local inn. When the food was bought to him, the landlord saw only Handel and commented that he had been led to understand Handel was expecting company. "I am the company," the composer told him, sitting down to work his way through both dinners.

William Parks, a colonial printer in Williamsburg, Virginia, publishes the first cookbook in America. *The Compleat Housewife, or Accomplish'd Gentlewoman's Companion*, is based on the fifth edition of E. Smith's *The Compleat Housewife*.

1745. King George II's reign is threatened when Bonnie Prince Charlie, the Young Pretender, lands in Scotland. The English king imagines his popularity might be increased by allowing his subjects to watch him eat in a public dining room at Hampton Court. Tickets can be brought to let his subjects watch the King and his family eat Sunday dinner.

1746. Apple pies, formerly called house pie by the poor, have become so popular a dessert in America that Yale College is serving them every night at supper.

1747. Hannah Glasse, in her book *The Art Of Cookery*, names the newly developed northern English pudding made from batter placed underneath meat being roasted on a spit to absorb the juices, "Yorkshire Pudding."

Andreas Marggraf, a chemist in Berlin, discovers the presence of a white substance with a sweet taste in the root of sugar beets and it can be extracted in crystalline form. At present the sugar beet is being grown as a garden vegetable and as animal fodder. Marggraf believes the amount of sugar in beets is inadequate to provide an incentive for further development of the techniques needed to extract sugar.

1748. Shepherd's pie is being cooked by frugal peasant housewives looking for creative ways to serve leftover meat to their families. It originated in the north of England and Scotland where there are large numbers of sheep, hence the name.

DIET IN EIGHTEENTH-CENTURY EUROPE

IN eighteenth-century western Europe cookery and nutrition were improving as a result of the greater range of foodstuffs available. More vegetables and meat were being eaten as farming and preserving techniques got better and many new kinds of tropical fruits were being introduced from abroad. French cuisine was influencing cooks throughout Europe who tried to enhance the taste of foods by using spices in a subtler way. For wealthy Europeans food and cookery had become an important part of their lives. They would compete against one another to employ the best cooks who produced new recipes and beautiful dishes that increased their employer's social status.

In Britain venison was the superior meat. If a person could serve venison, it meant that he was of the highest social status. Only a very select group of wealthy people could afford fruit and many of the British feared uncooked fruit; they thought it would give the person who consumed it indigestion or even the plague.

1756. A sauce made from olive oil and egg yolks has been invented by the French chef of Louis François Armand de Vignerot du Plessis, duc de Richelieu. While the duke was defeating the British at the successful siege of the English-held St. Philip's Castle, his chef was creating a victory feast that included a sauce made of cream and eggs. When the chef realized that there was no cream in the kitchen, he improvised, substituting olive oil for the cream. Located in Mahón, port city and the capital of Minorca, the successful siege has resulted in the French's gain of the entire island. The chef has named the new sauce "Mahonnaise" (or mayonnaise), in honor of the Duke's victory.

Frederick the Great's Prussians defeat the Austrians at Battle of Lowositz. His favorite lunch is spiced soup, Russian beef in brandy, Italian maize with garlic, and savory eel pie.

―――――――――

1759. Voltaire publishes his short prose romance, *Candide*. Though a meat eater himself, Voltaire is sympathetic to the philosophy of vegetarianism. The viewpoint has come increasingly into vogue due to the publication by Antonio Cocchi of the teachings of the ancient Greek vegetarian Pythagoras.

King Louis XV of France loses Quebec to General Wolfe of Britain. It is claimed that King Louis returned late one night to his hunting lodge, and all that was on hand was onions, butter, and champagne. He mixed them together, cooked it and thus invented the first French onion soup.

―――――――――

1760. In Yorkshire, England, a Pontefract chemist, George Dunhill has had the idea of making a new type of licorice candy by mixing juice from licorice root with flour and sugar.

1762. John Montagu, fourth Earl of Sandwich, has invented a new snack. A notorious gambler, he often goes from pub to pub in London on gambling marathons. To satisfy his hunger, while continuing to gamble, he orders roast beef between pieces of bread for a snack while he is at the gaming tables; it allows him to keep one hand free to play while he eats. It has become known as the "sandwich."

1763. Deserted by Britain, Frederick the Great has made peace with Austria at the Treaty of Hubertsburg, thus ending the Seven Years War. Several years earlier the Prussian ruler ordered his people to plant and eat potatoes, as a deterrent to famine. The people's fear of poisoning led him to enforce his orders by threatening to cut off the nose and ears of those who refused. Unsurprisingly, this was effective and now potatoes are a basic part of the Prussian diet.

1765. The first restaurant, by that name, is being run by a Parisian soup vendor Monsieur A. Boulanger, the owner of a Parisian cafe. Originally he was unable to make fully cooked dishes such as stews, as he didn't belong to the guild of caterers, the only ones allowed to sell them. The sign above his door advertised restoratives, or restaurants, referring to the soups and broths available within. However, he decided to serve "pieds de mouton a la sauce poulette" (basically sheep's feet in white sauce enriched with egg yolks), then won the case against the protesting caterers because Parliament decreed that because the sauce was made separately and was poured onto the meat, his dish is not a stew. Now his is the first establishment other than inns and taverns to offer a menu with a choice of dishes.

———

1768. A nine-year-old Scottish boy called Robbie Burns is the eldest son of a poor peasant tenant. His mother earns extra cash by making soft white cheese. Young Robbie exists on fish, cheese, potatoes, and oatmeal.

———

1770. Captain Cook has claimed the East Coast of Australia for Britain. To counteract scurvy on board during the long voyage he has introduced lime and lemon juice, carrot marmalade, sauerkraut (cabbage preserved in brine, an unpopular food due to its German origins), and brewers' malt extract.

In Australia aborigines are cooking bat and lizard meat. Kangaroo-tail soup is considered a delicacy.

———

1773. Captain Cook discovers Easter Island, New Caledonia, and Norfolk Island and ends up in the Antarctica ice. The portable soup, which is sustaining him and his crew on this three-year voyage, is made from pease flour and the long boiling of the most rotten parts of the meat so that it is reduced to the consistency of glue. Some sailors are refusing to eat this concoction and are being flogged.

1775. Dr. Johnson publishes *Journey to the Western Isles of Scotland*, which records his visit with Boswell to Scotland. A lover of good food, he claimed whilst in the Hebrides "A cucumber should be well sliced and dressed with pepper and vinegar and then thrown out, as good for nothing." He dislikes fish as due to his poor eyesight he has to eat them with his fingers in order to locate the bones. His favorite dish, which he takes at the Cheshire Cheese inn off Fleet Street, is a vast pudding containing beefsteaks, kidneys, mushrooms, oysters, and larks. He once claimed, "There is nothing which has yet been contrived by man by which so much happiness is produced as by a good tavern or inn."

Louis XVI of France has reduced the tax on fish substantially to help the poor people and also encourage the rather lapsed observance of Lent.

1776. Adam Smith has published *Wealth of Nations*. Notoriously absent minded, the Scottish economist once put bread and butter in his teapot and brewed bread and butter. He deplores the English disdain of potatoes, a crop that has apparently proved its value as a food in Ireland.

1778. A young French agriculturist and chemist, Antoine Augustin Parmentier, has made it his mission to popularize the potato after his experience as prisoner of war in Prussia where potatoes were part of his diet. He is writing books and pamphlets to dispel the beliefs of many that potatoes cause leprosy and fevers and has even persuaded the queen, Marie Antoinette to wear

CHOCOLATE

THE Maya people who lived in Central
America from around AD 300-900 were
fond of liquid chocolate drinks with a foamy,
frothy top but the consumption of chocolate was
mainly restricted to the society's elite. The drink
was made by mixing the roasted, crushed cocoa
beans and ground maize with a little water.
Later the Aztecs made their own version of the
drink, indeed they considered the cocoa plant to
be so precious that they sometimes used it as
money. They called it "xocalatl" meaning warm
or bitter liquid. Cortez took the drink to Spain
where it remained a Spanish secret until the
middle of the seventeenth century when it spread
rapidly to France, Britain, and the rest of
Europe. In 1780 Irish chocolate-maker John
Hanan who was importing cocoa beans from the
West Indies into Dorchester, Massachusetts
opened the first American chocolate factory,
Walter Baker and Co., with the financial help
of American Dr. James Baker.

potato flowers to ornament her dress. Parmentier is achieving his goals; potato dishes are being created in great variety and the potato has become a delicacy enjoyed by the nobility. Meanwhile the French populace is coveting potatoes for themselves.

———————

1781. In the American War of Independence General George Washington forces the surrender of General Cornwallis at Yorktown. A planter at heart, he has wheaten bread made for his many European guests (but doesn't eat it himself). The general is fond of cracking Brazil nuts between his jaws, which is causing his teeth to loosen. His favorite dessert is trifle.

———————

1782. A French cook, Antoine Beauvilliers, has founded in Paris La Grande Taverne de Londres, the first luxury restaurant. His eating house is the first to list the dishes available on a menu and serve them at individual tables during fixed hours.

———————

1783. Catherine the Great annexes Crimea. The Russian Czar maintains her own hothouses, in which fresh vegetables and fruit are grown at substantial expense throughout the long frozen Russian winter.

———————

1788. King George III of England has his first attack of madness. The King and his queen eat sparingly; the King prefers plain fare such as bread and potatoes for supper whilst Queen Charlotte eats gruel. On seeing workmen tucking into plates of beans the King has decided to try some.

He is so impressed that he has decreed there should be an annual "bean-feast."

Marie Antoinette, the wife of Louis XVI of France, is being nicknamed the baker's wife after her husband distributed bread to the starving Parisians during the current bread shortage. On being told that the people had no bread to eat she has untactfully proclaimed "Qu'ils mangent de la brioche" ("let them eat cake)". The Queen has a sweet tooth; she loves meringues, even making them with her own hands. Marie Antoinette is also partial to a pastille stuffed with chocolate paste.

———

1789. After serving as ambassador in Paris, Thomas Jefferson has brought back with him to America ice cream, which he delights in serving to his guests. The statesman has also introduced to the Americans the joys of fried potatoes after sampling them in Paris. He describes them as "potatoes, fried in the French manner" with beefsteak. In addition he serves macaroni or spaghetti made by cutting rolled dough into strips, which are then rolled by hand into noodles.

———

1790. Marmalade is being made commercially in Britain for the first time by a Dundee trader, Robert Keeler. He had wrongly been sent an assignment of bitter oranges from Spain and his wife, an expert jam-maker, decided she could make use of them.

———

1791. The French revolutionary Robespierre is being criticized by his comrades for his luxurious tendencies as he has had pyramids of oranges served to guests. In northern Europe oranges are still a rarity; they are usually made into preserves, used for table decoration or offered as luxury gifts.

In France oxtail soup has been created as a result of slaughterhouses sending the ox hides to the tanneries without cleaning them, leaving on the tails. A French noble asked for a tail, which was willingly given to him, and he created the first oxtail soup. Now the tanners are charging for the tails because of the constant demand that has been created for them.

A Marie Harel, from the Auge region of Normandy, has developed a new cow's milk cheese by combining the method used in Normandy with that used in Brie. His daughter has set up herself up in the local village of Camembert to sell the cheeses.

1795. Napoleon Bonaparte, who at the age of 25 is already a general in charge of the French army of the interior, has offered a prize for a practical way of preserving food for his marching army.

The Italian Giacomo Casanova in his prime achieved the reputation as the world's greatest lover. Now tired and dejected, he is employed as a librarian by a wealthy Bohemian count. A gourmet, between his amorous adventures he would often make a detour to taste fine food such as Leipzig's skewered larks. He once invented a special vinegar to season hard-boiled eggs. The reputation of oysters and truffles as aphrodisiacs are largely down to him.

CHEESE

THE *last two thousand years has seen a number of different cheeses being introduced, including:*

❖ **AD 879.** *Gorgonzola, an Italian cows' milk (and sometimes goats' milk) cheese, was named after the village of Gorgonzola which is north east of Milan. The soft cheese developed from the migration of cattle from the Alps to the south of the plains of Po. Tired from their journey the cattle rested in Gorgonzola.*

❖ **AD 900.** *In Gruyères, a small town in the Swiss Alps, cheese was made in pots that cooked over small piles of burning wood from the forest. When cheese makers needed to buy more firewood, they would use their cheese as payment. Recognizing the connection between the cheese and the forest, the cheese makers named their product Gruyère, which was not only the name of their village but also the Swiss word for "forest."*

❖ **1050.** *Parmesan cheese was developed in Parma in north Italy.*

❖ **1411.** *Charles VI of France gave sole rights to the ageing of Roquefort cheese to the village of Roquefort-sur-Soulzon.*

❖ **1722.** *The blue veined cheese, Stilton, took its name from the village of Stilton, Huntingdonshire on the Great North Road, though it wasn't made there. The coaches traveling from London to Scotland and the northern cities often stayed at the Bell Inn, a coaching-house inn in the village of Stilton, where Stilton was sold. The village became the center market place for the cheese with thousands being sold every week.*

1796. *American Cookery* by Amelia Simmons of New Haven is the first American cookbook. Although it borrows from English cookbooks and is only 47 pages long, it is the first cookbook to recognize and use American wares and customs. For instance, she has included the first recipes using corn meal as the basic ingredient and has combined English baking techniques and local ingredients to create "Pompkin" pie.

Simmons is the first cookbook author to suggest a stuffed turkey recipe and that cranberries be eaten with roast turkey.

In Britain a new pudding, apple charlotte, has been created. The name has been bestowed in honor of Queen Charlotte, a patron of apple growers.

1800. A new thinner type of pasta, spaghetti, is being produced on a large scale in Naples, with the aid of wooden screw presses, the long strings are then hung out to dry in the sun.

Chutney, from the Hindustani *chatni*, meaning strong spices has been discovered and enthusiastically adopted by the British in India.

1801. Joseph Berchoux, a French solicitor, has written a long poem in four cantos entitled *Gastronomie ou L'Homme des Champs a Table*. This is the first use of the word "gastronomie" in the French language.

1802. Franz Achard, a Prussian chemist and former student of Andreas Marggraf, has perfected an industrial process for the extraction of sugar from beet and has established the first sugar factory, in Kunern, Silesia, Germany with the encouragement of Frederick William III of Prussia.

1803. 28-year-old Jane Austen has sold her first novel, *Northanger Abbey*, to publishers for £10. Typically for this time, her parson father who is of moderate means, farms a small holding where he keeps cows, pigs, and sheep and grows wheat for making bread. Her mother keeps fowl and looks after the orchards, herbs, and vegetables. She has taught her daughters how make butter, cheese, jams, and pickles as well as how to cure bacon and hams.

1804. The visionary English artist and poet William Blake has written his poem *Jerusalem*. If his wife Catherine thinks that her eccentric husband is spending too much time with his visions and angels and not enough earning his daily bread then at mealtime she places an empty plate at his end of the table.

Napoleon proclaims himself emperor, and is crowned Napoleon I by Pope Pius VII. His code of French civil law is forced on all conquered countries. Napoleon eats very rapidly; he never takes more than 20 minutes to finish a meal, often eating with his fingers. He usually finishes long before anyone else. Sometimes he eats in reverse order starting with a sweet and finishing with a starter. The sweet-toothed emperor is very fond of licorice – indeed his teeth are almost permanently black from chewing it.

Before the French Revolution, aristocratic French households maintained luxurious culinary arrangements, but the Revolution reduced the number of private households offering employment. Consequently many chefs and cooks have found employment in eating establishment kitchens or have opened their own restaurant, of which there are currently 500 in Paris alone. Many of these are winning devoted followers among the French bourgeois, who are eager to display their elevated tastes in food and fashion.

1806. The British Prime Minister William Pitt dies, crushed by the overthrow of his coalition against Napoleon. Very fond of veal pies his last words included "I think I could eat one of Bellamy's meat pies."

Britain's first curry house, the Hindostanee Coffee House, has opened in Portman Square, London. The owner, Dean Mahomet is an Indian and is known as Mr Vindaloo.

1810. 15 years earlier, Nicholas-Francois Appert, a French maker of conserves of fruit, heard about the government prize being offered for improved methods of preserving food. On hearing of this potential reward, Appert started experimenting with cooking food in open kettles, then sealing it into glass jars using waxed cork bungs, wired into place. The jars were then heated by submersion in boiling water for varying lengths of time. Using this method he has succeeded in preserving dairy products, fruits, jellies, juices, marmalades, and vegetables and is now claiming the 12,000 franc prize. He has published a book, *Art de Conserver*, which has generously made his process available to all.

John "Johnny Appleseed" Chapman, a frontier missionary, having earlier started collecting apple seeds from cider presses in western Pennsylvania, has now embarked on a long trek westward, walking barefoot, planting a series of apple nurseries from Pennsylvania to central Ohio and beyond. He is selling away thousands of seedlings to pioneers, resulting in many acres of productive apple orchards.

1812. Nicholas-Francois Appert is using the prize money he won to establish the first commercial cannery, the House of Appert, at Massy. He is using jars and bottles as his containers.

Meanwhile, in England Bryan Donkin, a versatile British industrialist, has set up a factory for preserved foods for the Royal Navy. He is using the heat-sterilization process invented by Appert to produce tin canisters made of iron coated with tin to pack canned meats, soups, and vegetables.

Sam Wilson, a meat-packer from Troy, New York is shipping meat to the government. It is being stamped "U.S. Beef." Soldiers fighting in the current war with Great Britain are beginning to call this beef Uncle Sam's beef.

Thomas Jefferson has planted some of the first Brussels sprouts in America. A remarkably progressive Virginia farmer as well as statesman, Jefferson also grows tomatoes at his Monticello home, not to eat but as a curiosity. Not many

DIET ON BOARD A SLAVE TRADER

THE conditions on board ships carrying slaves from Africa to Europe or North America were disgraceful. The unfortunate slaves on board were fed twice a day, at eight o'clock in the morning and four in the afternoon, mainly with boiled rice and yams with beans boiled to the consistency of a pulp and sometimes a small quantity of beef or pork. If they refused to eat their unappetizing fare hot coals were put on a shovel and placed so near their lips as to scorch and burn them, and if they persisted in refusing to eat they could be forced to swallow these coals.

Many of these unfortunate slaves ended up running the kitchens on southern plantations, and they played a major role in inspiring much of its cuisine. Amongst the dishes and cooking techniques they introduced were hot, spicy sauces, frying grains and vegetables into fritters, and boiling leafy green vegetables.

colonists realize tomatoes are edible, indeed many Americans still fear tomatoes to be poisonous.

Britain's first curry house, the Hindostanee Coffee House has not proved a success, the menu is not popular and many have been misled, as despite the restaurant's name, it does not sell coffee.

The poet Lord Byron finds it repulsive to watch women eat. He has been enjoying a growing romance with a visiting Italian opera singer called "La Pulcella." However, he is being put off his stroke by watching her devour enormous dinners. Night after night he sees her fill her mouth with chicken wings, custards, peaches, and sweetbreads.

1813. The writer Jane Austen's main contribution to the household is preparing breakfast. The sweet-toothed writer has written in a letter "Good apple pies are a considerable part of our domestic happiness." She also writes, "You know how interesting the purchase of a sponge cake is to me."

The rebellious poet Percy Shelley has written a poem, 'Queen Mab', in which he declares the only hope for this world lies in reason, nature, virtue, and vegetarianism. Shelley vehemently disapproves of meat eating as it is an unnatural habit producing disease. He claims that as humans don't have the teeth that predator animals have it is normal to assume we should not eat animal food. The poet, who would be happy to just live on bread, believes people should consume only the food produced in their own native country because they are raised in that natural environment and are adapted to it. Consequently he refuses to use Indian spices amongst other foreign foods.

––––––––––

1814. Currently in the Western world there are a variety of methods for making toast, such as putting bread on multi-purpose toasting forks and holding it over a fire. Alternatively ornate, hinged bread holders can be attached to the side of a fireplace and swung into the flame.

––––––––––

1815. Jane Austen has included the first literary mention of soft-boiled eggs in her new book *Emma* when the heroine's father, Mr. Woodhouse, announces that "an egg boiled soft is not unwholesome."

The Duke of Wellington has defeated Napoleon at the Battle of Waterloo. His number one rule is to look after his men's stomachs. The Duke himself is indifferent to food.

The Congress of Vienna is held to discuss the reconstruction of Europe after the Napoleonic wars. Charles-Maurice de Talleyrand, representing France, proclaims Brie the king of cheeses at a dinner during the congress. This is in response to the Austrian foreign minister Prince Von Metternich identifying his pastry cook's rich chocolate sponge cake as the king of cakes. Talleyrand is a connoisseur of good food and his banquets are legendary. The French politician carves the meat and poultry himself and serves his guests according to their status.

The heir to the English throne, Prince George, has employed Marie-Antoine Carême, currently the most celebrated chef

THE DIET OF
COLONIAL AMERICANS

AMERICAN food began to distinguish itself from its European and British origins at the end of the eighteenth century. Cooks were creating new recipes reflecting the use of the continent's many native ingredients, such as cranberries, maize, and squash. There was soon an abundant and varied American cuisine.

In seventeenth- and eighteenth-century Europe grain was used mainly to bake bread. Americans, however, had enough land to feed their grain to animals, then eat the animals, instead of the grain. Pigs in particular were kept in abundance; their meat could easily be preserved as bacon, ham, or salt pork. The day began with breakfast, then dinner, the main meal, was taken midway through the afternoon and there was a simple supper in the evening. Dinner generally had two courses, each of which combined meat, fish, puddings, vegetables, savory and sweet pies with jellies, preserves, and pickles. By the end of the century the courses became more recognizable: most of the meat dishes being served in the first course and sweet dishes such as the popular apple pie, fruit, and cheese for the second course.

around. The sumptuous food being cooked for him is giving the prince almost permanent indigestion. The gargantuan excesses of Prince George greatly exceed any other royals.

1816. A Cape Cod, Massachusetts farmer, Henry Hall, has noticed that cranberries are larger and juicier where a layer of sand from the dunes blows over the vines. He is using this sand layering technique for his cranberries and is their first cultivator.

1818. The British industrialist Bryan Donkin's factory is producing cans of preserved meat and vegetable soup by the thousands and he is now an established naval supplier. Unfortunately no one has invented a device for prying off the lids so people have to use a hammer and chisel.

1819. Lord Byron publishes the first part of his epic poem, *Don Juan*. Inclined to put on weight, fearful of getting fat, for days on end he refuses most dinner invitations. During this period all he eats are biscuits and soda water, chewing tobacco to keep his mind off hunger and occasionally treating himself to a mixture of fish, greens, potatoes, or rice drowned in vinegar. (He takes vinegar to lessen his appetite.) The poet has adopted original slimming strategies; for instance he has been known to play cricket in half-a-dozen waistcoats.

1823. In the early days of colonial Australia most of the cooking is improvised. Pieces of meat, especially kangaroo meat, are jammed on sticks and cooked over an open fire.

In Japan a man named Hanaya Yohei has conceived of the idea of fresh, sliced, raw seafood, served on small fingers of vinegared rice – an instant improvement on the more traditional sushi dishes. The stall he has opened in the bustling Ryogoku district of Edo has caught on at once.

1824. Four years after a man from Nantes, Joseph Colin, had the idea for canning sardines in oil, the first sardine canning factory starts business there.

1825. George Stephenson is appointed engineer of the Stockton and Darlington Railway, the world's first public railway. The talented engineer once invented a cucumber straightener, a transparent glass tube open at one end in which a half-grown cucumber is placed and as it continues to grow it straightens.

1827. In Sansepolcro, Tuscany, Italy, Giulia Buitoni is turning her talent for making exceptional homemade pasta into a business. She has mortgaged two tracts of land and pawned her only heirloom, a pearl necklace, so that she can buy a few basic machines, adapted to make pasta. Her Buitoni pasta, made from high quality durum wheat semolina, is already receiving much praise.

1828. Poor Mexicans of San Antonio in Texas are eating a spicy stew of pork or beef, pinto beans, and chillies which they call chili con carne. "Con carne" means with meat.

The Cross brothers of Montpelier, Vermont, USA are producing unsweetened dry cracker biscuits. Shopkeepers are giving them away to customers buying cheese; a barrel of 1,200 crackers provides a year's worth of snacks and meals for many a rural family. Farmers are supping on these crackers crumbled in a bowl of milk and served with a chunk of Cheddar cheese.

1829. After the initial failure of his opera *William Tell* the Italian composer Gioachino Rossini has given up writing opera and decided to concentrate on cooking. He has already produced some inventive recipes such as thrush and chestnut soup and has devised a way of stuffing macaroni with *foie gras* by means of a silver syringe.

1830. The first pizza shop, Port 'Alba, has opened in Naples. The oven in which the pizzas at Port 'Alba are being cooked is lined with lava from Mount Vesuvius.

1831. A Leicestershire pie-maker, Edward Adcock, had the idea of transporting pork pies to London. In the capital they are becoming fashionable among the hunting fraternity, who have developed a liking for the portable, pocket-sized snacks on the annual Melton Mowbray foxhunt.

KETCHUP

K ETCHUP, or catsup, originated in China
in 1690 as a pickled fish sauce called
ke-tsiap. British sailors took Asian catsup or
ketchup from Singapore to England but the
British were unable to duplicate the recipe so
they started substituting other ingredients,
including ground mushrooms, walnuts, and
cucumbers. Later the first recipe for "tomato
catsup" appeared.

1832. Lorenzo Delmonico has arrived in New York from Switzerland and has opened a restaurant, Delmonico's, which aims to introduce European standards to New Yorkers.

Charles Darwin, a naturalist, is part of a surveying voyage around the world aboad the *Beagle*. He has described the meat of the agouti, a South American rodent, as "the very best meat I ever tasted."

1835. Sylvester Graham is an American Presbyterian minister who mainly preaches nutrition and wants to reform the eating habits of America and the world. He advocates vegetarianism and the use of only coarse, wholegrain flour. He also strongly recommended the reduction, if not total exclusion, of fats from one's daily diet. As a clergyman, he is deeply convinced that such a diet will bring man nearer to God. Graham has reached this conviction as the result of a bout of sickness he suffered. On his recovery, he gave much thought to the influence of diet on man's state of health and he has become a promoter of vegetarianism, stressing the advantage of eating a sufficient amount of roughage. The minister is embarking on a campaign to induce people to eat cereals and bread baked from coarse grain. Preferably, he suggests, the bread should be stale, as this will aid digestion.

Sir Marcus Sandys, a native of Worcestershire, returns from India with a recipe for Worcestershire sauce including a secret ingredient. He commissions a Worcester pharmacy owned by John Lea and William Perrins to produce it. The mixture is inedible and the jars have been placed to one side.

1836. Charles Dickens publishes his first novel, *Pickwick Papers*. His wife, Kate, is a lavish cook; Dickens loves good food and is especially partial to "lamb chops breaded with plenty of ketchup."

———————

1838. John Lea and William Perrins have rediscovered the jars of their Worcestershire Sauce, and have found that with maturity the taste has improved. They have brought the recipe from Sir Marcus Sandys, and have started manufacturing it. To help promote it they have arranged for cases of their sauce to be on all ocean liners that come in and out of British waters. They have paid the stewards to serve the sauce in the dining rooms, which is leading to passengers requesting to buy a bottle of this new appealing sauce to take home. The fame of Worcestershire Sauce is spreading very quickly indeed.

Sylvester Graham, now America's premier health-food promoter is traveling the country far and wide denouncing meat, potatoes, and pastries and extolling the benefits of fruits, vegetables, and bread made with only wholegrain, unrefined wheat flour. Bakers and butchers whose businesses he is threatening frequently harass him. He has developed Graham bread, a natural, wholegrain bread, which is proving successful. It is the first internationally consumed bread.

Charles Dickens makes the first reference to fried fish when he refers to a "fried fish warehouse" in *Oliver Twist*.

———————

1839. During the first Opium War, the Chinese believe the interruption of Chinese rhubarb exports will incapacitate British soldiers because of constipation. Their ploy is failing.

1840. In Britain, Anna, the seventh Duchess of Bedford, has introduced the idea of afternoon tea. Because the noon meal had become skimpier, and there was no other meal until eight o'clock dinner, the duchess used to suffer from "a sinking feeling" at about four o'clock in the afternoon. Adopting the European tea service format, she invited friends to join her for an additional afternoon meal at five o'clock in her rooms at Belvoir Castle. The menu included ham, tongue, or beef sandwiches, small cakes, assorted sweets, and tea. This summer practice proved so popular, the duchess having returned to London, is sending cards to her friends asking them to join her for "tea and a walking the fields."

Queen Victoria and Prince Albert marry. A giant wheel of Cheddar cheese has been given to the Queen for a wedding gift. It weighs 1,200 pound and two Somerset villages combined to make it. Their wedding cake is 9 feet around, weighs 300 pounds, and is 14 inches high.

In the U.S. Martin Van Buren, while campaigning for a second term of presidency, is said by his opponents to "wallow in raspberries," a shocking extravagance.

In Britain turkey is beginning to replace goose as the main Christmas dish. Only the white breast turkey meat is considered good enough for guests for their Christmas meal, the dark meat of the turkey legs is given to the servants or eaten by the family on the days after Christmas.

1841. In New York Delmonico's is now a chain of restaurants. Its fresh foods, large menu, and long hours are becoming widely copied innovations that are promoting a restaurant culture in American cities.

Prince Albert has longed to bring the familiar German Christmas observances of his youth to the British court. Albert is also extremely partial to the rich plum pudding he was served in England and Queen Victoria, as always, desires to please him. The resulting opulent Christmas table combines his German biscuits, special gingerbreads, and goose with the British boar's head and mince pies. The flamed pudding is given a place of honor.

1843. John Woodger, a fish merchant from north-east England, has after years of experimenting developed smoked kippers. He originally got the idea after the wooden shed in which he'd left some salted herring caught fire; the fish was rescued and found to be tasty.

1844. Joseph Turner paints *Rain, Steam and Speed*. The English landscape artist is discriminating when it comes to salads. Presented with one at his table, he comments to his neighbor "nice cool green, that lettuce, isn't it? And the beetroot pretty red – not quite strong enough; and the mixture delicate tint of yellow, Add some mustard and then you have one of my pictures."

VEGETARIANISM FROM THE THIRTEENTH TO THE NINETEENTH CENTURY

FROM the thirteenth to seventeenth centuries, when meat was largely a scarce and expensive luxury for the rich, an open vegetarian ideology was a rare phenomenon. Indeed, by the beginning of the eighteenth century it was common to torture animals before killing them in the mistaken belief it improved their taste in the cooking process. With the Enlightenment there arose a new assessment of man's place in the order of creation and moral objections were raised at the mistreatment of animals. In parallel with this many radical Christians were giving the cause of non-flesh eating great impetus in Britain.

They included John Wesley, the founder of Methodism, who believed in its health aspects. In 1809, the Reverend William Cowherd, the founder of the Bible Christian Church in Salford, asked his congregation to abstain from meat eating. One of his followers, a Mrs. Brotherton, published the first vegetarian cookery book in 1812. Two others of his followers, the Reverend James Clark and the Reverend William Metcalfe, emigrated to the United States in 1817 with 39 other members of the Bible Christian Church and formed the nucleus of a vegetarian movement in America. By the 1830s vegetarian communes were evident in the USA.

Alexandre Dumas writes *The Three Musketeers*. The French author loves melons so much, he once proposed to give to the municipal council of Cavaillon all of his present and future publications in exchange for "a life annuity of twelve melons per year."

───────────

1845. In Ireland, the potato crop fails. Potatoes are the mainstay of the diet of poor peasants, and the failure of the crop is affecting millions.

Eliza Acton's *Modern Cookery for Private Families*, published in London, is the first basic cookbook written for the housewife, rather than the trained chef with a full staff. Many people are calling this elegant, clearly written volume the greatest cookery book ever written in the English language. It includes the first recipe for Brussels sprouts.

───────────

1846. Belgian street vendors are selling thin fried potatoes called "Belgian fries" from pushcarts and now the French have adapted the idea and their version are known as "French fries".

George Sand writes her novel *La Mare au Diable (The Devil's Pool)*. She is fond of the sheep's trotters served at Magny's in Paris. A cordon bleu cook, the French novelist is particularly partial to chavignol (a soft goats' milk cheese).

───────────

1847. Fry and Sons of Bristol, under the leadership of the founder Joseph Fry's great-grandson, has discovered a way to mix some of the melted cacao butter back into de-fatted, cocoa powder (along with sugar) to create a paste that can be pressed into a mold. The resulting chocolate bar is, despite its bittersweet taste, such a hit that people are soon began to think of eating chocolate as much as drinking it.

The Bible Christian organization has taken the lead in establishing the first national vegetarian society which is formed at Ramsgate, England. At its inaugural meeting the word "vegetarian" is coined. The word should not be confused with the word "vegetable," it is derived from the Latin *vegetus*, meaning whole, vigorous, active. Meanwhile, in America the teenage Louisa Alcott's father is exchanging vegetarian recipes with his friends the essayists Ralph Emerson and Henry Thoreau.

The first novels by Emily and Charlotte Bronte, *Jane Eyre* and *Wuthering Heights*, are published. The Bronte sisters are keen on berries. They drink elderberry wine and like to eat blackberries, gooseberries, and elderberries.

1848. An expansive marketing campaign by a Pennsylvania tomato canning factory includes sending samples to the American President Polk and Queen Victoria. As a result of this campaign tomatoes are beginning to gain acceptance in America and Britain.

In Ireland, the potato crop crisis caused by late blight and the ensuing famine is extreme. The famine, which started three years ago, has devastated the crop and is depopulating the island. Some 750,000 people have died and over one million have emigrated, most of them to the United States. There is now a more cautious attitude toward dependence on potatoes.

Franz Joseph is arguing with his cook when he is told his father has abdicated and he is now Emperor of Austro-Hungary. His first words as ruler are: "I am the emperor and I want dumplings."

1849. The first self-service restaurants are appearing in San Francisco during the California gold rush. A selection of free food is being placed on the counter in saloons.

In Britain and its empire, the practice of the Duchess of Bedford, of inviting friends to come for tea in the afternoon, has been picked up by other social hostesses. Afternoon tea is becoming a daily social occasion for the aristocracy and buttered scones have become an important part of this fashionable "taking tea" ritual.

1851. The first cheese factory to make cheese from scratch has been started in Rome, New York by Jesse Williams. He is combining the milk from various dairy herds including his own to make one large cheese with unvaried taste and texture so he can manufacture large quantities. Other smaller companies use smaller batches of homemade cheese curd to produce cheeses with wide differences in taste and texture from one another.

1852. A part Native American chef George Crum has invented potato crisps. He did it by accident, thanks to a fussy customer. Industrialist Commodore Cornelius Vanderbilt came to the Moon Lake House Hotel in Saratoga Springs, New York, and ordered "thinner than normal

French fried potatoes." He kept sending them back to Crum, protesting that they were too thick. Finally, out of spite the chef sliced the potatoes paper-thin, so that he wouldn't be able to eat them with a fork, then fried them to a crisp in oil, and splashed salt on them. Vanderbilt loved them. These "potato crunches" as Crum calls them are now a regular feature of the hotel's menu.

1853. Chicken meat and eggs are now mass-production commodities in Britain. Previously eggs were only laid in summer and were uniformly white in color. The arrival of Asian breeds of hens that produce large brown eggs 12 months in the year is revolutionizing British attitudes to poultry.

Cans used by the British Army in the Crimean War are large and very heavy and a hammer and chisel are needed to open them.

1856. In Britain, the streets are flowing with traders selling baked potato, meat pudding, fried fish, hot eels, pickled whelks, oysters, trotters, and pea soup. There are 500 London traders in hot eels alone.

1858. In America Ezra J. Warner has patented the world's first can opener, a cross between a bayonet and a sickle.

A 13-year-old French peasant girl, Bernadette, sees the first of her visions of Mary at Lourdes. She exists on mashed corn, the staple diet of the poorest, with occasional slices of wheat bread.

DIET OF AMERICAN PIONEERS

A TYPICAL *emigrant wagon set off for the west with provisions of flour, sugar, bacon, salt pork and beef jerky, beans, lard, spices, dried fruit, beans, rice, and perhaps even a keg of pickles (a popular and tasty choice for warding off the dangers of malnutrition). Trail cooks were not well trained and the food often consisted of barely warm beans or tough stew served with sourdough biscuits.*

Friendly Native Americans taught pioneers crossing the American desert how to cook insects.

Some pioneers fried Rocky Mountain locusts in oil until crisp then seasoned them with salt.

Once they had set up a home most obtained their fresh meat such as venison, wild turkey, squirrel, or fresh fish by hunting. However, once game was killed, it almost immediately had to be prepared or preserved. In summer months, meat could go bad in an afternoon.

In the mid-West corn was the most commonly used dietary ingredient. Corn meal in varying

forms was the basis of many meals such as
"hoe-cake," which was meal plus a shortening
of bear grease, butter, or lard, baked flat on
a board.

One basic food source for almost every settler
was the "kitchen garden." Frontier families
brought seeds with them to their new homes, or
bought them from the general store once they
arrived on the frontier. A spring garden would be
planted containing peas and radishes; later in
the summer beans, pumpkins, and squash would
be grown.

Lack of supplies and cash led to a great deal of
improvising as women tried to cook familiar
recipes with unfamiliar materials. Instead of
lemon, vinegar would be used and treacle
substituted for sugar.

Fur traders and trappers, when necessary, could
survive for days on berries and tubers. However,
they mainly ate meat which came from hunting
large game animals such as antelope, buffalo,
and deer; small game was less important
because it was seldom worth the effort. The meat
was roasted or boiled or sometimes even eaten
raw; boiled or roasted beaver tail was
considered a delicacy.

1860. One of the consequences of the Industrial Revolution is that adulteration of food has become big business. As a result the British Parliament has passed the Adulteration of Food and Drink Act, the first food legislation law. This is designed to prevent the widespread practice of corrupting expensive foods with inexpensive substances. Examples are the addition of chalk to flour and the sweet tasting but poisonous lead acetate to sugar. Powdered bones are frequently found in ground pepper.

The Italian patriot Giuseppe Garibaldi, a one-time spaghetti salesman, and his Red Shirts have seized Naples from the Austrians. In Britain his episodes are acclaimed to such an extent a biscuit has been named after him.

In London Joseph Malin has opened the first fish and chip shop in Cleveland Street, Bow.

Napoleon III of France has made a commercial treaty with Great Britain, which has opened France up to free trade. The emperor is particularly fond of barley sugar sweets, which are now very fashionable because of his liking for them. While passing through the Vallee d'Auge region of Normandy, Napoleon tasted the local Camembert cheese and found it delicious. He has named it after the village in Normandy in which the creator of the cow's milk cheese, Marie Harel, lived.

1861. In Britain *Beeton's Book of Household Management*, which contains recipes, diet and menu plans, and practical advice on running a home, has been published to great acclaim. The author Mrs. Isabella Beeton is an attractive 25-year-old wife of a publisher and the eldest of 21 children and her groundbreaking book costing 7s 6d is making her a household name. It was originally published in monthly parts as a supplement to the *Englishwoman's Domestic Magazine*, a woman's magazine founded by her husband and filled with recipes sent in by readers from around the world. It is now appearing in a single volume and already in its first year it has sold over 50,000 copies.

The first appearance of a jellybean is in an advertisement for William Schrafft of Boston that promotes the sending of jellybeans to soldiers in the Union Army. The jellybean center is a descendent of the Mid-Eastern sweet, Turkish delight, which dates back to biblical times. The shell coating is an offspring of a process called panning, first invented in seventeenth-century France to make Jordan almonds.

1862. In America jellybeans are quickly earning a place amongst the many glass jars of "penny candy" in general stores where they are sold by weight and taken home in paper bags.

1863. Abraham Lincoln gives his Gettysburg address after the Battle of Gettysburg, which has turned the American Civil War. The thin and gaunt president cares nothing for food and has to be prodded to eat; however, he enjoys entertaining and he and his wife Mary give large dinner parties.

Many Civil War soldiers are suffering from "camp diarrhea." A Dr. James Henry Salisbury has devised a "meat cure" advocating they be fed a diet of chopped beef patties cut from disease-free animals' muscle fibers. He is recommending this same diet for all Americans, advising them to eat beef three times a day for health benefits.

Dr. James C. Jackson is a follower of the Seventh Day Adventists, who wish to avoid consumption of animal foods, and of health food nutritionist Sylvester Graham. At the Western Health Reform Institute in Battle Creek, Michigan, Jackson has created the first ready-to-eat breakfast cereal, which he is calling "Granula." Granula is wholegrain flour dough baked into dry loaves, broken into chunks and baked again, and then ground into still smaller chunks. But it is far from convenient; it has to be soaked overnight before it is even possible to chew the dense, bran-heavy nuggets.

1864. The popularity of chips in England is on the increase as a result of fish and chip shops such as Joseph Malin's in London. The previous year a Mr. Lees opened the first fish and chip shop in the north of England. He is selling fish and chips from a wooden hut in the market at Mossely, near Oldham, Lancashire.

Queen Victoria has adopted the new craze for tea parties. The Queen and her ladies adopt formal dress for the afternoon teas. The Victoria sandwich cake, named after her, is one of the queen's favorites.

1865. In New York City's Bowery district, German immigrants are selling from pushcarts "dachshund sausages." They often place them in a milk roll with a serving of sauerkraut and mustard on top.

In England for the first time the cost of white bread has dropped below that of brown bread. A contributing factor is the frequent dilution of white bread flour with meal made from other cereals or vegetable seeds.

1866. Domestic can openers are being made in America. They are called Bull's Head tin openers, as they have a cast-iron handle shaped into a bull's head and tails and are sold with tins of beef.

1867. In Vevey, Switzerland, Henri Nestlé has been working on a concentrated infant food formula, which requires that he find a way to treat milk so that it would not spoil while in storage but can be quickly reconstituted for use. The result of his efforts is a nutritious sweetened condensed milk product for babies that can be used by mothers who are unable to breast feed.

Karl Marx writes the first volume of *Das Kapital* in London. The Marx family likes to picnic on Hampstead Heath but they are not well off and they are often forced to survive on bread and potatoes.

Charles Ranhofer, the chef of the famous Delmonico's restaurant in New York, has created a new sponge cake covered in ice cream to celebrate the American purchase of

AMERICAN FIRSTS

H*ERE is a selection of American firsts:*

❖ **1548.** *Mexican green chili peppers were introduced to New Mexico from Mexico.*

❖ **1565.** *The Spanish established the first permanent settlement at St. Augustine, Florida. At St Augustine there was the first introduction of cattle, horses, pigs, and sheep into North America.*

❖ **1643.** *The first American restaurant opened in Boston.*

❖ **1711.** *Pretzels arrived in America with the first German and Dutch immigrants to settle in Pennsylvania.*

❖ **1763.** *Oysters were served to the public in America for the first time when a primitive saloon opened in New York City in a basement in Broad Street.*

❖ **1769.** *Spanish missionaries introduced the orange to California.*

❖ **1776.** *The first ice cream parlor in America opened in New York City.*

- ❖ **1790.** *Pineapples were introduced to Hawaii.*

- ❖ **1823.** *A Frenchman, Count Odette Phillipe, planted the first grapefruit trees in Safety Harbor near Tampa, Florida.*

- ❖ **1837.** *The sandwich was introduced to America in a cookbook by Elizabeth Leslie. A recipe for ham sandwiches was suggested as a main dish.*

- ❖ **1851.** *The first large-scale commercial ice cream plant was established in North America in Baltimore, Maryland, by Jacob Fussell.*

- ❖ **1866.** *George Busch and Lorenzo Dow Baker carried the first cargo of West Indian bananas to America.*

Alaska from the Russians. It was, at first, called Alaska-Florida cake, but has now been changed to baked Alaska.

_____

1868. Maria Ann Smith, a gardener who emigrated to Australia from England a few years ago, has developed a new apple. An all-purpose apple with green skin, firm, crisp flesh, and a tart flavor, they are named Granny Smith apples after her. She is selling them with great success on the Sydney markets.

The buffalo has been decimated east of the Mississippi River, thus removing a major source of meat. The extension of railroads across the Great Plains has led to the destruction of the huge herds that foraged on the vast grasslands there. One hunter alone, William F. Cody who is nicknamed "Buffalo Bill," has killed 4,280 animals in 18 months while supplying buffalo meat for railroad construction crews.

In America General Ulysses S. Grant is elected president. Grant is extremely fond of cucumbers and he frequently dines on just a sliced cucumber and a cup of coffee.

In America the first railway dining car (named Delmonico in honor of the New York restaurant) has been introduced. The introduction of the railway system throughout Britain and America means that food can now be carried hundreds of miles and arrive at its destination still fresh. In America the result of the national network of railroads is that meat and produce from the West and mid-West can be shipped to densely populated eastern cities.

_____

1869. A new cooking fat has been created by the French chemist Hippolyte Mège-Mouriès in response to a commission by the Emperor Louis Napoleon III for the production of a cooking fat for the French Navy that would be cheap and would keep well. To formulate his entry, Mège-Mouriès uses margaric acid, a fatty acid component that was isolated by the Frenchman Michael Chevreul over 50 years ago and named because of the lustrous pearly drops that reminded him of the Greek word for pearl, "margarites." He adds skimmed milk and water and a strip of udder to mimic the way butter fat forms in a calf's udder.

1870. In America a misplaced decimal point in a set of published food tables has made spinach appear to contain ten times more iron than other vegetables. This is creating the belief that spinach makes you strong.

Louis Pasteur has identified and produced germs and introduced the science of microbiology. His experiments with microbes involve work with rotten meat; the French chemist's laboratory is often filled with putrid smells. "Public usefulness ennobles the most disgusting work," he says. Pasteur is not an adventurous eater: every Thursday he consumes hot sausage garnished with red kidney beans, the other six days of the week he has a mutton cutlet with sautéed potatoes.

French canned bouilli (boiled) beef, is being fed to the French army in the Franco-Prussian War. It is ideal for soldiers on the move; they can eat it cold straight from the can.

During the Siege of Paris, the citizens are eating rats, which are sold for 10-15 sous each in the Place de L'Hotel de Ville.

Shortly after the McIlhenny family, who run the McIlhenny Company, returned to Avery Island, Louisiana, from self-imposed exile during the Civil War, Edmund McIlhenny obtained some hot pepper seeds from a traveler who had recently arrived in Louisiana from Central America. McIlhenny planted them on Avery Island, and then experimented with pepper sauces until he hit upon one he liked. He has now received a patent for his singular formula for processing peppers into a fiery red sauce. The family has created a brand name "Tabasco" for this new product.

A few weeks before his death Alexandre Dumas completes his 1152-page *Grand Dictionnaire de Cuisine*. A gourmet, Dumas often prepared his own salads seasoned with almond milk, a liqueur, or champagne.

1871. Giuseppe Verdi writes his opera *Aida*. When the composer needs inspiration, he has a bowl of noodle soup.

1872. Lewis Carroll, an Oxford don, publishes *Through the Looking Glass*, his follow-up to *Alice in Wonderland* in which he made several references complaining about dining hall food in Oxford. *Through the Looking Glass* contains the poem, 'Beautiful Soup' in chapter four.

"A loaf of bread," the walrus said

"Is what we chiefly need.

Pepper and vinegar besides

Are very good indeed."
The don does a great deal of entertaining and keeps a track of menus in his diary so that his guests will not have the same dishes too frequently.

Henry Tate, an English sugar merchant, has patented a method of cutting sugar into small cubes.

Three years ago, Charles A. Pillsbury bought a share in a Minneapolis flour mill. After the purchase of additional mills and several improvements to the milling process, his firm has now been reorganized as C.A. Pillsbury and Company.

George and Richard Cadbury, the sons of John Cadbury, are marketing the first box of chocolate candies, packed in a box decorated in the current sentimental Victorian style.

———

1873. In California the commercial potential of raisins has been discovered by accident. An unusually hot spell withered the grapes on the vine. One resourceful San Francisco grocer advertised these shriveled grapes as "Peruvian Delicacies" and these raisins have proved to be very popular.

In Britain sellers on the streets are selling a round and flat light textured roll called a muffin. These sellers carry trays of them on their heads, ringing a hand bell to call their wares.

———

1874. Hanson Gregory, a sea captain from Camden, Maine, has a passion for doughnuts which leads him to instruct the ship's cook to keep him constantly supplied on long voyages. During a brutal storm, Captain Gregory requires both hands to hold onto the ship's wheel. Unable to hold onto his

DIET IN WESTERN EUROPE IN THE LATE NINETEENTH CENTURY

IN Europe greater efficiency on farms and better food-distribution systems were preventing the onset of food shortages and famines. But although people rarely died from lack of food any more, this did not necessarily mean that they were well fed. The poor in towns and the countryside received food from charities to offset their hunger. In Britain falling food prices meant that meat, jam, and butter were making a more regular appearance on working men's tables.

Also dishes like shepherd's pie were becoming more widespread as mincing machines made the shredding of meat easy and popular. Meanwhile the rich enjoyed varied diets. Meals were often social events and new foods were being introduced at a phenomenal rate.

doughnuts, he pushes them onto the spokes of the wheel. Thus, the ringed doughnut is born.

In Paris horsemeat is all the rage. Apparently, the Parisians were forced to eat it during the Franco-Prussian War when beef was unavailable, and discovered they liked it.

Laws forbidding the sale of sweets and delicacies on Sunday have prompted William Garwood to invent the ice cream sundae in Evanston, Illinois. A mixture of ice cream and fruit coated with jam or syrup it can be served on the Sabbath with no fear of the law being broken.

1876. Queen Victoria becomes Empress of India. The Queen has an excessive liking for beef marrow, which she eats on toast for tea every day. She also enjoys roast beef and Yorkshire pudding followed by mind-numbingly cold ice cream. The Queen has decreed that only roast beef or mutton, followed by milk puddings, are suitable fare for her children and grandchildren. She loves picnics. After a gentle ramble around her Balmoral estate, she heads for a spot under the trees where an army of footmen and maids has set out the provisions on fine china, all on a white linen tablecloth.

Henry Heinz, a second generation German-American, in partnership with his brother and cousin, has founded a company at Sharpsburg, Pennsylvania to prepare and market horseradish. He is already mass-marketing the first commercially manufactured pickle products to the American public and is planning to make the first mass-produced and bottled tomato ketchup. Heinz Ketchup is exhibiting at the U.S.

Centennial Exposition in Philadelphia. Also at the exhibition many North Americans are getting their first taste of bananas. Each banana is wrapped in foil and sold for 10 cents.

Alexander Graham Bell is exhibiting his telephone at the exhibition. The Scottish inventor has the odd habit of drinking his soup through a glass straw.

1878. The German composer Johannes Brahms writes his *Violin Concerto in D Major*. The composer enjoys eating out in Vienna's cheap cafes and restaurants. Brahms falls ill and his doctor instructs him to go on a diet... "But this evening I'm dining with Strauss" he protests "and we shall have chicken paprika." "That's out of the question," the doctor tells him. "In that case" says the composer, "please consider that I did not come to consult you until tomorrow."

1879. During the 1860s, the Swiss chocolate manufacturer, Daniel Peter, tried repeatedly to create a chocolate bar flavored with milk, to lessen the bittersweet taste, but he couldn't manage to produce a smooth mixture of milk and chocolate. However, Henri Nestlé's sweetened condensed milk is turning out to be perfect for Peter's purposes; the low water content makes it possible to mix it with the pressed cocoa bean to create a chocolate bar that does not spoil and is less bittersweet. Peter and Nestlé have amalgamated to form a company – Nestlé.

Rodolphe Lindt of Berne, Switzerland has invented the "conching" machine that heats and rolls chocolate in order to refine it. After the chocolate has been conched for 72 hours and had more cocoa butter added to it, it is possible to create smoother and creamier forms of chocolate than before.

1880. The Empire Cheese Company of New York has begun producing Philadelphia Cream Cheese in its protective wrapper for a New York distributor called Reynolds.

A chipboard cheese box for housing Camembert cheese has been patented. Now these cheeses can be dispatched long distances and sales are taking off.

1882. The first consignment of mutton from New Zealand has arrived in Britain. The meat is presently the most eaten meat in British homes.

Thomas Edison designs the first hydroelectric plant, which puts electric light in the streets and houses in one square of New York. The inventor believes in a good hearty breakfast to work upon but doesn't eat much else apart from the occasional meal of sardines or lamb chops and vegetables. Most of the time his wife and children dine alone as Edison only eats when hungry. "A pound of food a day is all I need when I am working," he says. During a formal dinner Edison was finding the company to be so dreary that the inventor made up his mind to escape to his laboratory at the earliest opportunity. Unfortunately his host waylaid him as he lingered near the door. "It certainly is a pleasure to see you, Mr. Edison," he said. "What are you working on now?" "My exit" responded Edison.

Bouillon cubes, compressed, concentrated cubes of dehydrated meat or vegetable stock, are being made commercially by the Swiss flour manufacturer Julius Maggi. He is producing them so the poor living in city slums (who cannot afford meat) will have a cheap method for making nutritious soup.

1884. Having discovered the soda cracker in America the previous year William Jacob, the founder of W & R Jacob along with William & George Bewley, has launched Jacob's Cream Cracker in Dublin, Ireland. They are the first crackers to be packed in airtight containers.

General Gordon returns to Sudan to deal with Mohammed Ahmed (the Mahdi's) revolt. He takes a simple meal when alone, consisting of bread and milk or for variety bread soaked in a slop bowl of strong tea.

A new sponge cake made with apricot jam has been named a Battenberg cake in honor of the marriage of Queen Victoria's daughter Princess Victoria to Prince Louis of Battenberg.

1885. Only men are allowed to eat at the first self-service restaurant on the east coast of the U.S., the Exchange Buffet in New York. Customers eat standing up.

Mark Twain publishes *The Adventures of Huckleberry Finn*. One of Mark Twain's favorite meals is pan fried porterhouse steak with mushrooms and peas. The American novelist once quipped "A banquet is probably the most fatiguing thing in the world except ditch digging. It is the insanest of all recreations."

DIET OF COWBOYS

A NINETEENTH-CENTURY breakfast for an American cowboy included salt pork or bacon, and eggs, which, being shipped west for considerable distances, sometimes went bad. Dinner (the noontime meal) and supper were similar to breakfast, with the addition of beef and beans and canned or dried fruit for dessert. Cowboys everywhere liked fresh beef, especially steaks, fried well done in a cast iron skillet, piled high. Accompanying this would be soda biscuits made from sourdough, and gravy.

During cattle drives, cowboys often had to make do with less appealing cuts of meat such as pork butt, pork ribs, beef ribs, venison, and goat.

These tough pieces of meat were slow cooked at a low temperature for five to seven hours over wood or charcoal.

Charles Cretors of Chicago, Illinois invents the first popcorn machine, which he operates outside on the street. The bulky machine with its gasoline burner is becoming a familiar part of the outside scent.

Two years ago the German Chancellor Otto Bismarck was very bloated, over 17 stone, which made him ill and very bad tempered so for months he lived on a diet of herrings. Now he has made a full recovery, and is down to 14 stone.

1886. Oysters are plentiful and cheap in North America. Over 150 million lbs of oyster a year are being harvested and oystering supports large numbers of families. On the north eastern seaboard, the wealthy flock to eat in oyster houses. Other classes eat them up to three times a day at home or in oyster bars, oysters cellars, oyster houses, oyster parlors, oyster saloons, and oyster stalls. They are baked, fried, frittered, pickled, roasted, scalloped, stewed, skewed with bits of bacon, and used in puddings and soups.

Henry Heinz has sailed with his family to England. Included in his luggage is a Gladstone bag packed with "seven varieties of our finest and newest goods." In London, he calls on Fortnum & Mason, England's leading food purveyor, whose buyer tastes and promptly accepts all seven products for distribution. Now he sees the world as his market.

William Gladstone resigns as Prime Minister after his Irish Home Rule bill is defeated. He likes to entertain at breakfast guests from literature, politics, and the church, who turn up at 10.00 at Gladstone's home. Gladstone habitually chews each mouthful of food 32 times before swallowing it, one chew for each tooth.

1887. An 18-year-old South African Indian Mohandas Gandhi is sent to London to study law at the University College. He initially vowed to his mother that he would observe vegetarianism but at first he struggles, his friends warning him that it would wreck his studies as well as his health. Fortunately for him he comes across a vegetarian restaurant and he is able to feed himself amply rather than nearly starving himself. Vegetarian restaurants are becoming increasingly popular in London, offering cheap and nutritious meals in respectable settings.

1889. A baker called Raffaele Esposito of Pizzeria di Pietro from Naples, Italy has baked pizza especially for the visit of Italian King Umberto I and Queen Margherita. For one of the pizzas he has added ingredients representing the colors of the Italian flag, namely green (basil), white (mozzarella cheese), and red (tomato sauce). Despite normally being considered a peasant's meal this new pizza is favored by the Queen and it has been named Pizza Margherita in honor of her.

1890. The leader of the Salvation Army, William Booth, writes *In Darkest England and the Way Out*, which contains proposals for the physical and spiritual assistance of the great mass of down and outs. He writes, "A starving man cannot hear you preaching. Give him a bowl of soup and he will listen to every word."

George A. Bayle Junior, a St. Louis doctor and owner of a food products company, has developed peanut butter. The doctor had been looking for a nutritious protein substitute for his patients with bad teeth who can't chew meat and he had experimented by grinding peanuts in his hand-cranked meat grinder. Now he has mechanized the process and is selling peanut butter out of barrels for about 6 cents per pound.

A young Pole, Marie Curie, joins her sister Bronia in Paris studying at the Sorbonne. As a student in Paris young Marie is so poor and absorbed in her studies that she finds herself fainting through lack of food. Often her meals consist of buttered bread and tea.

The first cafeteria has been set up in the Y.W.C.A. in Kansas City, Montana. It provides cheap, self-service meals to working women and is modeled on a Chicago luncheon club for women where some aspects of self-service are already in practice.

Count Pavel Stroganov of St Petersburg is a noted gourmet as well as a friend of Czar Alexander III. A recipe called beef Stroganoff has been in the family for some years and has been brought to the notice of many due to the count's love of entertaining. A chef, Charles Briere, who is working in St. Petersburg, has now submitted the recipe to *L 'Art Culinaire*.

John Harvey Kellogg, a Seventh Day Adventist surgeon, is the superintendent of the Battle Creek Sanatorium. Kellogg is interested in nutrition, and he is earnestly striving to develop bran-rich foods that aren't too bland. A vegetarian, he wishes to replace meat on the breakfast table.

1892. In Russia there is a terrible famine and Leo Tolstoy has set up 370 kitchens feeding 16,000 daily. The great Russian novelist is now a strict vegetarian; he believes that meat is not a suitable diet for humans as it excites the mortal lusts and involves pain and death for animals. Tolstoy now exists mainly on oatmeal porridge, bread, and vegetable soup.

In Britain a new biscuit, Mcvitie's digestives, is being sold. It got its name because the baking soda in them is thought to be good for indigestion. They are mixed by hand, by hundreds of women using huge mixing bowls.

The previous year William Wrigley went to Chicago as a soap distributor and there he started offering baking powder as a premium with each box of soap. When baking powder proved to be more popular than soap, he switched to the baking powder business. Then one day Wrigley got the idea of offering two packages of chewing gum with each can of baking powder. The offer was a big success. Now he has decided that chewing gum is the product with the potential he has been looking for, so he has began marketing it under his own name.

1893. A Denver, Colorado lawyer, Henry Perky, who suffered from indigestion and had become converted to health foods, has invented a new product, Shredded Wheat biscuits, and a machine for making them. His original

HISTORY OF
CHEWING GUM

FOR centuries *Native Americans chewed
spruce tree resin, to ease hunger pains.
On arriving in the New World the colonists were
soon copying them.*

❖ **1848.** *State of Maine Spruce Gum, invented
by John B Curtis, was the first chewing gum
to be sold commercially in America. However,
it was not a success as its taste was too harsh
and its texture too tough.*

❖ **1850.** *John B. Curtis started selling flavored
paraffin gums, which were more popular than
spruce gums.*

❖ **1871.** *The Mexican president, General
Antonio Lopez de Santa Anna, who led the
sacking of the Alamo fortress in San Antonio,
was exiled in Staten Island, New York. He
asked his secretary Thomas Adams to find a*

substitute for rubber. Adams experimented with chicle and while he found it unsuitable as rubber, it was superior to all existing chewing gums and he started manufacturing it.

❖ **1872.** A dentist, William Semple, added sugar to chewing gum.

❖ **1880.** John Colgan, a druggist from Louisville, Kentucky, added licorice flavor to chicle, thus introducing flavored chewing gum.

❖ **1888.** The first practical vending machine was introduced selling the Thomas Adams' Tutti-Frutti brand of chewing gum on an elevated platform in a New York subway station.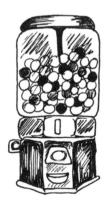

intention was to sell the machines, not the biscuits, which he gave out from a horse-drawn wagon in an attempt to market the idea. It was known at the time as The Cereal Machine Company. The biscuits proved more popular than the machines, however, so Perky has now opened his first bakery in Boston, Massachusetts.

———————

1894. After a long, hard night of partying, the New York Wall Street broker Lemuel Benedict confronts the Waldorf-Astoria *maitre d'hotel* and asks for the following hangover remedy: a piece of buttered toast topped with a poached egg, bacon, and hollandaise sauce. The *maitre d'hotel* complies but substitutes an English muffin for the toast, and ham for the bacon. So tasty is this combination the chef Oscar Tschirky has added this new recipe, called eggs Benedict, to the menu.

Mr. Milton Hershey, the owner of a candy company, became fascinated with German chocolate-making machinery on exhibit at the Chicago International Exposition the previous year. He bought the equipment for his Lancaster, Philadelphia plant and soon began producing his own chocolate coatings for caramels. Now the Hershey Chocolate Company has been created as a subsidiary of his Lancaster caramel business.

———————

1895. In South Africa Cecil Rhodes' ill-fated Jameson Raid ignites the Boer War. Once in answer to a question as to why he went to Africa, Rhodes replied it was because he "could no longer stand the eternal cold mutton."

John Harvey Kellogg, along with his younger brother and general office assistant at the Sanatorium William Keith Kellogg, have, after quite a bit of experimentation, developed a breakfast food that is easy to chew. It is a cereal flake made of wheat, which they are calling Granose. Meanwhile a former patient of Kellogg, Charles William Post, has developed Postum, a wheat and molasses based hot beverage. Post is advertising it widely claiming there is no limit to the number of physical and moral ills (even divorce or juvenile delinquency) caused by coffee, but it can all be improved with Postum.

Henry J. Heinz has started making baked beans. He is advertising them as "oven-baked beans in a pork and tomato sauce."

1896. The new Chinese ambassador to the United States, Li Hung-Chang, arrived recently in New York with a large staff including three cooks. He is determined to impress the Americans with the values of Chinese culture and cuisine and he gives a dinner party to which he invites distinguished members of both the American and Chinese communities. To make the event memorable, he instructs his chefs to include in the menu an entirely new course, which would appeal equally to western and eastern palates. The result is a mixture of chopped bean sprouts, celery, and meat in a soy sauce, all finely cut up and served under the name of chop suey, the English "chop" combined with Chinese "bits," spelled phonetically "suey".

Henry Heinz has created a slogan – "57 Varieties." Heinz actually is now manufacturing over 60 products but he

HISTORY OF DESSERT

IN ancient Rome and Greece meals generally ended with fresh or dried fruit, whilst sweet tarts or pastries were often served between meat courses. By the eighteenth century, once the main course had been completed at the banquets of the European courts, the table was completely cleared to make room for the last sweet course. Due to the now widespread availability of refined sugar and flour the meal would finish with an elaborate multitude of cakes, creams, fruits, jellies, meringues, pastries, puddings, and tarts admirably presented on tables decorated with flowers.

It was not until about 1850 that the word dessert took on its present meaning, referring to the "removal" of all plates and dishes from the table, from the French "desservier" meaning "to remove the cloth." By the end of the century in wealthy European and American homes there was a variety of different sponges, pastries, meringues, and ice creams for dessert.

believes the number "57" has a magical quality.

The disabled principal of Boston Cooking School, Fannie Farmer, has written *The Boston Cooking-School CookBook*. Farmer is the first person to standardize the methods and measurements of her recipes, rather than such vague terms as "heaping spoonful," assuring reliable results to her readers. Farmer has recognized in her comprehensive and organized book the relationship between good nutrition and health.

1897. A 24-year-old organic chemist who had trained in Europe, John Dorrance, is working in his uncle's canning factory, the Joseph Campbell Preserve Company, in Camden, New Jersey. He has outfitted a laboratory on the company premises out of his own pocket, which is reproducing the soups he enjoyed in Europe, but in condensed form. This is giving the company an advantage over competitors because by doing away with the water in canned soup shipping costs are much reduced, which is enabling it to offer a 10-ounce can of Campbell's condensed soup for just a dime. Also it makes it one of the first food companies to have national distribution.

The Sears and Robuck catalogue publishes the first recipe for brownies. The name "brownie" comes from the deep brown color of the confection. Its origin is with a housewife from Bangor, Maine who was baking chocolate cake one day and it fell. Instead of throwing it out, this thrifty cook cut the collapsed cake into bars and served it.

1898. Postum is a success, and now Charles William Post's Postum Cereal Company has an even greater achievement. Grape Nuts was a failure as a grain beverage, as Post originally marketed it, but it is turning out to be a very popular breakfast cereal. (It is sweetened with maltose, which Post erroneously calls grape sugar, and he thinks it has a nut-like flavor as a result of toasting, hence the name.)

During the Alaskan Klondike gold rush, potatoes are almost as valuable as gold. Potatoes are so esteemed for their nutritious content that miners are trading gold for potatoes.

Cesar Ritz, a Swiss hotelier, has opened a hotel in Paris, which bears his name. One of his innovations is to seat diners at small tables, as in a restaurant, as opposed to the traditional large communal table.

1899. Aunt Jemima pancake flour, invented at St. Joseph, Missouri, is the first ready-mix food ever to be introduced commercially and the first self-rising flour for pancakes.

Claude Monet visits London for the first time and paints views of the Thames. Whilst in England's capital city he has grown very fond of Yorkshire pudding. The French artist has an interest in cookery and claims to have originated ceps (an edible fungi) in olive oil. Back home in France he serves beautifully prepared homemade meals using whatever his garden or farmyard can supply.

Henri De Toulouse-Lautrec, the French artist, is painting with great psychological insight the personalities and aspects of Paris. An excellent amateur cook, he has created such original recipes as plums in rum and grilled grasshoppers, seasoned with salt and pepper.

In Britain the first packet of multi-colored Licorice Allsorts is created by accident when a salesman knocks over his tray of samples, scattering candy all over the counter. The customer likes the look of the different candy all mixed up and immediately places an order.

1900. Louis Lassen has invented the hamburger. He grounds beef, broils it, and serves it between two pieces of toast. It is derived from the thirteenth-century Hamburg steak that was introduced to the Germans by the Tartars. German immigrants arriving in North America are bringing this steak dish with them.

The Hershey Chocolate Company has introduced the first Hershey milk chocolate bar. It is priced cheaply enough to make this chocolate bar an everyday item.

1901. On a particularly cold day at a New York baseball game, no one is buying concessionaire Harry Stevens' ice cream, so he begins selling sausages and rolls. He starts calling out, "red hot dachshund sausages!" and finds they are very popular. Thomas "Tad" Dorgan, a sports cartoonist for *The New York Journal*, is in the press box and seeing this he attempts to draw a cartoon of a barking sausage steaming in its stretched out roll. He doesn't know how to spell "dachshund," so he writes "hot dog" instead, a name that is immediately catching on.

After the death of his mother, Queen Victoria, Edward VII becomes king of England. The new king is well known for his numerous extravagant court functions and his obesity. He faithfully records the height and weight of his guests after weekends at Sandringham to ensure they have eaten well. Breakfast for Edward is eggs followed by large thick slices of bacon then fish (turbot, lobster, or salmon) with finally steak or chops with a little game or poultry. He then has a ten-course lunch at 1.00 sharp. Dinner can be up to 12 courses. "Tum Tum," as he is nicknamed, especially enjoys grilled oysters and peasant stuffed with snipe all washed down with champagne. He also loves small whitebait. One man has the job of picking out the tiniest fish of uniform size for the king. When a footman accidentally spills a jug of cream over him, Edward retorts, "my good man, I'm not a strawberry."

British soldiers fighting in the Boer War have been issued with the first composite emergency ration packs containing two tins to be used only in extremity. One holds four ounces of beef concentrate and the other five ounces of cocoa paste.

1902. Robert Scott is on an Antarctic expedition. The food supplied to the ship is so bad that Scott and the crew are forced to eat seal (similar to beefsteak) and penguin (which has the flavor of jugged hare).

Father Clement Rodier, a French missionary, has developed the Clementine, a hybrid of the tangerine and the Seville or bitter orange, near Oran, Algeria. The demand for the nutritious citrus fruits has increased greatly as physicians have discovered their medical benefits.

1903. Horace Fletcher, an English importer, writes *The ABC of Nutrition*. In it he espouses the notion that Gladstone followed, that each mouthful of food should be chewed 32 times.

The ice cream cone is popularized at the St. Louis World Fair. On a hot day Ernest M. Hamwi, a pastry baker of Syrian origin, rolls up some of his Zalabia pastry and sells the cones to an ice cream concessionaire in an adjoining booth, who is running out of paper cups. There are around 50 ice cream stands at the Fair and a large number of waffle shops and many of them are now using cones. Some wits are calling it the "World's Fair Cornucopia."

Also taking off at the St. Louis World Fair is the hamburger. Fletch Davis is selling the ground beef patty sandwich at the amusement area, known as The Pike. Fairgoers are taking their taste home with them and are experimenting with the Hamburg steak tucked between two slices of bread.

Dr. Alexander P. Anderson developed the method for making puffed rice in New York two years earlier and is introducing it to the world at the St. Louis World's Fair. Anderson had made the discovery that rice kernels, after being heated to a high temperature then quickly cooled, would immediately expand to several times their normal size making a tasty breakfast cereal.

CUTLERY IN THE EIGHTEENTH AND NINETEENTH CENTURIES

IN the eighteenth century the Americans would either use their fingers to eat or spoons with which they steadied the food as they cut it and then passed the spoon to the other hand in order to scoop the food up. Meanwhile, four-pronged forks were being used by the French nobility at separate place settings to distinguish themselves from the lower classes, who still shared bowls and glasses. The additional prongs made diners less likely to drop food and the curves in the prongs served as a scoop so people did not have to constantly switch to a spoon while eating. By the early nineteenth century, these four-pronged forks had also been developed in England and were spreading to America. At first they were used mainly in restaurants or to hold meat while cutting it. Many were still suspicious: an irate American preacher told his congregation that to eat meat with a fork is to declare irreverently that God's creatures are not worthy of being touched by human hand.

By this time Sheffield, in England had become an international center of the cutlery industry. In 1840 the Englishman Elkington and the Frenchman Ruolz simultaneously invented electroplating. With the mass production of silver plating elegant dining utensils became widely available to American and British households with moderate incomes. Rather than using their fingers to eat many Americans were now using forks for everyday meals. Meanwhile in Britain the wealthy would show their wealth and status by collecting as many silver services as they could afford – the bigger, the better. In 1912 stainless steel, steel that was very resistant to corrosion and couldn't be hardened by cooling, was invented in England. This development made cutlery even more affordable.

1905. Gennaro Lombardi has opened the first pizzeria in North America at 53 1/3 Spring Street in New York City. Others are quickly following in the Italian communities around the city.

11-year-old Frank Epperson of San Francisco, California, has invented a frozen ice on a stick. One winter evening, he mixed some soda water powder to drink, but left it on the back porch overnight with the stirring stick in it. That night the city experienced record low temperatures. In the morning he discovered them frozen together. He is now selling the confection to his school friends.

Cadburys introduce to the world their Dairy Milk chocolate bar. The Quaker George Cadbury, the current owner of Cadburys, is an energetic social reformer. He devotes much of his time to improving education and housing for the poor.

1906. A new cereal, an improvement on the Granose idea, has been developed by William Keith Kellogg. This new product came about by accident: after some boiled corn was left alone, one of his cooks found it had broken into crispy flakes. The profit-minded younger Kellogg breaks away from his brother to found the Kellogg Toasted Corn Flake Company to market the cereal.

The Hot Fudge Sundae is created at C. C. Browns, a new ice cream parlor on Hollywood Boulevard in Los Angeles. Fudge originated in the last century when the sugar recrystallized after a mistake made during the manufacture of toffee.

1907. In the U.S. the bagel is appearing at Ellis Island, brought by Jewish refugees leaving eastern Europe. The recipe for bagels is being fiercely safeguarded.

A Swiss nutritionist called Dr. Max Birchner-Brenner has a raw food diet, which is high in fiber and low in fat. It includes oatmeal, grated apples, berries, and milk. From these mixtures the doctor has developed a mixture of cereals, nuts, and fruit. He is calling it muesli, which in German means "mixture".

1908. In Bern, Switzerland, Theodor Tobler, the son of the chocolate-factory owner Jean Tobler, and his cousin Emil Baumann have created Toberlone. The name is a play on Tobler and *torrone*, Italian for honey-almond nougat. The shape is inspired by the Swiss mountain the Matterhorn.

1908. George Smith is making lollipops, large boiled sweets mounted on sticks, in New Haven, Connecticut. They are named after a racehorse of the time, Lolly Pop. To help meet the demand a Wisconsin company has built for George Smith an automatic lollipop-making machine, which produces 40 a minute.

In the English county of Hampshire, the Cerebos salt company devises a dry powder which, when mixed with water and juices in the roasting tin, produces a thick, well-seasoned brown. It is becoming known as Bisto from the slogan, "Browns, Seasons, Thickens ... in One."

1909. The very first cereal gift offer is made available. The Funny Jungleland Moving Pictures Booklet is on offer with the purchase of two packages of Kellogg's Corn Flakes.

1911. Roald Amundsen is endeavoring to become the first man to reach the South Pole. At the Polar Plateau the 24 weakest dogs are shot, Amundsen's men then eat them before getting to the South Pole. Apart from dog meat, Amundsen and his men are surviving entirely on dried meat biscuits and chocolate powdered milk.

About 15 years earlier, a Dutch physician and pathologist, Christiaan Eijckmann noted that the frequency of the beriberi disease increased when there was a diet consisting entirely of polished white rice. Now the Polish chemist Casimir Funk discovers that a particular amine is acting as a preventive factor in unpolished rice, which Funk has suggested is named vitamin – for "vital amine."

1912. Seven years ago, a German immigrant, Richard Hellman, opened a delicatessen in New York. Salads sold at the delicatessen contained mayonnaise, which his wife made. The condiment itself proved very popular so now Hellmann has begun selling it in bottles and people are finding it especially quick and easy to use as a coleslaw (a dressing for shredded cabbage).

James Kraft, who started a wholesale cheese business in Chicago nine years ago, has developed a method to pasteurize cream cheese and this has led to the development of pasteurized Philadelphia cream cheese.

1913. Potato crisps are introduced to England. A Mr. Carter had discovered them in France and he has set up a company, Carter's Crisps, to manufacture them.

Henry Ford pioneers the moving conveyor belt assembly line to make the Model T Ford car. He is convinced that the soya bean is a promising raw material and it can be converted into products with commercial value. The American motor manufacturer is obsessed with diet; he maintains that eating sugar is tantamount to committing suicide as its sharp crystals cut a person's stomach to shreds. When he hears that the botanist George Washington Carver eats weed sandwiches every day Ford decides to do the same.

Marcel Proust publishes the first part of *Remembrance of Things Past*. The French writer was prompted to embark on his autobiographic novel by the smell of a tea-soaked orange teacake. He has said that fragrance is the most tenacious form of memory and the teacake evoked memories of culinary delights at Aunt Leonie's on a Sunday morning. These days he dines almost nightly at Place Vendome, Paris to observe the decadence about which he writes in *Remembrance of Things Past*.

1915. William Wrigley collects every telephone directory in the United States and mails three sticks of Wrigley Gum to every name and address listed. The ploy works and sales skyrocket.

Albert Einstein publishes his general theory of relativity. Whilst working on his theory the Swiss scientist lived on coffee, cheap sausages, and rolls.

AMERICAN DIET DURING WORLD WAR I

THREE special-purpose rations came into general use in World War 1 for the American soldier:

1. The trench ration to be used during trench warfare consisted mainly of canned roast beef, corned beef, salmon, and sardines plus potatoes and white bread which could be either prepared as a hot meal, or eaten straight out of the can.

2. The reserve ration was carried by a soldier on his person for when regular food was unavailable. A typical pack consisted of a one-pound can of corned beef, two half pound tins of hard bread, and some sugar and salt.

3. The "iron" ration, was a packaged unit of concentrated food carried by the soldier in a pocket-sized can to sustain life during emergencies when all other sources had run out. It consisted of three cakes of a mixture of beef powder and cooked wheat and three small chocolate bars.

Also in their ration packs was chewing gum, which they would share around with their French and British allies. As a consequence the gum was popularized in Europe.

The limited and standardized diet of meat, potatoes, and white bread served to American soldiers during World War I played an important role in uniting American food tastes into a more traditional British style.

Meanwhile, back in the U.S., because of food shortages, the food administrator Herbert Hoover called for one meatless, two wheat-less, and two pork-less days each week. Americans planted gardens and developed new recipes for cakes containing no eggs or butter and served wheat-free and meat-free meals.

1916. The prevalent food of the British army fighting in the Great War is corned beef. The "Tommies" are calling it "bully beef" because it is cooked beef, from the French bouilli for "boiled."

Clarence Birdseye, a Government field naturalist, is working as a fur trader in Labrador. He has noticed that freshly caught fish, when placed onto the Arctic ice by the Eskimos and exposed to the icy wind and frigid temperatures, freezes solid almost immediately. Yet when the fish is thawed and eaten, it still has all its fresh characteristics. He has concluded that quickly freezing certain items keeps large crystals from forming, preventing damage to their cellular structure. The field naturalist is intrigued.

1917. The British doctor, Dr. Charles Fearn, has been approached by President Wilson to assist the U.S. war effort by developing soybean. His resulting Soy-O-Pancake Mix is one of the first soy products to enter the U.S. market through health food stores.

1918. British food stocks are dangerously low because of German submarine attacks. To deal with the shortage of meat, the government has ordered restaurants to have two meatless days per week.

1919. The first airline meals, lunchboxes costing 3 shillings (approximately two dimes) each, are introduced by Handley Page on the London–Paris service.

1920. Yogurt is catching on in western Europe as Georgian and Greek immigrants from the World War are serving it in their restaurants and producing it on a small scale for local dairymen.

1921. Ernest Hemingway, a poverty-stricken young reporter in Paris manages to keep his family fed only by poaching pigeons in the Luxembourg Gardens in the company of his infant son. He lures a pigeon with some grain, wrings its neck, and then hides each one under the baby's pram blanket.

1922. Through innovative advertising techniques and improvements in the quality of the cereals, the Kellogg Toasted Corn Flake Company is prospering. They have now adopted the shortened name of Kelloggs as they are manufacturing cereals other than cornflakes.

Disregarding the lack of public support in the recent Italian election the Fascists march on Rome and install Mussolini as Duce. Mussolini is a vegetarian. His wife Rachele, whom Mussolini met when she was a local peasant girl, is still a countrywoman at heart. She bakes bread, makes her own pasta, and keeps chickens, geese, pigs, and turkeys.

1923. It has taken 18 years for Epperson to apply for a patent for his frozen ice on a stick, which his children have named the "Popsicle." He is selling them from a lemonade stand at an amusement park in Alameda, California.

An Australian chemist named Dr. Cyril P. Callister at the Fred Walker Cheese Company has developed a remarkable new spread from brewer's yeast blended with ingredients such as celery, onion, salt, and a few secret ones. It is a nutritious spread with an appealing taste and is a rich source of Vitamin B. Callister's Company runs a competition inviting the public to dream up a name for its new spread. A prize of £50 for finalists has guaranteed heaps of entries and from the pile a name is pulled: "Vegemite."

After years of experimenting after his time in Labrador, with an investment of $7 for an electric fan, buckets of brine, and cakes of ice, Clarence Birdseye has invented and is perfecting a system of packing fresh food into waxed cardboard boxes and flash-freezing under high pressure.

1924. Generally in America salad dishes are greens with a plain dressing of salt and vinegar and oil. Alex Cardini, an Italian Air Force pilot living in exile in Tijuana, runs a small restaurant, Caesar's Sports Bar & Grill Family Restaurant, next to an equally small hostel. Some hungry Italian Air Force friends arrive so Cardini, with the help of an old aunt of his who works in the kitchen, uses his leftover ingredients to create a salad. It contains cos lettuce, coddled eggs, garlic, lemon juice, olive oil, Worcester sauce, freshly grated Parmesan cheese, salt, and pepper. The salad is a success and with the addition of anchovies smoothed into a paste is put on the menu of not only Caesar's but many other restaurants. It is now known as Caesar's salad, after Cardini's restaurant.

Meanwhile California growers have started shipping crisphead lettuce covered with heaps of crushed ice. They are renaming it iceberg lettuce and it's proving popular in salads. Fresh green salads remained the exception well past the turn of the century. The shift toward green salad can be attributed to the development of refrigerated rail cars, which can transport perishable greens vast distances.

Clarence Birdseye has organized his own company, Birdseye Seafoods, Inc., at a plant near the Fulton Fish Market in New York City. There he has begun processing chilled fish fillets by packing dressed fish in cartons, then freezing the contents between two flat, refrigerated surfaces under pressure. This is the beginning of the frozen foods industry.

John L. Kellogg is developing a new cereal, All Bran. It is a convenient way of using up bran left over from other products.

———

1926. The Irish dramatist and wit George Bernard Shaw claims he is a vegetarian as "a man of my spiritual intensity does not eat corpses." He regularly frequents Cafe Royal, 68 Regent Street, London. The 70-year-old always eats small meals and has now, after nearly 60 years, switched from a diet of macaroni with beans and lentils in soups and porridges to one with more fresh fruit and vegetables, which is giving him health benefits.

A Mrs. Scudder, the owner of a potato crisp factory, has come up with a waxed-paper crisp bag, which will keep the crisps fresh inside. Every evening, she has women employees take home sheets of waxed paper and make them into bags.

HISTORY OF BREAKFAST

B *REAKFAST'S origins lie with early Christians who, prior to taking communion, were expected to fast from midnight. Only after the service were they permitted to eat and thereby to "break (their) fast."*

Up until the end of the eighteenth century a typical continental breakfast consisted of cold meat and cheese, whilst in Britain the upper classes breakfasted late (about 10.00), as befitted their leisured status. This distinguished them from the lower orders, who ate very early before going off to work at 7.00 to 8.00. The meal often lasted hours and it included cold roast beef, chops and steaks, fish, eggs, cheese, cakes, toast, bread, and butter. Meanwhile in America colonists had learnt to incorporate "new world" foods such as corn muffins and grits into their diets and immigrants had introduced traditional foods such as potato pancakes and doughnuts. A hundred years later

in upper class British households the full
Victorian breakfast had reached its zenith.
Now it consisted of a drawn out family meal
of bacon, eggs, kidneys, kippers, ox tongue, pies,
and sausages followed by fruit, honey, and
biscuits. Meanwhile the Americans were
beginning to eat a large English-style breakfast
light in fiber but heavy on pork and other meats.
The decline of the English breakfast only
happened when World War I arrived with the
ensuing shortages and a new horror of waste.
The standard English breakfast in the 1920s
was a more realistic egg and bacon, toast and
marmalade. Meanwhile many Americans, after
years of campaigning by
vegetarians and nutritionists,
were adopting a more healthy
option involving breakfast
cereals such as
cornflakes.

The next day the workers hand pack chips into the bags, seal the tops with warm irons, and deliver them to retailers. These freshly crisp potato crisps are quickly becoming popular.

1928. Walter Diemer is an American businessman who is working as an accountant for the Fleer Chewing Gum Co. Whilst experimenting during his spare time with recipes for a chewing gum base he has accidentally invented bubble gum, which he calls "Double Bubble". The reason the gum is pink is it is the only color the inventor has to hand.

1929. As a result of the current great economic slump, many are without work and have no money to buy food. Consequently kitchens distributing free soup to the needy are springing up in most large cities in the U.S. For the most part it is churches and charity organizations like the Salvation Army that provide food for the poorest.

Popcorn at 5 or 10 cents is one of the few luxuries down-and-out families affected by the American Depression can afford. While other businesses are failing, the popcorn business is thriving.

A new cartoon character called Popeye has appeared in cartoon strips. A long-term romance between Olive Oyl and Popeye has commenced with the latter overpowering his rivals with the help of spinach. The popularity of spinach is increasing rapidly because of Popeye. Another contributory factor is that nutritionists have recently found it has a high content of iron, vitamin A, and vitamin C.

1930. The birth of retail frozen foods has occurred in Springfield, Massachusetts. Birdseye has made 26 different vegetables, fruits, fish, and meats available to consumers in the "Springfield Experiment Test Market."

A new Los Angeles restaurant, the El Cholo Spanish café, has opened at 1121 South Western Avenue in a courtyard with a mission-style fountain. The proprietress Rosa Borquez's menu is popularizing Mexican food such as enchiladas and tacos. Another popular item they are selling is the burrito, meaning literally "little burro or donkey," which originated south of Los Angeles.

1932. In India Gandhi has started a "fast unto death" on behalf of the Untouchables. The Hindu and Untouchable leaders gather round his bed and arrange a compromise. The vegetarian Gandhi will not even pluck fruit from a tree as he feels this is too violent a gesture. He relies on gathering fruit once it has fallen to the ground. At one time he reduced his daily food to four ingredients: wheat, vegetables, a little oil, and fruit but he became very ill. So he added to his diet goats milk and salt. A teetotaller, he has a nightly enema (a fluid injected into the rectum) before going to bed just after 9.00.

1933. Three years ago sliced bread was introduced under the Wonder Bread label. Such is the success of the product that by now over 80% of Britain's bread is sliced. Not only are sales of sliced breads taking off but also toasters are becoming a popular vehicle for toasting sliced bread.

Franklin Roosevelt introduces the first New Deal – a Relief and Recovery program. His wife Eleanor Roosevelt eats three chocolate-covered garlic balls every morning. Her doctor prescribed this diet to improve her memory.

1935. The trademark for the name "cheeseburger" has been awarded to Louis Ballast of the Humpty Dumpty Drive-In, in Denver, Colorado. They were first served last year at Kaolin's restaurant in Louisville, Kentucky.

1936. In the U.S. Irma Rombauer's *The Joy of Cooking* is being published commercially. It is proving to be popular as many readers are attracted to the author's accessible style and personal touch. The success of this book is a sign that the Depression is loosening its grip.

1937. Two years ago Rowntree's launched their new two-bar wafer as Rowntree's Chocolate Crisp in Britain. Now it is being rebranded the Kit Kat Chocolate Crisp after the Kit-Kat Club, an eighteenth-century London political club named after Christopher (Kit) Catling who provided the venue.

Ruth Wakefield and her husband Kenneth own a tourist lodge, the Toll House Inn, near Whitman, Massachusetts. Ruth cooks for her guests and one of her favorite cookie recipes calls for the use of baker's chocolate. One day Ruth finds herself without the needed ingredient, so she substitutes a semi-sweet chocolate bar cut up into bits, but unlike the baker's chocolate the chopped up chocolate bar does not melt completely, the small pieces only soften. The guests like these new cookies with chocolate "chips." A few simple experiments later have led to her recipe for a chocolate chip cookie.

The American Hormel Foods Corporation has started marketing Hormel Spiced Ham but as it doesn't stand out from other brands Jay C. Hormel asks his New Year's Eve party guests to help and a Kenneth Daigneau comes up with the succinct "spam."

Marcel Boulestin has become the world's first television cook when he presents the first of the *Cooks Night* Out programs on the BBC.

Ernest Hemingway publishes *To Have and Have Not*. Whilst working on a novel he survives solely on peanut butter sandwiches.

———

1939. Adolf Hitler's Nazi Germany invades Poland thus precipitating World War II. The Anti Semitist Furhrer's cook is Jewish. A vegetarian, in a book on diet Hitler pencils a marginal note: "Cows were meant to give milk, oxen for drawing loads." He lost his taste buds during a gas attack in World War I and as a result he adores spicy food. He also has a passion for cream cakes and chocolate.

Hot dogs have gained an international reputation due to Franklin and Eleanor Roosevelt serving them to the British King George VI and his queen on their American tour.

Colonel Harland Saunders who owns a small restaurant and petrol station in Corbin, Kentucky invents his Kentucky Fried Chicken recipe with a secret blend of 11 herbs and spices.

FOOD DURING WORLD WAR II

BECAUSE *of general food shortages during World War II, the British were encouraged to "Dig For Victory" and grow their own fruit and vegetables. Because of rationing, the British people were forced to rustle up dreary meals from spam, powdered egg (eggs were rationed to one person per week), and home-grown vegetables. Food was often very scarce in occupied Europe and many went hungry. Luxuries such as shellfish and venison disappeared, everyday foods like fresh vegetables, oranges, and bananas became unobtainable. Meanwhile in the U.S. rationing meant the government limited each American to 28 ounces of meat per week plus restricting the amounts of butter, cheese, eggs, and sugar each household was permitted. As a result, sales of convenience and prepared foods increased in both countries and techniques of dehydration extended to eggs and other foods. Oven meals, in which all the meal was prepared in the oven at one time, became popular because they conserved fuel.*

1940. Bertrand Russell is living in the U.S. to escape World War II. The pacifist philosopher likes to eat at a certain cheap cafe that serves poor food. He explains the reason he eats there is "because I am never interrupted."

Brothers Dick and Maurice McDonald open a tiny hamburger restaurant on a street corner in San Bernardino, Los Angeles.

The American novelist Scott Fitzgerald dies of a heart attack listening to Beethoven's *Eroica Symphony* whilst eating a chocolate Hershey bar.

1941. On a trip to Spain during the Civil War, Forrest Mars Sr. encountered soldiers who were eating pellets of chocolate that were encased in a hard sugary coating to prevent them from melting. Inspired by this idea, Mr. Mars went back to his kitchen and now he has invented the recipe for M&M's.

A teenage Audrey Hepburn is surviving in occupied Utrecht, in the Netherlands, on a diet of turnips and tulip bulbs.

1942. In Britain during World War II there was a Ministry of Food campaign that used the slogan, "potatoes are good for you." This has been so successful that now a new campaign has started saying "potatoes are fattening."

1943. Ignacio Anaya, a chef at the small Mexican town of Piedras Negras, has assembled the first nachos, a combination of tortilla pieces with jalapeño peppers and melted cheese, for some Texan ladies who are on a shopping trip.

Ike Sewell of Chicago has created Deep Dish Pizza by combining traditional Italian pizza recipes with large quantities of the finest meats, spices, vegetables, and cheeses. He has opened Pizzeria Uno in Chicago as a restaurant specializing in his Deep Dish Pizza and already it has more customers than it can handle.

———

1944. Lady Eve Balfour, the daughter of a wealthy British family, has a keen interest in agriculture. Her research work in the 1920s and 1930s has resulted in the book *The Living Soil*, which is promoting organic farming. Two years earlier in the U.S. the organic gardening and farming movement was founded by Jerome Rodale.

———

1945. World War II is introducing an interest in international foods to America as soldiers bring home a love of the foods they have found in Europe and Asia.

———

1946. Lady Balfour's *The Living Soil* is generating much interest in developing organic food grown using natural farming methods. Organizations such as the Soil Association have been started to create healthy, nutritious foods while protecting and improving the environment.

———

1947. At Buffalo, New York, the U.S. Customs Court has ruled that despite rhubarb being botanically a vegetable, it is in fact a fruit as that it how it is normally eaten.

———

1948. It is common to see carhops serving those who want to order food from their car. Harry Snyder of Baldwin Park, California has had the idea of a drive-through hamburger stand where customers can order through a two-way speaker box. So Harry opens California's first drive-through hamburger stand, named "In-N-Out Burger."

Dick and Maurice McDonald replace the trained cooks in their San Bernardino restaurant with low-paid teenagers who simply flip burgers and dunk fries in oil. The menu is reduced to a few items and cutlery and china are discarded. Customers have to queue for their food and eat out of a cardboard carton with their hands. Prices are reduced, people pile in, and the fast food restaurant is born.

Cole Porter writes the musical *Kiss Me Kate*. The Broadway composer gets a kick from fudge. He has nine pounds of it shipped to him each month from his hometown.

1950. Elizabeth David of Britain studied at the Sorbonne, Paris, traveled to the Mediterranean, and spent the war years in Egypt picking up a love of French and Mediterranean cuisine. She returned to Britain four years ago and has now written *A Book of Mediterranean Food*, which is sparking off an increased interest in foreign cuisine.

1952. A new chicken dish, coronation chicken, is invented by Constance Spry and Rosemary Hume of Le Cordon Bleu School in London. It is served at a luncheon for heads of state visiting after the coronation of Queen Elizabeth II.

AMERICAN COOKING IN THE 1950s

THE idea of casserole cooking as a one-dish meal became increasingly popular in America as housewives learnt to create dishes by mixing together the readily available canned meats and fish, vegetables, and soups. Tuna-noodle casserole was a particular favorite. Meanwhile the man of the house was barbecuing steak, burgers, and spare ribs outside on his new charcoal grills. Beef stroganoff, with its rich sour cream sauce, was considered the height of contemporary entertaining.

Increased travel in the 1950s gave Americans a new appreciation for European-style cooking and a curiosity about international gourmet dishes.

1954. James McLamore and David Edgerton found Burger King. They are selling burgers and milkshakes for 18 cents each.

C.A. Swanson & Sons of Omaha, Nebraska introduces the first TV dinner to America. Executive Gerald Thomas came up with the idea when the company had half a million pounds of leftover turkey from Thanksgiving stored in 10 refrigerated railroad cars. On a visit to a Pittsburgh distributor he noticed a box of metal trays that an airline was testing as a way to serve heated meals on international flights. He saw a future for the unwanted turkeys. Their Swanson TV dinner is roast turkey with stuffing and gravy, sweet potatoes, and peas. It is selling for 98 cents and comes in an aluminum tray, so the diner can just open the box and heat the dinner in the oven.

1958. The first cereals for the sweet tooted are introduced, General Mills' Cocoa Puffs and Kellogg's Cocoa Krispies.

1959. Reuben Mattus introduces Häagen-Daz ice cream onto the American market. He chose the name because he thought a Danish sounding name would suggest a superior, exotic product to higher-income customers.

1960. A tin of Frank Cooper's Oxford marmalade taken by Scott on his 1911 Antarctic expedition and found in his tent is found to be still edible.

1962. In the U.S. Julia Child's cookbook *Mastering the Art of French Cooking* and her television show are almost single-handedly changing the way Americans cook and eat. Her detailed printed instructions for chocolate mousse and *coq au vin* are making these French classics possible for even a limited cook. Her widely popular recipe for the latter is being copied in millions of kitchens throughout America. A simple chicken dish, it is made with mushrooms, onions, bacon, and red wine.

Golden Wonder is introducing cheese and onion flavored crisps. They are the first British company to add flavors to crisps.

Five years ago Chairman Mao announced The Great Leap Forward, which he hoped would provide the pattern for the development of communist China. However, it is a stark failure, and as many as 30 million have starved to death. As a consequence Chairman Mao magnanimously gives up meat.

John Glenn is the first American to orbit the Earth when he does so three times in the Mercury spacecraft Friendship 7. Among the many tasks Glenn performs are the first American space experiments in eating food in the weightless conditions of Earth orbit. He reports that it tastes more bland than on earth. Glenn's flight does not last long enough to make eating a necessity, but future flights are expected to last much longer. His experience will help the design of future space food systems.

1963. President John F. Kennedy makes a historic speech in the city of West Berlin in Germany; he proudly proclaims in German "Ich bin ein Berliner!" which means literally "I am

a jelly doughnut!" He should have said, "Ich bin Berliner!"
or "I am of Berlin!"

1965. Pizza Express opens its first English restaurant at
Wardour Street, London.

Winston Churchill dies. He always sat at Table no 4 at the
Savoy Grill. Now he has passed away they intend to prohibit
other diners sitting there for a year as a tribute to the great
statesman.

In America the Immigration Act opens the doors to
millions of Asians and is responsible for the exotic
restaurants that are now springing up even in white
American neighborhoods.

1966. After World War II, as a result of chemical fertilizers,
increased mechanization, and the genetic modification of
crop species agricultural efficiency has improved immensely.
Now, it appears possible that soon most countries in the
world will be able to feed their population without importing
foodstuffs.

The Vatican has lifted the compulsory Friday fasting for
Catholics.

1967. An advertising slogan for Heinz Baked Beans, "Beanz
Meanz Heinz," is dreamt up by an advertiser Maurice Drake
in a London pub.

HISTORY OF
CHINESE FOOD

*F*OR *many centuries in China rice was the basic food, eaten whole in the south and in the form of flour in the north. But gradually Chinese food became more varied as different meats such as dog, duck, lamb, pork, and venison were incorporated. Spices such as aniseed, ginger, and peppers were becoming increasingly used. By the mid nineteenth century there were over 25,000 Chinese working on the American railroads. They ate exotic foods cooked by Chinese cooks such as cuttlefish, dried bamboo shoots, and dried mushrooms. Chow mein (from the Mandarin Chinese ch'ao mien, meaning "fried noodles"), a dish made of stewed vegetables and meat with fried noodles, particularly intrigued the locals.*

Chinese food became popular with sophisticated Europeans and Americans in the 1920s because it was considered exotic.

However, it wasn't until after World War II that Asian cuisines began to interest the ordinary western consumer. In 1947 Jeno Paulucci made Chinese food, under the Chun King label, available in American supermarkets nationwide for the first time and by the 1950s restaurants were springing up all over western Europe and America. However, the typical menu bore little resemblance to the foods the Chinese themselves ate. Egg rolls, barbecued spareribs, and sweet-and-sour pork were some of the many dishes created to appeal to the western consumer's palate.

1969. The Proctor and Gamble Company of Cincinnati, Ohio, has decided to take the technology for producing soap and apply it to potato chips. The result is Pringles potato chips.

1972. The French restaurant critics Henri Gault and Christian Millau have started a new cookery movement called nouvelle cuisine, which has been influenced by the Japanese style of food presentation. It is a method of preparing food in a simpler, less rich, and more natural way with detailed attention given to texture and detail. Fresh produce in very small quantities is prepared by grilling or steaming in reduced stocks. The resulting ultra-thin slices of meat or fish are artistically arranged on large plates with a colorful selection of crisp, only just-cooked vegetables in light fruit-based sauces.

Dr. Robert Atkins has rediscovered the high protein, low carbohydrate diet first made famous by an Englishman William Banting. His book, *Dr Atkins' Diet Revolution*, is selling millions of copies.

The Cuisines of Mexico, an influential cookbook by food authority Diana Kennedy, is drawing the line between authentic interior Mexican food and the Americanized Mexican food many eat at commercial Mexican restaurants in the U.S. Kennedy has begun referring to Americanized Mexican food as "Tex-Mex," a term previously used to describe anything that was half Texan and half Mexican.

1974. Richard Nixon resigns from the American presidency following Watergate. He is very fond of his wife's homemade meatloaf and has a liking for the curious combination of cottage cheese and ketchup.

1976. The British Prime Minister Harold Wilson entertains the Queen at 10 Downing Street. An unadventurous meal of beef, roast potatoes, ice cream, and cheese and biscuits is served.

1977. Elvis Presley dies at his Memphis home. The king of rock and roll devoured vast amounts of hamburgers and peanut butter and banana sandwiches. The last food Elvis ate was four scoops of ice cream and six chocolate chip cookies.

1979. One result of the nouvelle cuisine movement is the recognition of the chef as a creative artist. However, the dishes they design often look better than they taste. Colorful and attractive to look at, plate presentation rules but the best restaurants are charging a small fortune for tiny pieces of these exquisitely prepared delicacies.

1981. The newly elected American president Ronald Reagan is very fond of Jelly Belly candies. Reagan's passion for these jellybeans is a marketing dream, and has inspired the company to produce the blueberry flavor. As red and white colored jellybeans already exist now the three colors of the American flag can be served in jellybeans at Reagan's inaugural party.

1984. Balti food had originally been unknown outside north-east Pakistan but since an immigrant opened up a restaurant in Birmingham for the benefit of other immigrants 10 years ago the spread of Balti houses in England has been remarkable. Indeed throughout Europe and the U.S. there has been a great increase in the number of restaurants specializing in Chinese, Indian, Italian, and other national dishes. Each immigrant group has established its own type of restaurant.

1985. Despite the hope in the sixties that self-sufficiency would soon be possible for everyone, for several decades the gap between the western world and the developing world has been widening. While the Europeans and Americans are overproducing, in many parts of the third world due to a mixture of drought, poor management, and destructive western trading practices agricultural production is breaking down.

Richer countries have had a greater variety of foods available in increasing quantities since the end of World War II. Supermarkets are giving the consumer a vast choice of every type of food under the sun. At the same time, some regions of the globe, notably Africa, are regularly struck by terrible famines that decimate their populations. In eastern Africa the current famine has caused the death by malnutrition of millions. The vivid, shocking images coming from Ethiopia have prompted many westerners to attempt to do something about it. For instance, Bob Geldof, a rock musician, has arranged a pop concert at Wembley Stadium with all proceeds going towards famine relief.

1986. European and American law now stipulates that each food item must show clearly each food additive or e number (except for flavorings) on the label or packet rather than just quoting "colorings" or "preservatives" in the list of ingredients.

———

1987. In western Europe and America "yuppies" are seeking out the most fashionable food and the trendiest restaurants. These middle-class, two-income couples are over-indulging on frozen gourmet meals and the latest appliances. Yuppies don't have time to cook, at least during the week, but when they do throw a dinner party they like to show off for guests with flash recipes incorporating expensive ingredients.

An increase in food-poisoning cases due to salmonella bacteria is leading to government investigations in both the U.S. and Britain, and advice that eggs should be thoroughly cooked before being eaten.

———

1988. BSE or mad cow disease is made a notifiable disease in Britain and the compulsory slaughter of BSE-infected cattle begins.

———

1990. McDonalds opens its first restaurant in Moscow. It is now America's biggest employer of unskilled labor and has over 10,000 branches in around 50 countries. This is another sign of an increasing worldwide standardization of food.

A photograph of British minister John Selwyn Gummer feeding his daughter a British beefburger has appeared in many newspapers. Because of the growing anxiety about BSE the British minister is keen to show the world that British beef is safe.

1991. In Europe and America everyone is fitness crazy, jogging is the vogue, gyms are in. Meanwhile food manufacturers are finding ways to make everything reduced fat, low fat, or fat-free.

1993. In America almost 30% more married women are working or looking for work, compared with 20 years ago. The decrease in the number of traditional homemakers means that the one-dish prepared meals now being sold in supermarkets are flourishing. Specialized food items specifically designed to be cooked in the microwave are especially increasing in popularity.

1994. Controls of export of British beef to the continent are imposed due to fears of contamination from BSE. The livelihoods of many British farmers are affected. Such health scares are contributing to the increasing number of consumers who are turning to vegetarian options. There are now around 4 million vegetarians in Britain.

1995. The potato becomes the first vegetable to be grown in space. NASA and the University of Wisconsin, Madison, have created the technology with the goal of feeding astronauts on long space voyages, and eventually feeding future space colonies.

A HISTORY OF
SPACE FOOD

The early Mercury astronauts had bite-sized, freeze-dried foods, and semi-liquids in aluminum tubes where the food was squeezed out like toothpaste. They found it very unappealing. Later, condiments, spices, and sweeteners were included to try to satisfy hungry astronauts' taste buds. The Apollo missions had on board meals like chicken and vegetables and for the first time hot water was available to rehydrate the food, making them for the first time bearable.

Food on board the space shuttle was nutritious and appetizing and familiar late-twentieth-century fare. Crew members normally congregated in the mid-deck area for their meals, which were served in special trays that separated the different food containers and kept them from lifting off and soaring around in the weightless cabin. Each tray was secured to the crew member's leg during meal time with springs and Velcro fasteners. There was a freezer for foods with an oven to heat them up but most of the shuttle foods were dehydrated, saving on time and storage space.

In America Martha Stewart publishes *The Martha Stewart Cookbook*. Martha, who has a syndicated weekly television show that celebrates old-fashioned domesticity, is championing the skills and values of the traditional homemaker..

1996. A tomato puree is Britain's first genetically modified food to be sold in supermarkets. It contains tomatoes that are genetically modified to prevent ripening, thus preventing wastage.

President Bill Clinton is well known for his fondness for junk food but he also absolutely adores spicy Indian dishes. The White House kitchen cooks some for him and his wife Hilary at least once a week. Frequently when they get the opportunity to eat out, the Clintons go to a local Indian restaurant for a chicken tandoori.

1997. Many Americans and western Europeans are turning to low-fat and low-calorie foods on a regular basis. However, confusion exists on what constitutes a healthy diet. Each time a new scientific study points to a link between food and disease, people turn to something different. They switch from beef to chicken, from butter to margarine to olive oil, but still many of the foods they eat are highly processed with many additives. Research by the U.S. Department of Agriculture has found that throughout the world the foods that people are advised to eat and those they actually eat are different.

In Britain the voters of the United Kingdom have dispatched the Conservative Party into opposition after 18 years in power and replaced it with the Labour Party and a new Prime Minister,

Tony Blair. All things to all men, Tony Blair has told a Labour Party magazine that his favorite food is fish and chips and the *Islington Cookbook* that it is "fresh fettuccine garnished with olive oil, sun-dried tomatoes and capers."

1998. Worldwide, salt is the only edible commodity that hasn't vastly increased in price over the last 150 years.

1999. The British government is testing the effect of genetically modified crops on food eco systems. Over a five-year period British farms will be split evenly between traditionally grown and genetically modified (GM) crops. Many are anxious about the hazards of GM and protesters are trampling on and destroying many crops.

There is now a worldwide standardization of eating habits. For instance, an Indian dish chicken tikka has been voted the most popular meal in Britain.

2000. With the World Wide Web we now have instant access to millions of recipes from around the globe.

Recipe swap sites and online food magazines on home computers are providing a new source of culinary information. In Britain Tesco became the first supermarket four years ago to offer Internet shopping and now in many places in the western world housewives can buy groceries without ever leaving the house. And if a novice cook doesn't know how many minutes one should boil cabbage for, he or she can quickly look it up on the Web.

2001. Nestlé SA of Switzerland has been the world's largest food producer for several years. Meanwhile the McDonald's fast food brand is the most famous, and the most heavily promoted, on the planet.

––––––––––

2002. Consumption of fast foods and convenience meals are increasing considerably throughout the world.

Fried foods, which are attractively priced due to the low cost of large-scale frying, are particularly popular. Each day one in five Americans eats in a fast-food restaurant.

In the western world many barely know how to cook. With frozen foods that just need to be heated up and the ready availability of takeout foods, they no longer have to. In addition in the West the increase in different members of a family working different shifts and a growing number of single households is resulting in nearly half of all meals taken at home now being a solitary experience. Frequently dinner is a ready meal heated up in a microwave and consumed in front of the television.

Whilst many in the western world have a calorie intake of over 3,500 per day, a thousand above the amount recommended as healthy by nutritionists, two billion people in the world suffer from chronic under-nutrition and around 40 million die each year from a lack of food.

––––––––––

THE FUTURE OF FOOD

*S*OME *thoughts and predictions regarding the future of food.*

1. Meat and milk from cloned animals will probably be available by the end of the decade. At present a handful of farmers are already milking cloned cattle in the U.S. but they have had to dump the product. However, the huge cost of cloning, over £10,000 a time, means that the technique will most likely be used for breeding animals and their offspring will be slaughtered for their meat. Also consumers are likely to be suspicious of eating meat that may have hidden abnormalities.

Another process is transgenics, the process of introducing genes from one species to another to give it a desired characteristic. This could be used to produce larger animals or extra-tender low-fat meat, or cows that yield milk low in lactic acid and eggs that protect against heart disease.

Many crops and livestock are already genetically modified, often to yield more food, resist pests, or enhance nutrition. One development could be corn that can be harvested for medicine.

2. *Organic foods will grow increasingly popular as more and more are able to choose what they can afford. In 2002 in Britain for the first time sales of organic products reached £1 billion whilst in the U.S. it approached $20 billion. Sales of organic meat in particular are likely to increase with every report of contaminated meat.*

3. *The goal for many food manufacturers is fat-free, high-vitamin meals, which taste delicious. There will be many more variants on healthy nutritious foods such as natural yogurt.*

4. *There will still be a love for traditional home cooked foods such as apple pie. However, proper home cooking will continue to become a hobby rather than a necessity as we rely more and more on convenience foods.*

5. *Seafood will become more expensive as there is a very real concern that the world's seafood supplies are running out due to over-fishing. The exceptionally high stock of fish such as cod and haddock in the 1960s and 1970s has been followed by a decrease over the last couple of decades.*

6. Since the middle of the twentieth century many have had ideas for new foods such as dried milk and soya mince, which it was hoped would resolve the world's hunger crisis. Many will continue to develop new products.

7. Ethnic populations will continue to have an impact on local cuisine and Thai, Vietnamese, Indian, Japanese, and Chinese foods will continue to grow in popularity. Look out for Malaysian food and, from another continent, Brazilian.

8. The trend for dining out will continue. In America in the last decade alone there was a nearly 15% growth in the number of meals eaten away from home whilst in Britain spending on restaurants increased by more than a third in the past five years. Diners will continue to look for convenience and quality.

9. Despite the tragic possibility of mass starvation as population outstrips resources, gluttony will remain in places where food is readily available and easily affordable. We are naturally greedy eaters, and only strict discipline can keep us from unnecessary overeating.

5.62
3
p. 130
. 34
. 145
. 150

THE

SAVAGE

AND

BEAUTIFUL

COUNTRY

THE

SAVAGE

AND

BEAUTIFUL

COUNTRY

ALAN McGLASHAN

Imagination is the star in man
—RULAND THE LEXICOGRAPHER

HOUGHTON MIFFLIN COMPANY BOSTON

FOR ROBIN

CONTENTS

FOREWORD

PROSPERO's island was full of bewildering lights and noises: to Caliban a confusion, but carrying to the eye and ear of Prospero clear signals from a different order of experience. A far more mazing medley of light and noise is characteristic of the world we live in — and not even of a constant kind, but rising, in the unendurable manner of crowded cocktail parties, to a screaming and insane crescendo. It is for contemporary man to choose whether to turn tail on it all like howling Caliban or to develop new powers of attention and perception capable of orchestrating this mad music.

There are two ways of making the attempt. One is by a movement of self-recollection, closing the eyes and shutting the ears, treading the lonely ascetic path of the monk, the anchorite and certain of the mystics. Let no one doubt the courage and sincerity of this solution. It could be that it is the only true path, and to reject it may be the measure of our incapacity for sacrifice. The second, with which this book is concerned, is to re-awaken the pristine human power of regarding the phenomena of the external world in a certain way: in such a way that they begin to grow translucent and to reveal something of the mystery that sustains them.

In illo tempore, once upon a time, we were able to do this. The earliest myths and legends, which express man's first magnificent leap towards meaning, are all alight with this quality of translucency. Now alas, we know better. But although the archaic vision of life has been driven out of contemporary consciousness into the shadows, into a cobwebbed corner of the human mind, it lives on there with spiderish tenacity. For the archaic vision embodies, despite all its limitations and absurdities, a valid aspect of life's meaning which may be devalued or simply forgotten, but can never be completely canceled.

It would be more than foolish to fly to the opposite extreme and start deriding and belittling the staggering triumphs of the objective-scientific attitude. But it may be permissible to suggest that man has been for some centuries now sufficiently self-impressed by the public image of himself as scientist-explorer — standing as it were like a fatuous big-game hunter with one foot planted on the conquered body of Nature — and that it is time some attention were paid to his less premeditated postures. This book is an attempt to perform such a service. It portrays contemporary man not in any of his well-defined attitudes, scientific, religious or philosophic, but in his spontaneity, in his vagrant fancies, nostalgic memories, idle and unvalued daydreams; in the unnoticed motivations of his inventions and discoveries; and perhaps most revealingly in the fantastic images which throng around him in the hours of sleep.

This may sound like a belated echo of the Free Association method, as enacted daily on a thousand Freudian couches, and as currently exploited by the stream-of-consciousness schools of literature. It is not. Those readers will be disappointed who look either for an exposé of the egocentric, vainglorious little daydreams that tug like naughty children at the coat sleeve even of genius, or for the sexual preoccupations, often of the oddest kind, that flicker behind the modest façades of maiden ladies. Such phenomena have their interest and their therapeutic importance, but their proper milieu is the psychiatric consulting room.

Yet what the book is precisely about is hard to define. Its nearest analogy would be one of those peculiar journeys known as a photographic safari, from which the traveler returns with a series of brief "takes" of unsuspecting animals (in this case the human animal) in their natural surroundings.

Seeing humanity from this unfamiliar angle evokes a slight sense of shock, as when the first high-speed photographs were taken of a galloping horse — compelling us to note, in place of the lovely vision of rhythm and grace we always thought we had seen, a curiously stiff and haphazard arrangement of equine limbs. Nevertheless, far from being an essay in the popular art of debunking, the object of so displaying man is to concentrate attention on those movements of the psyche, normally passing unremarked, which reveal the human mind in the crucial act of transition — lit for a moment,

as by a star-shell, in the no-man's-land that lies between
two kinds of consciousness, the familiar and the translucent, still uncommitted to either.

Nothing in this book is presented in the idiom of a
specialist or technician. It is not written for "severed
heads," but for those who at whatever cost to their own
or others' technical advances insist on relating thinking
to feeling *at all times*, hold to the unity of head and
heart, and believe that, whatever else may be gained, if
this is lost human life becomes meaningless and insane.

Though it will probably be so labeled, such an attitude has nothing to do with anti-intellectualism. It is
opposed to feeling-run-riot as much as to thinking-run-
riot. But on this question contemporary bias can be exposed by the curious observation that while it would be
easy to gain general assent to the proposition that feeling should always be guided by thinking, the equally
valid proposition that thinking should always be guided
by feeling would raise cries of horror in many eminent
quarters. The autonomy of thought is a jealously
guarded dogma of our time.

In a vague unformulated way Everyman rejects this
dogma, and obscurely recognizes that there are fields of
experience which lie outside all systems of pure
thought; that *le coeur a ses raisons*. And in this intuition Everyman is right. But in his huge inarticulate rebellion against the over-intellectual attitude, he unfortunately opposes to the pretensions of scientism and
strict logic the deplorable pretensions of common sense
and gumption, thereby confusing the issue — and inci-

dentally bringing vulgarity into the world. "Vulgarity of mind," wrote Albert Dasnoy, a Belgian philosopher who should be better known, "comes . . . from the claim to reduce everything to the juridisdiction of common sense . . . and this is probably the core of all vulgarity."

Everyman, in fact, has failed to realize that those aspects of life which lie outside science and formal logic lie also and equally outside the range of the practical approach. They are not open to the hearty judgments of common sense, but require discriminating delicacies of perception of at least as high an order as those needed for scientific research — but of a different kind; qualities which are to be acquired only by sustained imaginative effort in a new direction. This book is an attempt to indicate the new direction. What is sought in these pages is not some flamboyant new form of consciousness that will seize men's minds and revolutionize the world, but an almost imperceptible inner change — a willed suspension of conventional judgments, a poised awareness, a *stillness*, in which long-smothered voices that speak the language of the soul can be heard again. It is a quiet secret.

But do not be misled by this. For it is also a terrible secret. The inner life of the mind has its nightmares, as well as its golden dreams and wayward fancies. To become purely receptive, to create an inner silence, is to unlock a dangerous door, opening upon a world from which faint hearts would do wisely to keep away. It is to set out on a solitary journey whose end is still unsure.

PART

ONE

The imaginative function . . . "hovers only round the reality of the past when it is entangled in the reality of the present."

Marcel Proust — *Jean Santeuil*

1

REMEMBERING
AND FORGETTING

PERHAPS the two most moving chords that can be struck from the human heart are contained in these four words: I remember, I forget. For the unheard anthem of our whole existence is created out of the antiphonal movements of remembering and forgetting; not only the remembering and forgetting of individuals, but of races and cultures. Perfect balance between this pair of opposites is the mark of maturity.

※

Memory, the psychologists briskly tell us, has two main aspects. The first is Reproduction — "not necessarily exact," as they concede with the *naïveté* which is the birthright of academic psychologists. The second is Recognition — that rainbow bridge flung in a magical instant between the present and the past. Recognition is the core of memory and of mental life. Without it nothing could be experienced, neither love nor hate, hope nor fear, beauty nor ugliness; and a merely vegetative existence would remain. Hardly even this perhaps; for as the physical world is held in being by the all-pervasive, unobtrusive force of friction, so without the act of remembering the entire architecture of the psychic world might at once disintegrate.

It is true, certainly, that according to the Common Law of England — that cozy little world of cobwebbed fantasies — memory begins with the coronation of Richard I in 1189. But this, alas, is too charming to have more than legal meaning, whatever that may be. Memory is, in fact, the mortar between all events, a veritable *glutinum mundi*.

This basic function apart, memory has other and more equivocal uses. It is, for instance, the guardian of self-love, the busy spider in the brain, interposing between past and present its invisible web, through which can pass only selected and fondly edited items into the specious records of the conscious mind. Memory has its graces, too, storing sharp images of happiness and grief, laying a soft patina on the past, giving to the unripe act of living what autumn's gold gives to the mellowing peach.

But if remembering is a vital function, so also is forgetting. To forget is essential to sanity. Like a clumsy mother the huge inchoate body of past events, recalled in their entirety, would overlay the infant mental life and suffocate it. Even if this were not so, the loss would be immeasurable if all things were clearly remembered. Experience would lack its chiaroscuro, and history's canvas would have the maddening facial iteration of a mammoth end-of-term school photograph. Not even historians would benefit from this, except that they would have more to argue about. Man owes more than he guesses to the gray waves of oblivion. Through forgetting comes much beauty into life, much richness and strangeness.

*

Since man must remember if he is not to become meaningless, and must forget if he is not to go mad, what shall he do? The dilemma, not logically resolvable, has been subtly resolved. Within man the past is perfectly contained — but he is allowed to live as if it were lost. He is tolerantly permitted to taste a naïve pride of discovery, a childish delight in new toys; as when William Harvey staggered the seventeenth-century world by his discovery of the circulation of the blood — in which he had been anticipated by Hwang Ti, Emperor of China in 2650 B.C., who quietly noted that "all the blood in the body is under the control of the heart . . . the blood current flows continuously in a circle and never stops." Or, to come nearer to our own time, when the recent discovery that the inner structure of the atom mirrors the structure of the universe is found to be but one more illustration of the fact long known to mystical thought, that the microcosm mirrors the macrocosm, "as above, so below"; each succeeding illustration of which will doubtless be celebrated by peal upon peal of contemporary trumpets.

Yet these pristine forms of knowledge are not wholly forgotten. Mixed always with the joy of new discovery is a shadow of disquiet, a teasing half-recollection of things long past — the secret penetration of the archaic into the present, of the timeless into the temporal. To the percepts of the conscious mind are added intimations from an unimaginably distant and forgotten past, still alive in the depths of the psyche. Nowhere is this more clear than in the magical quality of the enjoyment we derive from myth and parable and fairy tale. Good stories are very rare, and these are the three forms in which they are most often contained. The best of them have indeed been told countless times through history and prehistory. This would be intolerable were it not for the grace of half-forgetting, as children do, which allows us to receive with an ever-fresh delight tales first heard, perhaps, in some lake village of the Neolithic age. Like fascinated children, openmouthed and a little frightened, we listen to our songs and stories echoing faintly back from the walls of eternity.

The tragedy is that it is fatally easy to lose the precarious balance of these opposing and compensating functions of remembering and forgetting, whereby the imaginations of men are grouped and regrouped in endless intricate patterns of wisdom and folly, kindness and cruelty, insight and illusion. It is so hard to grasp the essence of this reciprocal movement. Human minds can only circle about such a concept as blinded moths round an invisible source of light. Equivocal, indefinable, slipping untouched through the most delicate web of words, it is perhaps this factor beyond all others that creates the lovely iridescence on the surface of life, the fathomless quality in its depth. Genius has sometimes known this, and to see life *sub specie aeternitatis* is no new thing. In his book *Cumaean Gates* Jackson Knight has suggested that the essence of genius "consists in the power to find contacts further back in time beyond the reach of others, and to evoke latent stores of feeling and of meaning in the collective mind of the present."

Genius is not the only guide. The evidence abounds, for it is inherent in all things. Even in the daily paper, that faithful mirror of disintegrated existence, faint intimations can be caught by an attentive ear. From what distant sources, and through what indefinable media, have lingered on such delightful and shame-faced fancies of the countryside, as that fresh earth from the grave of a baptized infant will make the blossoms of a plant larger and more handsome; that the cuckoo changes into a hawk at the end of summer; that driving rusty nails into a barren apple tree will cause it to bear fruit? All these, with many more, were seriously advanced within the last few years by correspondents to the English national newspapers.

There is a type of mind, otherwise intelligent, that reacts with a sort of snorting fury to these naïve beliefs, that feels outraged and genuinely shocked if such bucolic fantasies are not instantly dismissed with an impatient shrug. For many purposes, of course, they must be so dismissed. Science has built its high roads of fact and reason only by resolutely ignoring the lovely wayward blossoms of the countryside. Unfortunately for the not unworthy aims of the planning type of mind life is so constructed that resolutely to ignore a thing is to ensure being eventually tripped up by it. One of the gayest, saddest sights on earth is to see the good nag Rosinante carrying the scientific world on its back and confidently cantering along to its ultimate *quod erat demonstrandum*, suddenly put its foot in a *quod est absurdum*, and throw its illustrious burden: gay, because it is pleasant to see the rationalist with his heels higher than his fastidious nose for once; and sad, because he learns so little from his tumble.

In medicine alone there have been many such embarrassing *faux pas*. Not so long ago the doctors were loftily amused to hear of an old countrywoman who used to treat dropsy with decoctions of foxglove from her garden — and who was finally proved to have been, in fact, dispensing a hitherto unknown drug called digitalis. And it is only yesterday that the mold on damp cheeses, kept in many a farmhouse scullery in our great-grandfathers' time to make a rude plaster for infected wounds, was shown to be the source of penicillin. In the country they know that things are only half-discovered — and half-remembered. The precarious balance is unconsciously preserved, and with it the secret of the crude sanity of country life.

It is really amazing how blandly the scientific mind ignores these constant exposures of its own limitations. Like Theseus in the Forest of Arden, it "never can believe these antique fables, nor these fairy toys." Random proof, however startling, of the practical wisdom hidden in simple hearts seems only to serve as the origin of fresh distortions. With indecent haste the humble ladder is kicked away, and the thought to which it leads is separated, fatally, from the feeling that was its partner, and from the human context in which they quietly met and married.

For the essence of this earthly wisdom lies precisely in its slow, centuried synthesis of thinking with feeling, of remembering with forgetting. It cannot be invented or new minted from any single mind, but forms itself mysteriously, with the imperceptible accretions of a stalactite, in the tenebrous caverns of the collective mind. And we do wrong if we dismiss this process as merely passive. Such silent, patient waiting for truth, as Simone Weil has said, is an activity more intense than any searching.

The products of this activity are unlike the clear concepts of the classroom and the laboratory. It is neither very difficult nor very clever to prove them logically absurd. In any case, being a human process it is as fallible as all things human. But empty of value as many of these country tales undoubtedly are, childishly ridiculous as they all appear, they deserve a handling that is gentle and perceptive, as of an archaeologist with his broken relics, in virtue of the mystery of their origin. For these are the wayside flowers of another world than the everyday, the timeless paradoxical world of myth and fairy tale, of fantasy and dream; a world where startling absurdities and glaring inconsistencies are but secret signals to the instructed mind, bidding it note the crossing of an invisible frontier.

It would be well if man could recapture this richer, older mode of response to the enigma of existence, wholly lost to us these last three hundred years, which recognized that the final secrets of life may often be reached less by what we learn than by what we half-remember. What is needed is an extension of contemporary consciousness to include what can be defined as the translucent quality in all things; the quality by which an object or an event is seen not only as a thing-in-itself, but also as a membrane through which can dimly be discerned the foetal stirring of a different order of experience.

This once caught, even for a moment, transforms the sensible universe, investing all objects with a sharp intensity of being. The seeming-solid world grows permeable, beginning to transmit, not merely to reflect, the light. The quality of translucence is the key; a golden key that is the careless plaything of all children, and the conscious instrument of a few geniuses. In exceptional moments of their lives ordinary men and women may fleetingly hold it: in the first days of overwhelming love, in the final moments of overwhelming peril, in the presence of new life, and sometimes on the unheralded news of death.

At such moments a man stands on tiptoe, and may catch a startled glimpse of another level of being, where all values are changed, and everything is understood differently; the level of which Chekhov dreamed where "everything is forgiven, and it would be strange not to forgive"; that Goethe experienced when he murmured to his friend, "That fig tree, this little snake, the cocoon on my windowsill quietly awaiting its future — all these are momentous signatures"; the level touched in the Parables, the sixth book of the *Aeneid,* the "Ode to a Nightingale," and anonymously, and perhaps incomparably, in the mysterious golden light that shines through myth and fairy tale; the level of the kingdom of heaven that is within. It is a quality often missing in works of loftiest genius. Milton, for all the splendor of his planned achievement, and all the wealth of his well-chosen mythological themes, had not a trace of it; nor Shelley, despite his earnest preoccupation with eternity.

To become aware of this translucent quality in all things is no vague romantic goal. It is a sharply defined, delicately poised effort of mental vision, a state of harmonious balance of forces in the Pythagorean sense, born of the union of many opposites: of remembering with forgetting, of thinking with feeling, of the temporal with the eternal, of personal conscious perceptions with faint echoes from the remotest regions of the archaic psyche. It is the basis of all true science, the essence of ritual, the constant attribute of wisdom. It may be the nearest that human minds can reach to the meaning of meaning.

2

DAILY PAPER

PANTHEON

AT HEART modern man is lonely: isolated from all earlier generations by the brilliance, the power, the sheer mass of his own discoveries. Each new invention — drastically altering his life or dramatically changing his environment — fascinates him, yet leaves him secretly dismayed. He finds himself menaced by problems, undeniably of his own making, that are too large for him to handle. Looking round for reassurance, he discovers an almost total lack of guiding precedents, an almost total loss of the stabilizing sense of continuity with the past. In his haste to master new skills he has forgotten more than he can afford to forget.

In such a situation it may be well to look again at the contemporary scene, not — for once — in order to deplore or celebrate what is new, but to make a sustained attempt to reconnect with the past, to reestablish the sense of continuity.

So to look is to make an immediate discovery: the world of today is suddenly seen to be infiltrated in all directions with customs, ideas and beliefs which it fancied it had long outgrown. Contemporary man, in fact,

is by no means cut off. Between himself and men of
earlier times pass a thousand delicate threads of mutual
meaning. He is not even cut off from Nature — in spite
of the violent efforts of the neo-abstractionists to disown
the natural world. Between his own bold gambles with
space and time, and the patient experiments of Nature
itself through an unimaginable past, there stretch, as
will be shown in later chapters, unbroken lines of descent, not so much evolutionary as recurrent. It is a
clue which begins to make sense of the modern world.

To trace these lines, however, it is necessary to develop a sunny disregard concerning the current hierarchies of value. For over the unnumbered centuries
there have been some astonishing reversals of form.
Ideas and movements which engaged the finest intelli-
gences of their age have swiftly sunk to the level of
peasant "superstition," or dropped into empty vulgari-
ties; while others, disregarded for millennia, have as
swiftly emerged to be the hallmark of a whole civilization. The status accorded to an idea at any particular
time is a historical accident, and is irrelevant to the
question of its descent. It need therefore occasion no
surprise that in this and the following chapters matters
which are presently regarded either as vitally important
or as entirely negligible are given equal space and con-
sideration.

❋

We are often told that if God did not exist it would be
necessary to invent him. But this is true of many other

and lesser things. If, for example, so quaint a creature as the Loch Ness Monster did not already exist as a possibility, it would have to be invented. And if the monster were fished out of the loch tomorrow and *proved* to exist, it would be urgently necessary to find a similar phenomenon somewhere else. For the mythic monster in the still waters of the Highland loch carries, however crudely, an intuition of something that is frighteningly real — the image of destructive dragon powers within himself which man has always known to be hidden there. It really seems as if man needs an image of this kind. The Loch Ness Monster is the latest of a long line of hair-raising creatures, half mocked at, half believed in: Roman Cerberus and Briareus, Anubis the dog-headed death-bringer of Egypt, the savage Fenris-Wolf that roamed the Nordic world, his cousins the were-wolves of medieval Britain; these and a hundred others bear the burden of man's knowledge that crouched in the heart, biding its time, lies a ruthless predator. Even in so slight and recent a tale as *The Hound of the Baskervilles* the image was at once accepted in popular imagination, and outlives its author. In every age the more sophisticated have laughed at such things, but at the back of their laughter is often detectable a faint *frisson* of unease. And even by the hard-headed standards of Fleet Street, claims, however unauthentic, of having glimpsed the monster in the loch are eagerly accepted as news.

*

But there is more to read in the newspapers than news. Precisely because of the breakneck speed at which they are run off the presses, the hour-by-hour datelines which have to be met, certain concepts slip through — echoes of a remote past, intimations of things not yet known — that could never survive a more leisured and intellectual approach. There are ideas so dangerous and revolutionary that only in a naïve form can they be suffered to approach the human mind. All these "eyewitness" accounts of flying saucers, for instance, all these endless funny — but slightly hair-raising — stories of earth-visiting Martians . . . can this be a dramatization and projection onto images which we understand and can handle, of an idea which is invading our minds from somewhere beyond our familiar three-dimensional world, *an idea from psychological outer space,* as it were, which we *don't* understand and *can't* handle? Could it be that these feeble images and jokes are the nearest we can get to expressing our thrilled awareness of something "altogether other" on the verge of bursting through to us —something that may give the human mind a revised relationship to the external world? Is it the ferment in our souls that creates these childish visions in the sky?

*

Echoes of the long-forgotten past are to be found in the daily press even more frequently than intimations of the future. Nowhere is this more clear than in that curious and worldwide phenomenon the comic strip cartoon.

Millions of adults read the comic strips in the daily papers. Those who do not are amused, baffled or exasperated by those who do. Unhappily addicts are either dumb (in both senses) or evasive, and they never seem able to give valid reasons for their semi-secret vice. It is a minor sociological mystery, inviting minor research.

Even a first glance shows something interesting. Comic strips for adults, an offshoot from children's comic papers, are not homogeneous: they fall into three groups. Two of the groups, whose puppets satirically reflect the modern scene, are different in nature from the third, but nevertheless have their own compulsive attraction, and their own faithful, furtive band of addicts.

The first is nothing more than a tabloid version of the ever-popular thriller. In the second group, much favored in the U.S.A., the intention cuts deeper, and a mordant image of contemporary society is projected, either directly in the squabbles and adventures of a typical young couple such as the Bumsteads, or indirectly through the eyes of a child or an animal — both being, of course, Everyman in an easily penetrated disguise. Perhaps the two best-loved of all American strip characters in this group are Charlie Brown, that endearingly bewildered infant, and Pogo, an appealing little creature of indefinable zoological status. Both Charlie Brown and Pogo are simple quixotic characters who wander in the modern jungle of hideous opportunity, frustrated by either the malicious and the corrupt or by the self-righteous and the ineffably stupid.

Charlie Brown can be counted on to take the responsibility that none will take, and to fail miserably, humiliatingly in every pinch. He is the common man, and his Lucy is the comman man's Everywoman. In Lucy, a grim picture of a sexless life of unlove and mental tyranny is shown — woman, the ever-present executive assistant of life, undisturbed by the cancer of logic or the paralysis of doubt, who knows that she can do the job better. It is an unkind, unfair caricature — but recognizable.

Pogo, too, is an Everyman, adrift in a world too much for him. There are few problems in American life that he does not encounter. Pogo has been beset in his day by a wildcat, which bore a remarkable resemblance to Senator McCarthy, and a bear which dropped out of a plane and looked quite exactly like Khrushchev. There is Miz Beaver, who represents everything a man does not want in a woman, and Miss Mamselle, a juvenile skunk with a French accent, who is everything he does want — soft, eternally ingenuous, innocently sure that Pogo is good (as, of course, he is) and can in a crisis protect her from all harm. In this type of comic strip American society is laughing at itself, cynically and healthily.

But in the third group the comic strip moves into a new dimension, and draws its images from a more mysterious source. Distinguishable always by the presence of an element of the miraculous or magical, this form of strip has an attraction subtly compulsive, altogether different.

Examples of this third kind occur everywhere. For convenience may be cited a single British newspaper, the *Daily Mirror,* where till recently no less than four out of its six comic strips unmistakably belonged to it. These four comic strip characters have strikingly different personalities, and their adventures follow entirely different patterns. The first is *Garth,* a huge, honest, bull-necked fellow whose constant role is rescuing people and overcoming apparently hopeless odds by sheer physical strength. Then there is *Jane,* a highly seductive young woman who escapes by a hair's breadth — usually with the loss of most of her clothes — from a series of compromising situations. The third character is a gambling, drinking, rip-roaring, rather attractive scoundrel, *Captain Reilly-Ffoull,* whose exploits, however promisingly they begin, always end in his own discomfiture. Finally there is *Jimpy,* a curious little boy whose extreme politeness and humility conceal a startling capacity to work magic at just those moments when he and his companions are faced by disaster.

Garth and Jane, Jimpy and Captain Reilly-Ffoull: is it possible that someone on the staff of the *Daily Mirror* chose these grotesques with full understanding of what he was doing? It is wildly unlikely. Yet beyond this and the even less likely theory of coincidence there lies only one other possibility — that they were chosen by the uncannily accurate processes of unconscious selection, operating at the deepest level of the human psyche. If this fantastic hypothesis were true, they would be found to exert a curiously compulsive power, overriding rational repudiation, on the minds of multitudes. Which is precisely what they do.

For these figures are no casual products of the imagination. Faintly through all their exploits, vulgar and puerile as these usually are, sounds an echo of something unimaginably archaic: the adventure cycles of the early gods. The famous mythologist, Kerenyi, latest among many, has shown with high probability that such adventure cycles are the basic themes of human mental activity as far back as it can be traced, recurring endlessly in the likeliest and most unlikely places, the noblest and most degenerate forms.

Consider *Garth*, that beefy and bewildered giant, long-suffering, virtuous, strong, faced by a never-ending series of heroic tasks. Is there not more than an echo here of Hercules and his labors, much-enduring, far-traveled Ulysses, blinded Samson, Noah, Gilgamesh . . . and behind these the timeless image of the heroic principle in man, aided magically by Heaven in reward of faith and valor?

Garth, for all his crudity, is a hero in the classic sense. He uses his miraculous strength only to restore the balance of things disturbed by evil forces. If he were a Leader it would be of nothing more sinister than a Boy Scout patrol. He is a "verray parfit gentil knight." Indeed, with women his unwearying chivalry puts to shame many of the accepted heroes in their weaker moments. Calypso would have had no chance with Garth; Delilah would have charmed in vain. Even the colorless girl-companion of Garth's adventures, Dawn, is

only there on sufferance, a sort of little sister allowed
under strict rules — which she is always breaking — to
share her brother's manly expeditions. To friendly ears
it may be whispered that here lies the clue to this almost dismaying chastity: Garth's life is bounded by the
simple certainties of pre-adolescence; he has never
reached the mental age at which woman becomes a
sweet temptation.

Woman as temptress: the image leads straight to another strip character, the often excruciating *Jane,* beautiful but virginal, constantly wooed but never wed.
Above her — far, far above — does there not float, as
on vaulted ceilings of Venetian palaces, a company of
bright figures? Hainuwele the moon maiden, irresist-
ible Helen, Aphrodite from the wine-dark sea, flower-
gathering Persephone, and all the countless images of
Kore the maiden goddess — "La Belle Dame sans
Merci," the unpossessable yet eternally nubile she,
whose golden promises invest with a brief splendor the
too credulous heart of man. Does not Jane in *Fritzy* the
dachshund even possess her appropriate animal attribute, as Diana has her hound, and Cynthia her hare?

In *Captain Reilly-Ffoull* the echoing image is at once
more immediate and more remote. His life of shameless
gusto, full of shady triumphs and richly earned humili-
ations, rouses in us secret sympathies; for here is the
renegade, the lame god, our shadow-self, the dark and
unacknowledged side of brindled human nature. Even
the quaint title of his moated and battlemented country
residence — Arntwee Hall — hints at his common hu-

manity, and is clearly more than accident. Here is a god so close to us that even the shallowest modern still hears his bold licentious whispers, yet so remote in origin that without experience of him Man would not be Man.

Older than all these are the dim unfocusable forms that throng "like pageantry of mist on an autumnal stream" behind the enigmatic figure of young *Jimpy*. These dim shapes are indeed the Early Gods, older far than "the bright static hierarchy of Olympus," older perhaps than Time itself. They reach back, these primal figures, to those fluid ever-changing changeless archetypes that gloom and glow in the depths of the archaic psyche. Incredibly, little Jimpy is of their company. Eternally childlike, vague of parentage, he displays with startling fidelity the attributes of weakness and insignificance combined with mysterious power possessed by the dawn-image of God in the human mind. At one point in the Jimpy cycle an adult character says to him, "Is it true, then, you must always remain a boy?" It would be hard to devise a clearer modern evocation of the *Puer Aeternus*.

Perhaps the key to the whole mystery of the comic strip's compulsive force lies in this Jimpian paradox of weakness and smallness combined with magical, boundless power. For paradox itself, that disquieting insult to received opinion, is usually a pointer to the heart of things. The approaches to wisdom are paved with prickly paradox; hard going for bare rational feet.

"Smaller than small, yet bigger than big." In these ap-

parently senseless words are expressed the earliest concepts of the Divine in the history of the human mind:
the Little Copper Man, for instance, of the Finnish
Kalevala, "no bigger than the thumb and no higher than
an oxhoof," who yet could fell the giant oak tree that
covered the sun and moon with its branches, with the
happy result that "the sun shone again and the dear
moon glimmered pleasantly, the clouds sailed far and
wide and the rainbow spanned the heavens"; or *Naray-
ana*, the little Hindu boy asleep in the branches of the
nyagrodha tree, in whose belly lay "the whole world
with its lands and cities, with the Ganges and the other
rivers and the Sea"; or, a more familiar image, *the Babe*
laid in a Manger, in whose praise the morning stars sang
together and all the sons of God shouted for joy. In
widely differing cultures the same paradoxical weakness and strength is visualized: in David with his sling,
Hercules strangling serpents in his cradle, Eros armed
with fatal arrows, and — little Jimpy, deferential to
adults but gifted with his magic powers.

There is, of course, something both offensive and out-
rageous in these parallels of the sublime with the de-
generate-ridiculous. The association is lunatic and the
rational mind recoils from it at first in repulsion and dis-
gust. The rational mind should calm itself. There have
been in myth and legend many such divine *bouleverse-
ments;* as of Jove, Lord of an antique Heaven, dwin-
dling down to bottle-nosed Father Christmas among the
kitchen pots and pans; though later, it is true, promoted
to reindeers and a fur coat. That these cheap and paltry

images in the corner of a popular newspaper should have spiritual significance remains, nevertheless, a thing painful to contemplate. And yet, if accepted, it emerges as but one more illustration of a phenomenon to which, perhaps, the universe is subject: *enantiodromia*, the incessant inevitable turning of all things into their opposites. Heraclitus, as Jung points out, was first of European minds to express this concept philosophically, but it owns a far more ancient parentage. The *Tai-gi-tu*, Chinese symbol of unguessed age, conveys the same concept with incomparable wholeness and precision. A white fish with a seed of blackness at its center curves into a black fish with a seed of whiteness, to form a perfect circle; each fish changes eternally into its opposite. What was important carried within itself the seed of its own destruction, and is slowly emptied of meaning; what was derided carried a forgotten truth, and leads to a new valuation.

Seen by this light the values we now neglect, the stone which the builders have rejected, should be looked for in exactly such a place, in a despised, unhonored corner of daily life. It is a measure of our neglect that these values are forced to put on so mean a mask in order to reenter human consciousness. The comic strip by its very bathos and infantilism, by the derision it arouses, by its astonishing universality of appeal and crude vitality, fulfills the historic conditions for "the return of the repressed." The comic strip is, in fact, a ludicrous but valid symptom of our disease. For in one form or another "the return of the repressed" is precisely what is making the present century rock and quiver with premonitions of eruption.

Unpalatable though it may be to modern taste, the truth is that we cannot live without the Early Gods. It was said of Nature that even if you throw her out with a pitchfork she nevertheless comes back. So do the Gods. If cast out in the forms of Man's profoundest apprehensions of them — if Christ and Buddha and Mithra, if Ashtaroth and Pan are disowned — they nevertheless come back. However meanly and unrecognizably, they come back to the human heart whose inevictable tenants they are. And "there all smothered up in shade" they sit, radiating that strange compelling power which is Man's unconscious tribute to the Unknowable. In the comic strip may be concealed the indestructible germ of natural religion.

3

THE SUBTLE BODY

IT IS probably true to say that whatever a man's conscious philosophy may be, a certain part of his mind is ceaselessly concerned with spiritual values. One of the most curious expressions of this is revealed in the history of alchemy. For modern man the word "alchemy" holds a kind of quaint magic, and conjures images of bubbling crucible and sealed retort, of little furnaces in medieval chambers "well fastened against the light," and of bent fanatic figures peering hopefully, year on year, for the mythical gold they will never see. In another mood a reference to alchemy brings us the comfortable feeling of intellectual superiority. "How odd," we say, "that men should waste their lives in so futile an undertaking! Though it may be," we generously add, "that these misguided efforts have lit the way to the triumphs of our modern chemistry." If this were alchemy's sole claim to remembrance, it were best altogether forgotten. The accidental discovery of antimony by Basilius Valentinus — who was inordinately pleased about it — would be indeed a puny result for more than seventeen centuries of human effort.

Seventeen hundred years is a considerable span of time; during all those centuries the basic concepts of alchemy have fascinated the minds and engaged the powers of not a few of the profoundest and subtlest intellects of their succeeding ages. Heraclitus, the near-legendary Trismegistus, Paracelsus, Jakob Böhme, all felt their strange attraction. Even outside this enormous time bracket alchemy exists; on the far side its origins recede into Egyptian darkness; on the near, the *Tragedy of Faust* appears in the unmistakable shape of an alchemical drama. Ideas of such enduring vitality are seldom, if ever, ignoble. It is only in the last three hundred years — since the Age of Enlightenment, which put out so many lights — that the alchemical quest for the transforming symbol, the Philosopher's Stone, has lain rejected and forgotten in an undusted attic of human memory; until picked up again in our own day by a man of genius, whose name was Carl Gustav Jung.

Seen casually and superficially, alchemy, it is true, aimed at the vulgar hope of turning baser metals into gold — though even the casual might surely have noted the alchemists' own rejection of this greedy dream: *Aurum nostrum,* says the Rosarium, *non est aurum vulgi* — "Our gold is not the common gold." More ripely considered its aim emerges as a striving for completeness, for a symbol that includes and expresses the play of all possible opposites. But alchemy had still another aim, the rich consequence of its rigorous discipline: it tried to produce a *certain kind of man,* a certain kind of investigator. It is this, perhaps, which gives the long-devalued art of alchemy its curiously present-day relevance; for precisely this kind of man alone can hope to tackle the terrifying dilemmas of the modern world. Only he can do so, because only he can penetrate their bewildering antinomies. It is his *métier particulier,* this coming to terms with apparently irreconcilable opposites. For as Jung says, in his brilliant and scholarly work *Psychology and Alchemy* — "The problem of the opposites plays a great — indeed the decisive — rôle in alchemy, since it leads in the ultimate phase of the work to the union of the opposites in the archetypal form of the . . . Alchemical Marriage. Here the supreme opposites, male and female (Yang and Yin) are melted into a unity purified of all opposition and therefore incorruptible."

What kind of man, then, did the art of alchemy require as its adept? The profusion of detailed directions leaves no doubt. And from them steps out a figure remote indeed from the mumbling charlatan of popular fancy. Hear how Morienus Romanus in the sixteenth century speaks to Prince Khalid, his pupil in the art of alchemy: "This thing for which you have sought so long is not to be acquired or accomplished by force or passion. It is only to be won by patience and humility, and a most perfect love. For God bestows this divine and immaculate science only on his faithful servants. . . ." Another of the old Masters says that to acquire "the golden understanding" one must keep the eyes of the mind and soul well open, observing and contemplating by means of "that inner light which God has lit in nature and in our hearts from the beginning." The Rosarium Philosophorum is even more precise: "He who wishes to be initiated into this art and wisdom must not be arrogant, but devout, righteous, of profound understanding; humane, of a cheerful countenance and a happy nature. . . . " Finally, this single pearl from Ruland the Lexicographer: "Imagination is the star in man."

One who fulfills such requirements is worthy of respect, however strange his calling. The alchemist knew, what the world had since forgotten — until it was rediscovered by Einstein, and, from a different angle, by Proust — that for the profoundest questions the seeker himself is the essential instrument of the seeker. The alchemist also recognized that the inner harmony and wholeness of that instrument is a prerequisite before such questions can even be seen, much less answered. In our own day the psychologist has stumbled once more on this neglected fact, and begins to reach out his hand, a little shyly and uncertainly, to his fantastic brother.

Alchemy bred many charlatans and fools, of course, as does psychology. But at his best the alchemist grappled as honestly as he could with those dark questions that lie unanswered in the heart of every man. In particular he approached matter with a passionate conviction that it held a mystery, a *mysterium magnum*, the nature of which was different in quality and in essence from its material container; and that he himself was in the literal sense a redeemer destined by his work, and

with God's help (a point which was always empha-
sized), to release the imprisoned spirit, the *lapis invisibilitatis*. Psychologically considered, his work was a
profound and sustained attempt to release the spirit imprisoned within himself, though such a concept was beyond the range of most medieval minds. Not, however,
of all. "Transform *yourselves*," says Gerhard Dorn,
"from dead stones into living philosophical stones!"
And the prescribed discipline for meditation has an
oddly familiar ring to psychologists: "The alchemical
meditatio," says Ruland the Lexicographer, "is an inner
dialogue with someone who is invisible, as also with
God, or with oneself, or with one's good angel." Today
we would add — "and with one's dark angel."

The actual technique of the alchemical opus was an
elaborate chemical process in three stages, the Black,
the White and the Red, by means of which the
"pneuma" or spirit was extracted from matter, as quick-
silver is extracted from ore. It culminated in the Alchemical Wedding, or union of opposites, symbolized as
King and Queen, *Sol* and *Luna,* from which finally was
born the precious Child of Wisdom, the Philosopher's
Stone. The thing sounds fantastic. Yet in reality it was
no new idea: the Gnostics had long before seen the necessity of releasing the *Nous* from the entangling em-
brace of physical nature; earlier still the Greeks had
made pictures of Hermes conjuring winged spirits from
the dead matter in a funeral urn; and Christianity itself
is the story of the Son of God, symbol of Spirit, entering
the world of matter in order finally to free Himself —

and us — from the dominion of physical death. It is not, indeed, impossible that this tremendous concept exists independently of space and time, constellating itself over and over again in images of majestic and numinous power.

These were the not ignoble preoccupations of the alchemist. Such servants of the Unseen, fortunately for the rest of us, will always recur in human history. There will always be those who must look into the dark in order to see, who must open the window of the little lighted world of men, and lean out to gaze entranced at the featureless night. . . . Leaning out so, the world sees only their back view; and it must be admitted that from this angle they are more than a little ridiculous, reminiscent mainly of those curious persons on piers who turn their backs on sunlight and dancing waves to look into little machines that reveal, for a small sum, What the Butler Saw. The world laughs at these night gazers, indulgently or acidly, and may be pardoned for it, having no inkling of what such men seek, and have always sought, through the ages: Helen, the Golden Fleece, the Grail, the Diamond Body, the Corpus Subtile — the secret of "the treasure hard to attain" under all its lovely names and aspects.

What the alchemist sought for, he sought not with his intellect alone, but with his whole self. It is a mode of approach transcending limitations of period. Obscurely, but with unshakable certainty, man is aware of a goal which demands, and to which he can freely give, the whole of himself. There is a merchant in man unexpectedly ready to sell all that he has to buy the pearl of great price. In the meantime, it is true, he bargains cynically enough; though, as middle age is reached and passed, with a secretly sinking heart. The union of all opposites at which alchemy aims is a not unworthy adumbration of such a goal, which is the goal also of the great religions.

There was, in fact, a time when Hermetic philosophy was not felt to be in any way inimical to the Christianity of the Church. On the contrary, certain people regarded it as one of the mainstays of the Christian faith. In 1593 Francesco Patrizi, a Venetian humanist philosopher, addressed a plea to Pope Gregory XIV requesting him "to let Hermes take the place of Aristotle." The moment passed. But it was a crucial choice. It is fascinating to imagine what might have happened to European culture if the alternative path had been followed. Certainly no loss in Christian faith, and, perhaps, what shining gains! — above all in the transcendence of the dreary dichotomy of mind and body.

In the speculations of alchemists no such bleak division existed between matter and mind as till recently existed for us. Whether the alchemist was searching for that which actually turns baser metal into gold, or for its spiritual equivalent, is rather our dilemma than his. He was capable of conceiving a "subtle body" which could manifest itself equally in the mental and physical modes. It is a capacity we lost in the eighteenth and nineteenth centuries, but which now in the twentieth we may be in the act of regaining, confronted as we are by a physics and a psychology which are peering into an ultimate and frightening darkness undreamed of by our fathers and grandfathers.

Like the dragon that swallows its own tail, human thought has returned, by a circular journey of more than three hundred years, to the perilous watershed between the mental and the physical, and now stands, dwarfed and daunted by the immensities that surround it, at the approaches to the secret link in the structure of the universe. By a far different path the alchemist was there before us. As befits so dark a mystery he had many names for the quintessence which he sought: *lapis invisibilitatis,* he called it, Child of Wisdom, *Light above all lights,* the Subtle Body, *Mercurius;* and most naïvely but perhaps most perfectly of all — *glutinum mundi,* "the glue of the world," that which is the union of all that is humanly separate: mind and body, life and death, the eternal and the temporal. We seek again this glue. The aims of alchemy are precisely those of the delicate growing point of modern consciousness.

4

FAIRY-TALE
WORLDS

THE MIND of a child is a mystery and a paradox. Outwardly all clarity and innocence — *O ces voix d'enfants!* — all ignorance and dependence, all rainbow tears and laughter; inwardly the rapt secret communion with realities of another order, with opposites and correspondences of which the golden key is lost to us, with the world of witch and dwarf and monster: the archetypal Fairy-Tale World. A child lives largely in the Unconscious, and is more than a little mad.

Here is one playing alone in a garden: listen to the earnest dialogue with imaginary beings, watch the bizarre gestures and queer grimaces. For less than this adults have been put quietly away. And yet it is a madness which wisdom envies, for to a child the world is meaningful, is urgently alive with meaning. And this in the last analysis is wisdom's goal. Having in childhood possessed it, and lost it again, there persists in the adult mind a forlorn sense of estrangement.

John Keats once said that the life of a man of any worth is a continual allegory. It is the corroding certainty of having lost the key to this translucent kind of living, that eats the heart out on quiet summer evenings. In such an hour men and events seem contingent, pointless, formless; and Reason, that tireless choreographer of "the bloodless ballet of concepts," grows sick of its own success.

Three paths there are that lead out of this wilderness. One is a fatal path, with a fatal fascination. Through the iron gates of War man suddenly reenters the fluid and phantasmagorial world of the child and the madman. With what helpless dread and what infinite weariness the rational part of the mind, critic of millennial sad experience, watches the old stock figures strut confidently on to the stage, as the curtain rises yet again on the deadly, dreary drama! With what enormous distaste it foresees the futile finale before the opening word is spoken. Even the protagonists' names are hardly altered — Khan, Caesar, Kaiser, Führer — though the players' stature seems to shrink, the crown and robes to sit more grotesquely, with each preposterous reenactment. Everything is stale, false, seen-before, senseless. Beauty vanishes, darkness falls from the air. One man finds the perfect phrase: "The lamps of Europe are going out," said Sir Edward Grey in 1914; "they will not be re-lit in our time." To the eyes of reason War is the total eclipse of meaning.

Exactly here lies the inevitable paradox. While reason cries out on the insanity of War, feverishly searching out its causes, shuffling and rearranging its determinants, the Unconscious sees only this: that War allows the reappearance on earth of certain meaningful fig-

ures. Like Walpurgis Night it is a privileged occasion,
when the portals of the Unconscious swing wide. And
what a nightmare throng streams up through those un-
guarded gates! Monstrous and unreal they are, yet
charged with a terrible energy: Führers and Duces with
the implacable faces of blood-loving Baal and child-
devouring Moloch; women spies, the Lamias of the twilight hour, sliding like jeweled snakes through the ruined
cities; Renegades, loaded with infamy and shame, whis-
pering dark secrets to the enemy; and here and there,
crawling up from remotest swamps of the archaic psyche, furtive bearers of unnameable evil, men who make
bonfires of living bodies, women who make lampshades
of human skin.

Jostling these grisly figures come the shining band of
Saviors: hero generals haloed with golden legend; Unknown Warriors; triumphing martyrs; divinely compas-
sioned Mother-figures like the Lady with the Lamp.
The qualities of all things good and evil are fiercely in-
tensified. Opposites collide to form new truths and new
falsehoods. Faith blooms, born of despair; at Mons
once, ten thousand hopeless eyes see Angels close above
them. The whole world suddenly brims with clear and
terrible meaning. Silenced and appalled, the conscious
part of man looks on, while the Unconscious eagerly releases these tremendous avatars of good and evil, each
one a secret but immortal aspect of the human psyche.

War is the punishment of man's disbelief in these
forces within himself. It is the cruel reaffirmation of
those powers which the ego can never command or sub-

due. And disastrous as the cost may be, something in the depths of man is mysteriously assuaged by this release of daemonic and destructive energies. There is a fierce satisfaction in living under the rule of the Early Gods. There is a dignity in facing powers beyond us, and indifferent to us. To be blind to this, to fail to grasp its difficult meaning, is to let slip the golden Ariadne's thread that may lead man at last out of the stinking labyrinth of War.

In *The Green Table*, that terrifying ballet of the nineteen-thirties, the cause of War is shown to lie in the criminal futilities of power-politics. The intolerable blame is comfortingly projected on to wrangling statesmen. It may well be so. But causal chains belong to the conscious level, while War springs from the Unconscious, which is concerned not with causes but with meanings. And meaning, as Lao Tzu has said, is that which exists through itself: it is the Secret of the Golden Flower. War has causes — social, political, and economic — but it also has a meaning. To reach this meaning in time may be man's last and best hope. For in the moment it is reached, a question rises urgently in the heart: is there no other way to release these primordial powers, no other path to wholeness?

*

If indeed there were none, mankind could well yield to despair. But another does exist; a curious path, this one, that winds its secret way through very different regions, but leads there no less surely. Children, the pre-elected freemen of the world of the Unconscious, stray along this path — or perhaps are blown along it like brightly colored leaves. Swayed by intimations from an unknown source, the games and groupings of children left entirely to themselves have an unmistakable air of ritual. They seem to be half remembering something, and their movements, made often with the tranced certainty of sleepwalkers, awaken memories that have slept for centuries in the adult human heart. Absorbed and serious, they draw a circle in the dust that may be a quaint copy of the necromancer's *temenos*, or of the circular furrow cut by plough to mark the founding of some rose-red city of the pagan world. They weave little dances, secret and ritualistic, whose original patterns lie buried with the lost religions. And they sing strange meaningless snatches of songs that may be time-altered echoes from Eleusis or the Nile. "Nor you, nor I, nor anyone know, How corn and beans and barley grow," sing the children, intending only to find who pays the forfeit; not guessing, or indeed caring, that Demeter listens in the shadows with a warm motherly smile.

And not children only: kings and queens, priests and mystics, the very wise and the very simple, have always intuitively sought and found this path that leads to the fourth-dimensional world of meaning. From Delphos to Westminster Abbey, from shrouded oracle to impeccably laundered Archbishop, from primitive fertility rite to the crowning of a young and radiant Queen, the magic of ritual binds and releases the soul of man and reveals to him the world of meaning that logic can never reach.

In their final significance the forms of ritual are far more than forms: they are the intricate beautiful patterns, the delicate temporal webs, in which man has striven to enmesh that which lies outside his space and time. And sometimes with their help (as also sometimes without it, a sheer, lovely irrelevance) a door suddenly opens, revealing for an instant the timeless world of primordial images in whose depths the meaning of life is contained. As in the monstrous instance of War, the forces of the Unconscious surge eagerly through the momentary opening, and something in the heart of man responds, as always, with the deep, indefinable sense of assuagement.

How subtle a thing is this feeling of assuagement! The thirst it allays, the terrible thirst to find a meaning in life, is one of which a man is at first only obscurely aware. He feels only a vague deepening sense of discomfort, of missed harmonies as faint as the wave-music in a small seashell — which Science reassures us is nothing but illusion. O keep still, keep still, and listen. Once the inner ear is attuned to this music, there is no other it will wish to hear; no other reality in the world of time and space that compares with this "illusion" — this sweet assuaging harmony — heard only on that Everest-peak of inner experience where the temporal touches, however briefly, the eternal. "Man has come into this world," said William Law, "on no other errand than to arise out of the vanity of time."

There is no alternative. The more ingenious and determined the attempt to assign to life a purely rational value, the more cruelly and viciously will the irrational burst through to reestablish its own neglected values; on the social level by War, on the individual level by neurotic conflict, on the intellectual by such epileptic reactions as the Surrealists and the neo-abstractionists. Humility is the key. Man must return to his origins, personal and racial, and learn again the truths of the imagination. And in this task his strange instructors are the child, who has but half-entered the rational world of time and space, and the madman, who has half escaped from it. For just these two are in some measure released from the remorseless pressure of daily events, the ceaseless impact of the external senses, which burdens the rest of mankind. They travel light, this curious pair, and go on far and solitary journeys, sometimes bringing back a gleaming branch from the Gold Forest through which they have wandered. "Nor you, nor I, nor anyone know," sing the wise children. "I know more than Apollo," cries foolish Tom o'Bedlam, crooning to himself his mysterious Song,

> *I know more than Apollo,*
> *For oft while he lies sleeping*
> *I behold the stars at mortal wars,*
> *And the rounded welkin weeping.*

Such things as these, the fantasies of the child, the intuitions of the madman, are more than moonshine. Concealed within them are realities, though of a different

order from those of which guns and computers are
made.

It is no accident that John Custance, who has written
a travel book of a new kind, has given it the curious title
of *Wisdom, Madness, and Folly*. It records a grim,
heroic journey of the spirit through the fear-haunted
realm of lunacy; from which he is perhaps the first modern ever to return strengthened and enriched. Time
and again on his wild Odyssey he comes to perilous regions where the madman and the child are the only
companions that Wisdom has, or can have. For these
three know, what we have fatally forgotten, that we
carry within us that which must, at however tragic a
cost, keep its contacts with the world of myth and fairy
tale, the world beyond human space and time, beyond
human cause and effect. It is man's chief aim. We have
come into this world on no other errand.

*

There is a third path — unfashionable now, and unfre-
quented — along which dark elements of the soul, the
monstrous apparitions and wild pageantry of the inner
world, are allowed for a few dream-like days and nights
to irrupt into conscious life. For that brief period law
and order abdicate, and all the forces of the irrational
make hasty holiday. In Catholic countries this strange
interlude in men's lives has been christened Carnival,
and its culminating day — *Mardi Gras,* "Fat Tuesday"
— is a shrewdly permitted license to the faithful on the

eve of Lenten austerities. But its origins are worldwide, and more ancient by many centuries than Christian belief.

Carnival is a phenomenon of cultured societies. Primitive man had no need of it, for the return of chaos loomed over him every hour of his life. But as soon as men began to create for themselves conditions of stability and some measure of the rule of reason, at once the necessity for a compensating period, however brief, of anarchy and license became manifest. In all ages and in all parts of the earth, from China to the Amazon — with the sole exception of the petrified, death-obsessed culture of Dynastic Egypt — the most intelligent societies have recognized this need and tried to canalize it, to contain it within the specified dates of their local calendar.

*

The history of Carnival is the history of the socially unacceptable impulses in human nature, and their insistent demand to be admitted into life. In the Western world the response of Authority to this demand — by the institution of cannily controlled Festivals — has been only partially successful. For these Festivals had a disconcerting way of either turning themselves into a seething "cauldron of unholy loves" or petering out in childish fun which offered no release to the rebel impulses in man. They refused to stay as their originators intended, and swung through the centuries from one extreme to the other. It is, in fact, possible to trace the movement of this peculiar pendulum, to observe to what extraordinary excesses it can carry the human spirit, and to note that in the contemporary world it is once more, disquietingly, on the turn.

When first caught sight of, emerging in uncertain outline from the legendary past, the pendulum was already in an extreme position. The *Dionysiac Revels,* perhaps the earliest expression of the spirit of Carnival of which we know, was a pretty brutal affair, hardening finally into the far-famed annual orgy of the Bacchantes; when bands of maids and matrons streamed out of the civilized city of Athens in strange disguises and roamed the mountains for days and nights on end, tearing to pieces with their bare hands any living animal they met — including, it was whispered, man.

In later times the sophisticated rulers of pre-Christian Rome transferred this primitive cathartic device from conquered Greece to their own country, softening it to the *Saturnalia,* a festival for both sexes celebrated at the turn of the winter solstice. The emphasis here was laid on fun and reckless spirits rather than destructiveness, a humorous reversal of roles and hierarchies — slaves, for example, being served by their masters — and a general loosening up of the proprieties.

When Christianity was accepted by Rome the early Christian Fathers — then as now — tried to mitigate for the masses the shock of the sudden change by continuing many of the old pagan festivals as Christian feast-days. *Saturnalia* became *Carnevale* — farewell to flesh — and was moved to the days preceding the fasting period of Lent. But then a curious thing occurred. Carnival became too successful. In the wake of Christianity it spread like flaming oil on water through the ancient city-states of Italy, and within a few centuries Rome and Venice, Milan and Naples became the centers of an annual festival which took on wilder, madder and more menacing forms in each succeeding year. The Church had innocently touched the lock and once more Pandora's Box flew open.

Swelling up from the Unconscious came horrid shapes that walked the streets — giants on stilts with hideous grinning masks, crudely fashioned dragons and misshapen beasts, children in the guise of evil dwarfs, men as painted and bejeweled ladies, women swaggering in the clothes of men. Carriages rushed by crammed with drunken revelers throwing flour and mud and dung in the faces of passersby. Maddened horses were set free to trample down the rioting crowds. Anthony Munday, a medieval traveler (quoted in Rattray Taylor's remarkable book, *Sex in History*, from which these scenes are taken), records how in Venice during Carnival he saw murder committed in the open streets with no one "taking any accoumpt either of the murtherer or of the slaine gentleman."

The Christian Fathers, dismayed, issued edicts and threatened punishments; but the pendulum was on the move once more, and for centuries no human power could stay its swing. The spirit of Carnival now began to spread more widely — to London, Paris, Madrid — and to assume an even more sinister form. In the *Feast of Fools,* condemned by the Council of Toledo in A.D. 635, obscenity and blasphemy were added to the general license. Priests and clergy themselves took part, electing a Pope of Fools, and appearing at divine service in masks, or dressed as women or panders. While the drunken celebrant was saying Mass they danced, played dice, and sang indecent songs.

By the thirteenth century it had become the *Feast of Asses.* An ass, or a man wearing as ass's head, was introduced into the religious revels, and during Mass the bawdy Song of the Asses was sung, accompanied by the congregation chanting "Hee-haw, Hee-haw." How far matters were out of hand may be gauged by the fact that the Chapter of Sens in 1444 issued a strict ruling that those couples who wished to copulate during divine service should go outside the church before doing so. A not unreasonable injunction.

The swing of the pendulum had reached its term. In Elizabethan England the *Feast of Fools* was at last suppressed, and its energies directed into the milder ceremony of the election of a Lord of Misrule, or Abbot of Unreason. He and his followers, mounted on hobby-horses, proceeded to the local churchyard, issuing absurd commands to all who met them on the way; and there the Leader set up his crazy Court, where they feasted uproariously and libidinously for a short season. In France the *Feast of Fools* was similarly replaced by a ceremony called the *Société Joyeuse,* led by a man, often a priest, known as *La Mère Folle* and dressed in women's clothes.

In passing, it is interesting to notice how constantly Carnival is connected with the phenomenon of *transvestism*. The interchange of clothes between the sexes is part of the essence of the Carnival spirit and reveals a curious link between Carnival and one of the earliest ideas to enter the mind of man. For in many primitive societies the primordial gods and the first human beings were believed to be androgynous, and only after the fatal separation of Heaven and Earth — the Fall of Man — were the sexes set apart. Primitive festal rites were often designed to undo this "inferior" arrangement and restore the original state of completeness, in order to make possible a new beginning, a transcending of one's everyday self. Many centuries later this strange concept was still alive, and still related to festive occasions. Plutarch recorded with astonishment that in Argos a bride wore a false beard for the marriage night, while in Cos it was the husband who put on woman's clothes to receive his wife. In the fragment of a lost play by Aeschylus, the bisexual god Dionysus is greeted by cries of "*Where have you come from, man-woman? What is your country? And what is that garment?*" — questions which incidentally might well be addressed to a contemporary teen-ager. This deliberate confusion of sexes is also part of the basic aim of Carnival which seeks, however crudely, a dissolution of the stiffened traditional order, a reversal of all accepted values, and a reactivation of the boundless power and creativity of the Beginning.

To return to the image of the pendulum: by degrees

even the relatively harmless excesses of the Lord of Misrule and La Mère Folle — still frowned on by the strengthening forces of law and order — quieted down, and slowly developed into such innocent customs as the *Christmas Mummers*, whose antics entertained our rude forefathers and provided an outlet merely for rough jokes and bucolic buffoonery. With the nineteenth century came April Fool's Day, and, at Christmas, paper hats, crackers and charades — pale survivals of the masked daemonic figures of medieval Carnival. The pendulum had touched its opposite extreme.

But it will swing back. The claim of the irrational forces for recognition will recur — *must recur*. In the contemporary world there are already signs of this among the adolescents of many countries. Boys with feminine haircuts and gaudy clothes, girls as masculine and bizarre as they can make themselves, are appearing in the streets, the harbingers of masquerade. Their outbursts of violence — still vaguely connected with public holidays — against each other and against the community and the police are, of course, an ebullition of youthful high spirits; but not simply that. There is also present, for those who dare to look for it, an unmistakable flavor of the sinister. What these adolescents are rousing is the sleeping urge to anarchy that hides not only in their hearts, but in ours. And we must somehow make room for its reawakening demands. It is a task of enormous difficulty. To crush these anarchic impulses by superior power is to invite catastrophe. Yet to handle them indulgently and "understandingly" is to risk, as in the past, the release of vicious mass frenzies of a kind that is fortunately peculiar to the human animal.

❋

We are compelled, nevertheless, to take the second of the two risks. For the truth is that these recurrent irruptions of unconscious imagery into everyday life express in their own fantastic terms a not unworthy aim: *to fling in the world's face the Dionysiac challenge* — life lived like a mountain torrent, sparkling and tumbling in the sunlight, carrying all before it, crowned with beauty in the instant of its own destruction . . . Over against it forever stands the Classic attitude, marmoreal, calm, clear thinking; verbalized once and for all in the sonorous syllables of St. Augustine — PAX, ORDO, LEX, SOCIETAS; the four great pillars of Apollonian life.

No one in his normal senses would wish for the total victory of either side. A world of Romantics would end in unendurable chaos, a world of pure Classics in a static perfection; and "perfection," as Kenneth Clarke has said, "closes the door." Both attitudes are valid and indeed complementary. What is deplorable is that each, in its brief moment of victory, can treat the other with such savagery and lack of comprehension.

Perhaps after all, Carnival, the answer given by so many earlier civilizations, is the best we can do. For all its look of lunacy and its inherent dangers, it is an answer that rises up from the deepest levels of the psyche. The giant phantoms of Carnival are direct, unmediated creations of the dreaming mind. Set free for a time they release and act out its negative, non-conforming aspect. Swaying monstrously past startled eyes, the figures of Carnival grant us a warning glimpse of the iconoclastic impulses of man's unconscious mind — as War reveals its homicidal madness, and Ritual hints at its fragile and inexpressible beauty.

5

MAN AND HIS BOMB

IN CONTRAST to the universal fear of personal death, men seem to look forward with a kind of relief to an eventual end of the world they live in. Every major religion has its teleological goal. Even Hinduism, with its concept of eternal reincarnation, includes an escape route for the enlightened spirit from the horror of infinite recurrence. In cities everywhere, men are to be seen with banners that proclaim the imminent doom of mankind. We smile at the banner-carriers (a little uneasily these days), but the fact is that like them we are all concerned with eschatology, the doctrine of Last Things.

The human mind, misapprehending Time as an ultimate reality, recoils from the vision of a world without end, a ceaseless procession of births and deaths with no final cataclysmic event to give the long, long story at least a retrospective meaning. The end, it is said, crowns the work. And Time without its crown would seem to many as unsatisfactory as a bowler hat in like condition.

If such a belief expresses, as it seems to do, a valid

aspect of the religious impulse, contemporary man is, in one sense, profoundly religious. For to our generation the end of the world as it now exists is an immediate practical possibility — some would contend, a probability. To say that we live in the shadow of the multi-megaton bomb is no figure of speech. Day and night, patrolling in the air above us are machines whose monstrous cargo is ready to be dropped at a word from Washington or Moscow. The Bomb reigns in our sky like Jehovah of the Israelites — vengeful and observant. It is the supreme symbol of our time.

Like all true symbols it is double-faced. One of its two faces is the most terrifyingly concrete fact in our daily existence; the other points, beyond all trivialities of time and place, to a central and still unsolved mystery, to the meaning of life and consciousness. For terrestrial life, developing at first blindly through thousands of centuries, has reached in our time a critical degree of consciousness: it is now confronted, through the bomb, with the inescapable choice of coming to terms with itself, or destroying itself. Mother Nature has at last brought into existence a progeny that dares to rebel against her. The human race has suddenly come of age and asserts the right to follow its own destiny, even — if it so wills — to self-destruction. As with the dangerous passions of adolescence it must be left free to make its own choice; and the whole world shudderingly awaits the outcome.

The parallel with unbalanced adolescence is precise. For when neurotic youth is hell-bent on suicide no external influence or loving care can permanently prevent

a tragedy. Only an inner force, born in the moment of
crisis, can sway the issue between life and death; and
only its victory can bring back meaning into that individual life. Luckily it is a force of such enormous
strength that suicide in adolescence, relative to the
numbers involved, is a rarity.

What is this inner force, and where is it to be found?
These are questions worth asking, for the human race
as a whole has urgent need of it. Indeed, it could be
said that on this elusive factor alone now depends the
fate of the world.

To attempt an answer is to be at once confronted by
an enigma, the *location* of consciousness. There are two
contemporary views about this — or three if we include
the average man's conviction that his consciousness
must be situated somewhere among the convolutions of
his brain. Apart from this naïve concept, the question
is still open whether consciousness is constellated only
within the individual, or transcends individual limitations.

Nature is prolific of apparent examples of the second
possibility. The hive and the anthill are illustrations of
a group-consciousness which manifestly exceeds the
limited consciousness of the individual insect. So much
so that these insect communities are regarded by some
entomologists rather as one purposive individual than
as a swarm of separate insects.

This phenomenon is relevant to man's present predicament. For it is impossible to imagine any threat to the
existence of, say, a beehive or an anthill — a threat created by a specialized group of insect-workers in the

same way that the thermonuclear bomb has been created by human scientists — being allowed to endanger for a single moment the life of the community. The mysterious power of the insect group-mind, intent on preservation and continuance of the community, would nip such insanity swiftly in the bud.

If consciousness can transcend individual limitations at the insect level, it is conceivable that it could do so at the human level. This suggests one escape route from the peril which looms over us: by the evolution (as in the nightmare vision of Père Teilhard du Chardin) of a super-intelligence, not set up in some international center, nor lodged in any single mind, but permeating the community; an all-powerful, prescient group-consciousness whose decisions are blindly obeyed by the individual. Such a super-intelligence would be permanently unchallengeable, for it would rule from inside as well as outside each individual. It would be everywhere — and nowhere. There is after all nothing new in this. The collective intelligence which controls the hive or termitary has this mysterious, unquestionable power. And deep in the heart of the dedicated bureaucrat may lie an unconscious longing to rule from that invisible, unassailable throne.

On the human level these things have not happened yet. They could be nearer than we think. One contemporary writer has seen humanity caught already in the grip of an unseen yet pervasive power with which it is impossible to contend; and it drove him to despair and death. Kafka's tremendous, suffocating books communicate perfectly the panic horror of the moment when man begins to guess that the very essence of himself, the power to will, to decide, to feel, even to realize the loss of these faculties, is slipping out of his grasp and sliding smoothly into invisible waiting hands whose purposes, perhaps hostile, at best indifferent, must be for ever unknown to him . . .

*

Two possibilities, therefore, seem to be open to modern man. On the one hand we can continue as we have started — bombing, poisoning and infecting each other till death do us part, leaving Life a free hand to begin again with the remnants of the human race, or to experiment with some entirely different species. Many already believe this to be the destiny of our world — and try not to think about it. On the other we can make a voluntary sacrifice of individual values and move forward, along the lines of the insect "blueprints" which Nature has provided, towards the creation of a super-intelligent group-mind of which the individual is merely the acquiescent instrument. To the majority of human beings both these solutions are almost equally repellent.

When a problem appears to be insoluble, it is a safe assumption that the lines of approach are inadequate. Some factor of primary importance has not been taken into account. Could it be that the daunting difficulties now crowding in upon the bewildered human race are designed to awaken man to this fact? Is it possible that the monstrous menace poised above our heads — release of which could cause, it has been calculated, above a hundred million deaths — carries a numinous command that man must reach a new relationship to the world around him, and that to do this he must give priority, not to external problems, but to the *mind* that is considering them? For hardly a beginning has yet been made to bring the illimitable inner world that has recently been opened to us, the world of the unconscious, the world of the dreaming mind, into living contact with everyday life. Within the mind of Everyman there are untried forms of apprehension altogether different from waking consciousness, and free of the waking mind's anxious preoccupation with space and time.

They are indeed so different that he is rightly afraid of them. Yet this perhaps is the moment when man must take the incalculable risk of permitting his shadow-side to appear, the risk of allowing the dark sun of the unconscious to rise above the mind's horizon and irradiate the world we live in with "a new and terrible beauty." Dangerous as the remedy is (although there are certain contemporary painters and sculptors who show us that it can be done), the disease is equally dangerous. Our problems are plainly growing beyond conventional human control, and consciousness has no choice but to enlarge itself to meet them.

The trouble is, consciousness *per se* has not the power to do this. It must look beyond itself for help. At this point organized religions tend to present themselves as the answer; but surely an insufficient one, or religious war would be a contradiction in terms. Contemporary philosophy is even less helpful, shaking a wise head

over the follies of men, or busying itself with questions
of linguistics.

For modern man there is a new and promising possibility: to go down boldly into the darkness of the under-
world, and there to claim his bride, his shadow-self, his
wholeness. For the truth is, full human consciousness
has still to be won. It is waiting to be born from a marriage that has not yet taken place, that only *can* take
place at the deepest level of the psyche — the marriage
between thinking and feeling. In everyday life these
two functions tend to be antagonistic except in certain
moments of high crisis. And while this is so, human
consciousness is a crippled thing.

Moreover, when operating in isolation each function
is essentially destructive. The thermonuclear bomb is a
typical end-product of the kind of thinking that is disconnected from feeling. But feeling is also a mode of
consciousness. The kind of feeling that is disconnected
from thinking has as its end-product — war. Autonomous thinking provides the cataclysmic weapon. Autonomous feeling provides the setting in which the
weapon can be used. The appalling danger presented
by the operations of these isolated functions can be
countered at the individual level in one way only: by a
fusion of these two modes of consciousness so perfect
and indissoluble as to make it impossible for the human
mind ever again to use them separately.

They should never be so used. For isolated thinking
and isolated feeling are, in fact, classic forms of madness: they constitute the two dangerous, closed-in

worlds of the schizophrenic and the manic-depressive. But to marry thinking to feeling is not merely to restore sanity to the operations of the human mind; it is also to open new and urgently needed dimensions in human consciousness.

Out of the royal union of thinking and feeling will be born the inner force that alone can pull man back to safety from the high and narrow window ledge on which he now stands, screaming silently.

Feel with your brain
Think with your heart

PART

TWO

"Heavier-than-air flying machines are impossible."
Lord Kelvin, President of the Royal Society
1890–5

"I'm all for the cosmos. I'll go, too — but with a rose in my hand."

Young Russian girl, 1965

6

THE DRAMA OF
SPACE AND TIME

ADDED to his sense of isolation, twentieth-century man feels scared. For this is, beyond all question, the Promethean century of human history. The contemporary spirit of adventure admits no bounds; even the sky is no longer the limit. We live now in a world which is developing more and more the improbable qualities of a dream. And as in a dream, we find ourselves suddenly cast in the leading role of a tremendous drama — but with a sick awareness that we have had no time to study the part.

It is a drama in three acts, and its title is *Space and Time*. Gamely we have struggled through the first act, whose theme is conquest of the air, acquitting ourselves with a kind of trembling success; but before we can draw breath the second act is upon us, in which we have to fling ourselves recklessly into the abyss of outer space; and looming straight ahead is the apocalyptic third act, where we are committed to the fantastic dangers of tampering with the mystery of Time. . . .

Let us run through the story of this peculiar play, where all the classic rules of drama are flouted, and every act ends in a gigantic question mark. It is worth doing. For even at this eleventh hour it may be possible, with the help of memory and imagination, to infuse some meaning into the part we are, in any case, compelled to perform.

ACT I: *Fear and Flying*

Flying is remarkably safe. Statistics show that its accident rate per passenger mile compares favorably with most other forms of public transport. The insurance rate, that unemotional guide to real danger, is roughly the same for travel by land, sea or air. Yet many people — and many more than will admit it — are secretly afraid of flying. Some will stoutly confess their fear. The rest casually produce rather more reasons than are necessary to account for their preference for other kinds of transport. "Flying is so noisy," they say; or "Flying is so boring, so cramping, so dependent on the weather — besides it makes me deaf for hours — and in any case I don't feel it is entirely *natural* to be whisked from one country to another without time for readjustment . . ." They will brush aside the reassuring accident rate as if these figures were quite irrelevant to their state of mind. Which, of course, they are. It is the tragic error of bureaucracy to believe that one can overcome feeling with figures.

What, then, are the psychological factors behind this latent sense of fear?

They can be said to fall into two groups — the Rational and the Irrational. The rational factors are obvious enough to any intelligent person. It is plain, for instance, that an air crash has the elusive quality of News Value; even when no one has been killed it hits the headlines of the daily papers, while a bus accident of similar kind gains a mere paragraph in the middle pages. In a plane accident the total helplessness of the passengers strikes chillingly on the mind; no one has ever suggested holding the legs up, or climbing into the luggage rack — as in train accidents — to avoid disaster. Added to all this is the terrifying risk of fire. Finally, while the vagaries of land and sea have been explored and tabulated by countless generations of adventurous men, the element of air is still a zone of unpredictable mystery, whose well-meaning servants the meteorologists are the daily butts of its sardonic humor. In short, the imagination has in every sense more to play with in an air catastrophe: for though it is equally fatal, to fall 60 feet is less frightening than to fall 6,000 feet. And indeed there is some sense in this, for there is more time provided for anticipation — and anticipation is the kernel of fear. All these factors, and many subsidiary ones, give food for the reasonable apprehensions of imaginative men; though each can be effectively countered by rational argument.

But deeper than any of these, far below the reach of reasonable counter-claim, lie the irrational factors. For countless centuries men have longed, not only in their waking lives but in their dreams, to soar into the air and sweep across seas and continents. There is a direct and simple symbolism about flying, and our language and ways of thought are steeped in it. We try to "rise above" our troubles, and "aspire" to greatness; in human imagination angels are always fitted with wings, and heaven is always in the sky. Man seems to have felt more frustrated by the law of gravity than by any other of his physical limitations. He has ceaselessly dreamed of defeating it. To our generation belongs the almost unbelievable privilege of actualizing this age-old dream.

Like all privileges, it must be paid for. This brave adventure of flying stirs deep roots, wakens ancient echoes in the heart of man. It rouses archaic hopes and fears, ancestral doubts, that cannot be explained away by figures from a Department of Statistics, but must be accepted as inherent in the meaning of life. For in the dark unconscious basis of the human mind there is an eternal collision of opposites. The positive creative forces urging upward towards more light, more life, more consciousness, are confronted by the negative destructive powers stubbornly opposing them. At every forward step of the human race something in the heart of man rejoices, and something recoils in fear and anger — for anger is the child of fear.

When we fly, and still more when we hear of air crashes, we are experiencing once again the eternal conflict between the heroic principle and the powers of darkness, in which man himself is the inescapable battleground. In the classic world this conflict was felt directly as a dangerous invasion of the realm of the gods, inviting fatal retribution unless undertaken in a spirit of humility and wisdom. In countless myths and legends — those fadeless records of what transpires in the human heart — the perils of overboldness are vividly expressed, and the need shown for the essential qualities of humility and wisdom in all such heroic ventures. They tell of Prometheus, who stole fire from heaven for man's use, and paid a terrible price for the rashness of his method; of poor young Icarus, whose wax wings melted when he flew too near the sun, so that he plunged into the Sicilian sea and drowned, while Daedalus, his wiser and more cautious father, flew lower and escaped disaster; of Phaethon, the vainglorious child of the sun god Helios, who insisted on driving his father's sun chariot across the sky. Too late he realized he was neither old enough nor strong enough to control its mighty team of untamed horses; and to avoid destruction of all that lives his own father was forced to have him struck down by a thunderbolt and cast flaming into the sea.

These are not old men's fireside tales. Far-off echoes of them still reverberate in the mind of modern man confronted by the morning news, with his paper propped against the coffee pot. He reads of hydrogen bomb explosions, and is filled with an indefinable sense of dread; he reads of air disasters, and becomes strangely uneasy — particularly so if it is an "unexplained" disaster. For this attacks his cherished conviction that if only we were clever enough and organized enough we should understand everything. Modern man longs above all for explanations, and on the rational level he is entirely right to do so, and not to rest till he has found them. But when all the probing and explaining is done there remains at the back of his mind, in the depths of his heart, a formless suspicion that just possibly another factor is involved. *Perhaps we have gone too far*, he thinks — and the next instant laughs at himself for the foolish idea. But this idea is not foolish, and not to be laughed away. It is as old as man. It is the dark aspect of the bright heroic venture, and must be met with understanding and courage. In psychiatric work people will often dream of flying, and its meaning is almost always the same: a warning that the dreamer has lost touch with some part of reality, of the solid ground of common sense, and that he had better, not necessarily come back to earth, but — watch where he is going. It is a question always worth asking, for to become aware of these ancestral fears is the only way to draw their dragon teeth.

The irrational factors in the fear of flying are therefore nothing to be ashamed of. Indeed, those who boast of having none are admitting that they no longer hear those age-old counsels of caution and humility that speak from the depths of man's unconscious mind, and have providentially warned him again and again on the long, rough road. But to hear them is one thing, to be controlled by them quite another. For these counsels are born of the unnumbered failures, frustrations and false starts of human beings since the dawn of the world. Their warning note — faint and forlorn as a bell-buoy heard in the dark of the sea — must sometimes be ignored to make room for the emergence of the heroic principle in man, the vital gesture that can be victorious even in failure. The antique tale of Phaethon tells of such an act, and its perfectly balanced close could be the epitaph of all brave men: "Phaethon fell from his father's chariot, but he lost not his glory, for his heart was set on great things."

ACT II: *Man in Space*

The predicaments of a man in outer space and a child in the womb have a startling resemblance. Both are carried in sealed capsules through a potentially hostile environment, both are ingeniously cushioned against external shocks and extremes of temperature, both nourished by highly specialized feeding arrangements. The atmosphere of outer space, inconceivably thin, inconceivably cold, would be instantly fatal to the astronaut — but not more so than the air we ordinarily breathe to the embryo; neither could maintain life for a moment apart from the elaborate and precarious protective devices with which they are surrounded. And for the astronaut, almost as for the embryo, there runs, in the to and fro radio beams, a kind of invisible umbilical cord, along which floods a ceaseless stream of delicate adjustments, corrections, assistances from the ever-watchful maternal organization.

But perhaps the most curious of their shared experiences is concerned with gravity. On his astral journeys man in space is weightless and unencumbered. For him gravity, least understood of all natural forces, is suspended, and it does not matter to him in the least which way up he happens to be. Intra-uterine life also possesses this engaging quality. For months on end, as never again in our terrestrial lives, we are about equally content to stand on our heads or our heels, with, if anything, a slight preference for the former.

There is, of course, one big difference. The womb is "natural," the capsule "artificial." But what precisely do we mean by these terms? Space capsules are constructed by human intelligence, and the human brain (I speak of *brain* — not *mind*, which is a mystery) is itself an evolutionary achievement of Nature. On this particular level, therefore, which seems still to be the most readily acceptable to modern man, the level of life seen as an evolutionary process, all products of the human brain, however technical — jet planes, electronic computers, sputniks and the like — are in the last analysis works of Nature created by Nature's latest and most highly evolved instrument, the human brain-box.

Now, if this striking parallelism between the astronaut and the embryo were all, it would be fascinating — and unimportant. But it is not all. These complicated capsules, each guarding and enclosing a single spark of living substance, carried with maternal care, or thrown hopefully into space — have we not seen this before? And when there was neither human nor animal eye to watch, has it not all *happened* before, millions and millions of times through millions and millions of years: the acorn falling softly to the forest floor, the sycamore seed equipped with tiny helicopter wings to

further its flight from the parent tree, the horse-
chestnut capsule pronged and spiked like any sputnik
. . . I suggest that the manned space ship is only the
latest of an almost infinite series of such attempts: the
ceaseless, compulsive efforts of Life to propagate itself,
to survive somehow, somewhere, to find new lodgments
and new possibilities of growth; efforts stretching backward to the first unicellular stirring in some primeval
mud bank, and forward to the unimaginable hybrid life-
forms of intercommunicating worlds.

Seen in this light there is no real break in continuity
between man flung into outer space in search of a hos-
pitable star and a single spore blown by the winds of
chance on to some remote and alien, but accepting,
soil. Both are means of propagation, crazily irrational,
hazardous, magnificent, dauntless: Life dicing against
the forces of destruction, pitting her almost illimitable
wealth of fertility against destruction's astronomical
odds; losing a game here and there with the extinction
of this or that species, but usually winning in the end,
often with a truly desperate gambler's throw. In this
giant game of chance the space ship can be seen as
Life's current wager.

Like all gambling games, this one is tediously repeti-
tive in essence, but infinitely variable in detail. Life's
simple and recurrent aim is the protecting and then the
scattering of seed: the founding of new centers and
colonies of healthy growth as far as possible from the
parent organization. But success in this is no simple
matter. It is a fierce game that Life plays against the

Fenris-Wolf of destruction — a contest of bewildering complexity against an opponent who never rests and never surrenders, in which all that can be hoped for is, not final victory, but fleeting touch-and-go triumphs wrested from the enemy by sheer courage and tiptoe alertness, by sharp surprise attacks, brilliant improvisations, and above all by the readiness to risk everything on a single, freakish chance.

Luckily for all creation Life is a born gambler. Some of her improvisations have to be seen to be believed: the means, for example, she uses to complete the life-cycle of *Dibothriocephalus Latus,* one of man's rarest and least attractive of parasites, the length of whose name is well matched by the length of its body, which, full grown, can be anything up to 26 feet. Seen in early embryonic life the prospects of *Dibothriocephalus* reaching maturity are, actuarially speaking, far from rosy. Consider what has to happen if this ungainly monster is to survive: an infested freshwater crab has to excrete on some river bed where a trout comes nosing for food; this particular trout has to be caught by a fisherman, *inefficiently cooked,* and eaten by a human being; the excreta of this human being must then be somehow carried to a stream that happens to be the habitat of a freshwater crab, which has to pick up the worm segment in its food — and so complete the cycle. It is rather like a biological variant of the House that Jack Built. "This is the Girl that cooked for the Man that caught the Trout that swallowed the Worm that came from the Crab that ate the . . ." The odds against all

these events occurring, at the right time and in the right
order, must be incalculable. Yet *Dibothriocephalus,*
perhaps unluckily, has not become extinct. Sufficient
numbers of them fulfill these next-to-impossible demands — reminiscent of the tasks the Wicked Witch
sets the unhappy Princess in the fairy tale — to keep the
species in existence and hundreds of human beings in
peculiar discomfort.

This is, of course, an extremely wasteful method of
propagation. The hopes and lives of myriads of bud-
ding *Dibothriocephali* are blighted for one that succeeds. It is here recorded simply as an example of the
odds Life is prepared to take, if necessary, in order to
win even one small, difficult point of the game. In less
harsh conditions her fancy takes wind, and she throws
up a glittering wealth of invention, a virtuoso display of
ingenious and delightful mechanisms for seed-scatter-
ing — many of which have an uncanny resemblance to
our own current devices for the exploration of space.

There is, for instance, the Balsam Plant, whose seeds
are shot out as if by a catapult when the sun-ripened
capsule explodes; or the Wild Cucumber, whose fruit as
it matures becomes full to bursting-point of liquid, till a
moment comes when a weak spot at the distal end of
the fruit suddenly splits open and the pressurized fluid
within shoots into the air, scattering the wet seeds like
silver spray from a fountain. This was before Life hit
on the admirable idea of giving her creations fins and
wings and legs so that they could do their own seed-
scattering — an improved facility of which certain spe-

cies, including Homo Sapiens, have taken the fullest
possible advantage.

Undazzled by this triumph, however, Life continues
to look after her earlier sessile forms. One still has only
to lie drowsing on the Sussex Downs on a hot day to
hear, like Lilliputian pistol shots all round, the bursting
gorse-pods firing their seeds a few reckless inches into
the summer air. And farther afield, in the silent forest
depths of Brazil, there is a tree called *Hura Crepitans*,
the Sand-Box Tree, with a truly remarkable launching
apparatus. Its large woody fruit, about the size of a
tennis ball, on ripening not only bursts violently apart,
launching its seeds at high velocity into space, but also
accompanies this with a bang that can be heard half a
mile away — for all the world like a miniature Cape
Kennedy . . . All discovery is at the deepest level re-
discovery. In the long-established laboratories of Nature the manned space ship, pride of the mid-twentieth
century, is no more than the modification of an archaic
prototype.

The present attempt, nevertheless, has its unique feature. For the first time in the history of the world man
is consciously cooperating in the great gamble. Life has
coopted the human brain-box, her latest improvisation,
to help in the most daring and imaginative of all her
earthly ventures — the attempt to fling her precious
seed across the monstrous abyss of outer space, and find
a new lodgment for it among the stars.

And now that we have taken a deliberate hand in it
the game has altered. Life's prodigality as a gambler,

recklessly flinging in her pawns by the hundred thousand — like blood-lusting old war generals on the
Somme — does not suit modern man at all. Conscious,
in this sole sense, of his individual importance, he
hedges his attempts on outer space with every conceivable precaution, and risks but one or two lives at a time
in place of the holocausts of the past. Though in this,
too, he is perhaps only following Life's own lead. For as
her creations advanced in complexity and inner organization, so her previously lavish views on their expenda-
bility diminished, until at the mammalian level Life
changed her approach entirely; and began to guard the
individual embryo with almost as much care and anxiety as Man now devotes to a Gagarin or a Glenn.

But, however cautiously, the attempt is actually being made; and it is an attempt whose grandeur makes
the heart stand still. Do not think of a space ship as one
more ingenious scientific experiment, whatever the
electronic engineers and astrophysicists may say. See,
rather, the image of this pale blue spinning ball on
which we live, this dancing dust-mote of a world, miracle of self-contained, self-sustaining life, hurtling vertiginously through the vast silence of interstellar space;
and daring at last to shoot out its infinitesimal seeds, its
atoms of living matter, towards other remotely spinning
worlds, pinpoint targets millions of miles away — in the
forlorn, crazy, inextinguishable faith of finding new
possibilities of survival and growth. The manned space
ship is no scientific toy. It is a unique and numinous
symbol — a union of opposites, of the very old and the

very new — whose ultimate meaning may one day reverberate through the galaxies and fatefully alter the
majestic pattern of the cosmos. To have a part in so
great a venture is an inconceivable honor for that handful of dust which is the mortal part of man.

But, of course, we go too far. With typical human
cocksureness we imagine it is all our own idea, that we
are free to carry on or give up this tremendous project.
Eminent divines warn us gravely not to pervert space
travel to evil and destructive ends; leading scientists
and politicians proclaim that, come what may, man
must never turn back from the gleaming road of human
reason and technology; power-drunk dictators nurse secret and insensate dreams; while poor Everyman shakes
his turnip head at the fantastic cost of it all, and proves
over a couple of drinks that the money would be far
better spent on hospitals and houses.

Everyman may well be right. None can know what
triumphs and evils may spring from this most literal
leap into the dark. But the fact is, we have no choice.
There is an infinite pathos about these anxious voices
that rise in automatic protest against every forward
movement of Life since Life began. The antique chorus
of frogs round any moonlit pond, which started before
man did, may be an endless antiphonal argument between those who press on to the brave amphibian life
and those who hold that it would have been wiser to
stay tadpoles. And earlier still, when the first crusta-
ceans struggled, clumsy and gasping, out of the thick
dark steaming seas into the unfriendly element of air —

precisely as man now ventures into the coldly hostile regions of space — their sorties were doubtless made to the accompaniment of admonitions from marine mothers urging them not to go too far up the beach . . .

We have no choice. By this contemporary adventure into space we are merely actualizing one of Life's basic drives, and are no more than the tools she has chosen, this time, for the job. Despite priest and scientist and homespun moralist alike, nothing is more certain than that we shall continue to fling human beings into the terrifying abyss of outer space, as blindly as ever the ancient Aztecs flung their children into the maw of cruel Huitzilopochtli. We are driven on this desperate course by a need transcending human fear: Life's indecipherable need to find new breeding grounds for — Life.

ACT III: *Man in Time*

Beyond the faintly nightmarish vistas of the evolutionary process in which Time is taken for granted lies a more subtle field of research; for man from his first appearance on earth has been attacking not merely on one front but on two. It is self-evident that twentieth-century man has broken through the traditional boundaries of Space. What is perhaps less obvious is that he is also challenging the inhuman tyranny of Time. But here his task is infinitely harder. It may even be that its accomplishment involves the next advance in human meaning.

In the conquest of Space, as we have seen, Nature

had long anticipated man's efforts, and had even prefigured the design and performance of his modern space machines. In this great adventure man has been able to follow up, though largely unconsciously, hints and clues provided by Nature. He has, in fact, ventured into outer space as a child might venture into a moonlit forest, reaching out instinctively for his Mother's hand. But when he stands up and questions the meaning of Time the whole situation is dramatically reversed: man is now the adult while Nature dwindles from the huge, inscrutable, all-containing Mother to a bewildered parent, whose simple faith — that to procreate and to survive are self-sufficing goals — has been incomprehensibly brushed aside.

In challenging Time there have been no extra-human precedents to follow, since man alone has had this impulse. The assault on Time is a uniquely human occurrence. It is almost impossible to conceive of any form of earthly life, other than man, concerning itself in any way at all with Time. Even to speak of the blind obedience of the rest of creation towards it is to be anthropomorphic, because to the rest of creation Time is a "given" thing, a factor lying completely, or almost completely, outside their rudimentary range of consciousness — as indeed it lies largely outside ours. They cannot be obedient to it, for they have no inkling that it exists. But man throughout his history, even archaic man in the dawn of his precarious emergence, seems always to have known Time as his last enemy, and to have dreamed of its defeat.

He dreams of it still. To be concerned with Time.

and especially with escape from it, is the hallmark of the human spirit. And how colorful, how varied have been these dreams of escape! It is as if man alone in all creation knows himself to be a captive, and spends his days, like the nobler sort of war-prisoner, in ceaseless schemes to give his enemy the slip and struggle home. In the jargon of our day a silly word has been coined to cover this intuitive longing that is as old as the human race. It is called "escapism" — to be guilty of which is, in contemporary Humanist eyes, the sin beyond for-giveness. But there are two kinds of escape. There is the escape *from* something, motivated by fear; and the escape *to* something, motivated by longing. To confuse the second with the first is to confuse strength with weakness, courage with cowardice, love with fear. "All life," said the wise witch of Edmonton, "is a wandering to find home," and nothing will ever finally extinguish this conviction of the human heart.

Yet, strangely, there are those who dedicate their lives to the bleak attempt. Light flashes furiously from their horn-rimmed glasses, their thin lips open and shut in endless argument, shrilly they applaud each other's irrefutable logic: but the sheer stolidity of Everyman guards his inner truth from them more effectually than any counter-argument. He tips his hat back and by the grace of God can't rightly see what they are talking about; and returns to his age-old dreams of escape . . . the foolish dreams that he shares with Pythagoras and Plato, with Vergil and St. Augustine and Dante and Goethe.

Admittedly the imaginations of Everyman on this

theme lack the precision and coherence of the poets and philosophers, but they have always been authentic expressions of the same conviction: that Life is more than existence. There is evidence of this intuition from remotest antiquity. It is no accident that the earliest records we have of primitive man are concerned with an odd and peculiarly human phenomenon — care of the newly dead. To die is to acknowledge Time's victory over man, and from the beginning man has struggled naïvely against this by giving ritualistic values to the act of dying, and by ingenious efforts to preserve the integrity and continuity of the remains. *He tried, in fact, to arrest the flow of Time.*

Even on this simple level his efforts have been unceasing to this day, and have resulted in the fascinating pageantry of human burial rites through the ages; beginning with the stone piles of palaeolithic man and the Long Barrows of later prehistory, burgeoning then into a thousand fantastic ceremonies: funeral pyres of the Homeric Greeks, Arabian stone terraces of the dead, burning-ghats of India, the subtle necrophilic arts of the dynastic Egyptians, Roman urn-burials — "lavish caskets" which on occasion, as Sir Thomas Browne reported, could contain, as well as the ashes of the deceased, "above two hundred Rubies, many hundreds of Imperial Coyns, and three hundred Golden Bees . . . according to the barbarous magnificence of those dayes in their sepulchral Obsequies . . ." On and on through the centuries winds the endless slow pageant of the newly dead, carried humbly on men's shoulders down rutted country lanes, or borne through the streets

of hushed capitals on gun carriages and royal cata-
falques "with music and with fatal gifts of flowers";
moving on without pause up to and past the grotesque
set-pieces of the present day — the swathes of black
crepe, the ebony steeds, the sable-plumed hearses of
French provincial *pompes funèbres,* and the excruciating beauty treatments of the corpse in American Gardens of Remembrance. In these matters we have perhaps kept up with the efforts of archaic man. We can
hardly be said to have improved on them.

All these maneuvers, however, are protests on a childish level. Archaic man did something else to arrest the
flow of Time, of infinitely greater significance. By an
approach which his descendants only sporadically revived and have now for centuries largely discarded and
forgotten, he made a sustained, magnificent, and in
some ways successful attempt to give certain parts at
least of his life the quality of timelessness. His method
was to sacralize the essential human activities.

According to man's earliest beliefs, in the beginning,
in illo tempore, man lived in a timeless world on terms
of near-equality with the gods, with whom he freely
conversed; he could fly or climb to heaven at will; and
he possessed also the power of communication with
many of the lower forms of life, with birds and beasts
and even insects. To paraphrase these naïve beliefs in
contemporary terms, primitive man held that human
consciousness instead of being confined to its present
narrow range had once extended "upwards" into the
spiritual sphere and "downwards" to the animal level.
He believed — in company with certain modern phi-

losophers, notably Bergson — that this pristine range of consciousness had been lost, and that man's first aim must be to recover it, if only momentarily. To bring this about he tried in all his essential activities — eating, drinking, hunting, sleeping and waking, copulating, dying — to imitate the actions and attitudes, as known to him through oral tradition, of the superior beings from whom he believed himself to have descended. By so doing he tried to lift these particular actions out of the temporal and accidental into the timeless atmosphere in which these beings had lived. That is, he raised as much as he could of his daily life to the level of a sacrament.

Man has never since discovered a better technique. It lies at the root of all religious ritual, and is the basis of certain kinds of mystical experience. The difference between the archaic world and later generations in this respect is that the sacraments of primitive man were performed communally, and permeated the life of the entire group. In later times they became separated off from the life of the community and increasingly left in the hands of individuals and specialized bodies of religiously minded people, often bitterly at odds with each other on ritual issues. For the majority of human beings today the sacramental way of life is little more than a teasing memory.

In the course of human history occasional attempts — as with Confucianism in China and Bushido in Japan — were made to revive among certain classes of people this sacramental approach to life: and centuries later the Holy Roman Empire had for a time a more general success in this direction. But for the last three centuries, at any rate in the Western world, and now spreading like a forest fire in the Far East, human experience has become completely secularized and time-ridden. Man has almost forgotten the possibility of escape from his ancient enemy, and has almost accepted life within the straitened range of everyday consciousness.

Almost, but not quite. The desire to escape into timelessness being an integral part of human life is in the last resort coterminous with it. While man exists it cannot be destroyed, but only repressed and driven underground. Even in cultures where the major religions, which are among its finest manifestations, are denied or ignored, in a thousand devious ways this repressed desire struggled to the surface of daily life, often in puerile or degenerate forms. Contemporary man might be astonished if he recognized how constantly his private daydreams are preoccupied with this hope, how clearly his homely customs and celebrations — his housewarmings and birthdays and New Year aspirations — reveal it.

There is, curiously, a certain type of businessman who is shrewdly aware of this universal subsconscious nostalgia for a timeless Paradise, and of the financial advantage he can extract from it. Holiday brochures are drawn up by men who know what they are about. Their enticing descriptions of holidays — in a ship, on a tropic isle, in an ancient, historied city — all have this underlying leitmotif of man's archaic intuitions of another mode of being, and of our own contemporary fantasies of escape. These places, they suggest, are the golden lands where time stands still, summer never ends, food appears as if by magic, and *all is changed from the every day* . . . Far-away islands by their own nature have this quality. Good wine needs no bush, and islands need no brochure. At the very sound of their names an echo reaches us across unimaginable stretches of time. This may be the mythical island, it whispers, so sequestered and remote that all that has happened since the Fall of Man has passed it by, leaving it innocent and dawn clean. Here that part of me which knows itself to be an exile in the febrile, rat-race world might perhaps find its timeless home . . . "God," said Robert Sencourt, "has the strangeness of undiscovered islands." The power of this perfect image comes directly from that irrational but indestructible hope.

*

As human beings, then, it would appear that we are continually impelled, by forces outside our conscious control, to try to escape from or arrest the flow of Time. At our back we always hear Time's wingèd chariot hurrying near. But inevitably, following the inexorable law of opposites, there is an equal and opposing aspect of man's mysterious relationship to Time. The quality in Time which most deeply of all offends man's impatient spirit is not its swiftness but the maddening *uniformity* of its progress, moment following moment, hour following hour, tomorrow and tomorrow and tomorrow, while man looks helplessly on, unable to hasten or to hinder. No other single fact in all existence is so crushing to human ambition, so openly contemptuous of human values.

This aspect of man's subjection to Time is perhaps most clearly evident in the quiet processes of gestation. The seed in the earth, the embryo in the womb pursues its own unhurried rhythm. Man has learned how to start these processes at will, but for their fruition he must wait with what patience he can muster. And he has never been good at mustering patience.

Gestation was for the primitive a profound symbol. He saw the whole world — or rather that corner of it of which he was aware and which he mistook for the whole world — as the Great Mother, a living maternal power gradually perfecting the dark primordial materials in her womb by an immensely protracted process of gestation. As the centuries passed and men began to dig up more and more undreamed-of treasures from their mother earth, gold and silver and precious shining stones, the idea became widespread, as Mircea Eliade has shown, that metals "grow" in the belly of the earth, and that, for instance, "as the peasants of Tonkin still hold today, bronze if left long enough in the earth will turn to gold." And not only Oriental peasants, clinging to an ancient legend; for the same idea lay at the basis of the alchemist's transmuting art; and even the sophisticated John Donne could write,

> As men of China, after an age's stay,
> Do dig up Porcelane where they buried clay.

"After an age's stay" . . . but this was precisely the point. Man was simply not prepared to wait through patient centuries while the earth's slow pregnancies matured, while the humble embryonic ores were gradually changed, as he believed, into glittering jewels and bright gold. He wanted now, not to arrest the flow of Time, *but to accelerate it.*

This must have seemed an impossible demand. But miraculously a type of man arose to answer it; and was at once regarded with a mixture of veneration and terror. As well he might be, since he and his successors have between them transformed the face of the entire world, revolutionized the conditions of human life, and fatefully intervened in the destiny of man. This remarkable individual, this Promethean figure, was the Smith, the Metallurgist: the primal genius who first applied the transmuting arts of fire to ores and metals.

So far, so good. Primitive man with his unsleeping intuition for the meaning of life recognized the enormity of what he was doing, the temerity of his challenge to the Earth Mother and to Time itself. For what the smith was in fact doing was to take the law — and Time — into his own hands, hurry on the earth's slow process of gestation, and by mechanical means induce "birth" to take place before its natural term: impiety on a cosmic scale. The primitive therefore insisted that the smith should be an outstanding figure, divinely inspired, filled with an inner strength and integrity far exceeding that of ordinary men. He was usually given equal status with the shaman, sometimes even higher status. "Smiths and shamans come from the same nest," declares a proverb of the Yakuts, quoted by Eliade; and their myths also assert that the smith originally learned his skill from the evil deity K'daai Maqsin, the Master-Smith of Hell, "who lives in a house made of iron surrounded by splinters of fire . . ." Not perhaps altogether inappropriate as a residential background for the Managing Director of Vickers, or the Chief of Harwell. After all, K'daai Maqsin was not exclusively destructive; it was he who mended the broken or amputated limbs of heroes. Nuclear Fission, they say, has medicinal uses.

Many centuries later this concept of the sacred and dangerous nature of the smith's calling was developed, elaborated and subtilized in the esoteric processes of alchemy. Despite the packs of thieves and charlatans that collected round this arcane activity — which occupied much the same controversial and popularly misunderstood position as Depth Psychology does today, and which was nevertheless influential in human affairs in various parts of the world for at least two thousand years — the true alchemist always embodied the principle that the spiritual quality of the operator was as vital as his skill in the task of transmuting base metals into gold. The reason for this, as Carl Jung brilliantly demonstrated, was that the hidden aspect of alchemical work was, in fact, the symbolic transmutation of the "base metal" of diurnal experience into the "gold" of spiritual insight. *Aurum nostrum,* said Gerhard Dorn, *non est aurum vulgum* — "Our gold is not the common gold."

But this was a hindering and restricting qualification,

and man's impatience for quick results once more got the better of him. In order to hasten the work he dropped his standards. Gradually the sacredness of the metallurgist's activities and the spiritual quality of the operator became less important. Finally they became irrelevant. The smith's calling was secularized and, many centuries later, the alchemist's also. Metallurgy turned into engineering, Alchemy into chemistry and physics. The suggestion that a test should be made of a man's spiritual fitness to be a nuclear physicist would sound extremely peculiar to a modern ear. Only in relation to medical men (the engineers, chemists and physicists of the human body), with their still-operative Hippocratic Oath, is there left any trace of the archaic feeling that spiritual quality is as basic as skill. For the rest, in these three spheres of contemporary activity, the severance between head and heart is complete, and the Faustian bargain with the devil has been struck.

In one sense the bargain has paid off magnificently. Man's accelerated control of the mechanics of Nature is unprecedented in the earth's history, and has become a new and overwhelming factor in existence. In the field of performance modern scientific man has far outstripped the alchemist's and the primitive metallurgist's most daring hopes: today he can transform carbon dust into diamonds within a few hours, and has created countless new fabrics and substances, and a bewildering variety of new metals, incorporating in them just those qualities of strength, toughness, or resilience that he happens to require — syntheses that Nature herself

might take another million years to achieve. In this sole
sense contemporary man is indeed the Master of Nature
and of Time. Men of insight have often declared that
man's chief aim is "to escape from the vanity of Time."
Swelling with pride the twentieth-century Humanist
now claims to have discovered the trick of it, the talis-
man that saints and artists and philosophers have pa-
tiently searched for through the centuries. "Jump on
our bandwagon," cries the evolutionary Humanist, "you
silly, moonstruck crew! *We* have escaped from Time!
We are its masters! We have turned your impotent
dreams into shining facts. Come along with us!"

It is a plausible and a glittering temptation. For in a
sense the claim is true. The temporal acceleration of
discovery in our day is breathtaking. Whole sciences
spring up such as *bionics* or *moletronics,* unheard of a
few years ago, still unknown to many, and grow at once
to formidable importance. The expansion of science,
now firmly harnessed to the aims of Big Business and
Big Politics, is so incredibly swift that out of all the scientists the world has produced since the beginning of
history, *no less than ninety percent are now alive.* This,
far more than East-West tensions, is the explosive and
revolutionary fact of today. Like a new Golden Horde
the wheeling armies of research workers are sweeping
across the face of the world, reckless of race or creed or
color; and where they pass nothing can ever be the
same again. Their fantastic and exuberant discoveries
tear in shreds the fabric of the old familiar world, and
make mockery of Time.

But while this is true, precisely the reverse is also true: that man is becoming more and more the slave of Time. In the world of today man lives by stopwatch. His prosperity, even his life, depends on split-second timing and ever more precise chronometers. In large organizations he clocks in and out like an automaton — which in any case is rapidly replacing him — and in factories his movements are watched by experts to see if a few seconds can be lopped off his rate of work. (Even the contemporary Time-slave is vaguely affronted by this, and the watching has to be carried out surreptitiously to avoid "industrial unrest.") On the roads his clock-chasing speeds involve daily human sacrifice on a scale that leaves the holocausts of the Aztecs and the Inquisition far behind. In Western societies it is regarded as a serious moral defect not to be anxious about time. Some railway authorities in America are said to pay their passengers — that is, fine themselves — for every minute their express trains run late. Time is the acknowledged Master of the modern world, the only god to whom all civilized humanity — Catholic and pagan, Communist and Capitalist alike — bends a submissive knee. His tyrannic rule is resented, but never defied.

And the process is accelerating. On a recent orbital space flight a part of the automatic mechanism short-circuited, and the astronaut had to bring back his craft to earth by hand. He succeeded magnificently, landing just four miles from the mid-Pacific rendezvous. As he was traveling at twenty miles a second, this meant that

he was only one-fifth of a second out. His life and the
success of his mission depended on this degree of precision. It is plain that the old standards of service no
longer suffice. The tyrant grows bolder and is beginning to demand of his slaves an almost superhuman accuracy — on pain of death. Time is a jealous god.
Time is not mocked.

*

This is the paradox of the contemporary world, to be at
once the masters and the slaves of Time. And there
seems to be no way out. It is clearly impossible for man
to turn his back on the thrilling discoveries of his own
ingenious brain. We are impelled to increase our mastery, and by so doing to increase our slavery.

There is, of course, a way out. Child and artist and
mystic all escape from the lunatic dilemma. And something hidden but valued in the heart of man applauds
this solution, since buried within every human being
are traces of these three. Privately, we incline to agree
that here is the only true and perfect answer. But having honored it, we reject it. Ruefully admitting we can
neither remain children nor all become artists, still less
saints and mystics, we turn back, regretfully but mas-
sively, to the time-ridden world.

It is not, however, mere cowardice that leads contemporary man to turn away from the mystic's solution as a
final answer to the mystery of life. There is integrity in
the rejection. For the possibility is beginning to emerge
that the mystic, for whom Time is the Great Illusion,

and escape from it the beginning of wisdom, may have laid hold after all not on Truth itself but on an aspect of truth. It is becoming plain that the religious intuitions, even of genius, from earliest recorded times to the beginning of the present century, however valid in themselves, have rested on childishly inadequate concepts of the illimitable cosmos now coming into view. The old bulwarks against an evolutionist-humanist attitude to life will no longer serve, and the challengers grow bolder. "The time is past," writes Russell Brain, "when philosophers *ex cathedra* could issue naïve views on the nature of knowledge, brain and mind, reality and appearance . . . without penetrating the physiological aspects of these problems in detail." The spiritual certainties of former days, untroubled then by a gross factual ignorance of which we have now become uncomfortably aware, have lost, for us, their numinous power. Contemporary man urgently requires an adequate intellectual framework for his inner life.

But if the mystic's rejection of Time is only an aspect of truth, so also is the evolutionist's wholehearted acceptance of it. To the partisan of the evolutionary theory Time is the Great Reality; for him all meaning will emerge in the course of Time. By measuring it backward he reaches the origin of things; by tracing it forward he arrives at the shape of things to come. The Theory of Evolution is based on Time as a measurable datum. The extent to which this theory in its broad outlines has been accepted is all but absolute among civilized peoples. It is the mental climate in which we and our fathers and grandfathers were born and bred. And it is, of course, true; demonstrably and irrefutably true. But like all other human truths it obeys the Law of Opposites. The evolutionary theory is only one aspect of a polarity whose opposing aspect has a precisely equal validity. But there are fashions in thought, and this other aspect is for the time being extremely unfashionable; with the result that the contemporary technologist is at least as childishly ignorant of the meaningful world of the primitive, saint and mystic, as ever they have been of his.

All this is nothing new. Evolutionist and mystic, Time-worshipper and Time-scorner: these two archetypal figures face each other today as under variant names they have always done, each pointing his half-truth as if it were a sword at the heart of the other. They may pretend to find, or even believe that they have found, a *rapprochement;* but in the end it turns out to be the only kind of agreement possible between boa constrictor and sheep — that one finishes up inside the other. They are natural antagonists. And so they will remain, unless and until there is a break-through of the accepted frontiers of our awareness, a sudden mutation — whether willed or chance — of human consciousness, transcending the world of opposites. Till then these two must stand, ignorant of each other's essence, in mutual mistrust, part of the changeless, ever-changing iridescent interplay of opposites, as of a fountain in sunlight, through which human life at its existing level is manifested.

But to see life so, *sub specie aeternitatis,* is the idio-
syncrasy of philosophic minds. To Everyman these opposing attitudes to Time appear to be immediate stark
alternatives, as indeed to him they are. He stands between them, rather bewildered and uncertain, like a
ploughboy at a country fair clutching his last half-
crown and wondering on which final treat to spend it.
"Come with us!" call the high-riding Humanists, whirling vertiginously above his head on their gaudy roundabout. Half-deafened, half-delighted by the brassy
music, dazzled by the blaze of lights and the blurred
glimpses of his clever friends swooping past on their
scarlet and gold heraldic animals, Everyman stands hesitantly, one foot on the short flight of steps that leads to
their bright company . . . *"Come with us!"* call hidden
voices from a quiet corner of the fair-ground; clear and
urgent voices, these, though a mere whisper, hardly to
be heard above the noises of the fair. But Everyman
hears them, too, and pauses again, irresolute. It is a
fateful and historic moment of decision . . .

Yet perhaps, after all, not so fateful. For whether
Everyman elects to join his gay companions on the
roundabout, or his quiet friends of the inner world, is of
little final account. He will still be in the same old
fair-ground, where man's boldest external achievements
and his highest spiritual affirmations are no more than
half-truths waiting to be surpassed by the visionary
power of an expanded human consciousness. To reach
this is Everyman's personal task. Not by saint, scientist
or philosopher, those three curious mutations from the

mainstream of human life, but by Everyman himself
must be accomplished the daring leap, the *salto mortale*,
to a new level of awareness. And for this great adventure he must use the homely tools that are available to
him, not the recondite instruments of intellectual and
spiritual experts.

It is within his powers. The task is simple, though
not easy. Pompous, pseudo-scientific terms such as "expanded consciousness" and "a new level of awareness"
could intimidate him, but need not. They are nothing
more than attempts to express a way of living which has
not yet risen to general recognition — though now it is
very near: the habit of paying as much attention to the
fringes of an experience as to the experience itself; of
keeping all parts of the mind so attuned that every impact which life makes upon it evokes not a note but a
chord; of understanding, in T. S. Eliot's phrase, "what it
is to be awake, to be living on several planes at once";
in a word, the habit of seeing everything, and especially
Time itself, translucently. In all such apprehensions
Everyman starts nearer to the truth than any specialist.

This indeed is the fateful decision he has to make.
For if he misses the opportunity and remains at the fair-
ground level, inexorably the old cycle of events will be
reenacted. A time will come once more when the whirling machinery will grind to a halt, the harsh music
cease, and the roundabout riders step down stiffly from
their apocalyptic beasts. Looking round for his friends
of the inner world, Everyman will see them, too, in
troops of gray shadows, slipping silently away. One by

one the lights of the fair-ground will go out, and Every-man will be left at last, as at the shadowed close of so many earlier civilizations, to find his own way home, by himself, in the dark.

Epilogue

Not all plays end at the third act; and for this particular play a fourth can still be written, carrying on the story in a new and exciting direction. Whether it ever will be written, and eventually acted, depends on our reluctant hero, Everyman. At the moment, faced by these two opposing aspects of Time, both of which he has the honesty to accept, all he seems capable of doing is to shrug his shoulders — and get on with life. The trouble about this unheroic solution is — and in his heart he knows it — that life with this basic dilemma shrugged off is emptied of significance.

But suppose he began to be aware of Time in another sense? For this is possible. Time can be seen as an irreducible fact, or as an illusion; *but it can also be seen as a symbol* — the word "symbol" carrying here its modern meaning as that which unifies, by perfect fusion within itself, what reason can apprehend only as irreconcilable opposites.

To see Time in this way is to become immediately aware of the presence of a new character in the drama . . . a strange archaic figure . . . *Janus,* the two-faced Roman god, legendary guardian of doors and gates, who stands on the threshold between two worlds; one face looking toward the tumbling multicolored torrent of the outer Ten Thousand Things, the other toward an inner world where life and death, youth and age, space and temporality are suddenly irrelevant; the Janus-guardian whose two faces, at once unitary and antagonistic, compose a single ultimate meaning. Here is the missing character without whom the fourth act can never be written.

Janus is the spirit of the threshold, poised forever on that razor edge between outward and inward life where every object in the universe has its secret center, and where man himself must learn at last to stand. In varying measure all forms of being radiate this Janus-quality: the greater the being, the more intense the radiation. In none is this more evident than in the greatest being the Western world has known. Jesus Christ has a Janus-face. On the one hand is the Jesus-face, gentle pastor of his sheep, wise moralist, golden sun of the noonday world; on the other the terrible Christ-face, numinous, indecipherable, eyes fixed irrevocably on the abyss of the Timeless. No wonder the parson and his little flock stick to the Jesus-face. The Christ-face once seen, if only for a moment, would empty as by magic all those prosperous pews.

To most human beings, however, this Janus-quality in life is simply a source of embarrassment. In relation to the outer and inner worlds they are roughly in the position of those birds and fishes whose eyes are set one on each side of the head so that they cannot look straight forward and are continuously presented with two entirely separate and unconnected pictures of their environment. What birds and fishes do about this disconcerting situation, I do not know. The human solution is to look out of only one eye. And not always the same one. In Christian lands many people by careful training accomplish the remarkable feat of looking out of one eye for a couple of hours a week and out of the other eye all the rest of their lives. Plainly an unsatisfactory solution to the problem of the two worlds.

This, however, is not surprising, since the search for the true solution is one which has continued from the beginning. It is, in fact, the never-ending treasure hunt which under many lovely names — the Plant of Immortality, the Golden Fleece, Aladdin's Cave, the Pearl of great price, the Rhinegold — has been the quest of legendary heroes in all times from the beginning. And it continues still, because every man must attempt it for himself anew. For to seek this treasure is to try to find the central point within oneself; the secret threshold where the world of the senses and the world of the psyche meet in mutual simultaneous recognition. Man has always intuitively known of its existence, and sought for it. It is his Center, tantalizingly close yet immensely hard to find, guarded by magic so that mere shrewdness will never find the way.

In the earliest records we have of primitive man there is evidence of a tendency to call his dwelling place the Center of the World. That he was not speaking spatially or geographically is plain from the fact that he was perfectly content that his neighbor's dwelling place should also be so regarded. Moreover, any hill or rock or tree that acquired sacred significance in his eyes immediately became the Center of the World. The Center, in fact, was everywhere. (Incidentally, this archaic concept of the center being everywhere at once has recently been advanced as perhaps the essential characteristic of a four-dimensional universe.) These sacral "centers" were all that really mattered in the life of primitive man. In comparison with them everything else was trivial and in the last resort meaningless. For him the Center was the only place where meaning could exist.

The tense of that sentence can be amended, for primitive man here grasped a truth that we have somehow contrived to forget; *the Center is the only place where meaning can exist.* This is why it endlessly appears and reappears in antique myth and fairy tale, and in the visions of saint and mystic, as that hidden treasure which the heroic principle in man is born to seek. And lives on, degraded and unrecognized in present-day fantasies of a Football Pools fortune, or a right answer (shades of the riddling Sphinx!) to the Sixty-four Thousand Dollar Question.

Moralists must, of course, decry these "vulgar" modern passions. But unguessed by devotee and moralist alike, they derive their strength from the power that belongs to the other Janus-face of treasure-seeking — the certainty in man that by courage and risk-taking he can miraculously transform his everyday life. It may indeed be preferable for men sometimes to pursue this goal even in such degenerate and illusory forms than to give up the quest. For many it is the only form in which they could understand it at all. To dismiss the longing of unnumbered millions to get-rich-quick as a sorry victory of the material over the spiritual is altogether too smug an attitude. This longing for the almost impossible to happen has affinities, however tenuous, with a basic human aspiration. For the supreme value of the Hidden Treasure, which is the Center, is that it exists, it can only be found, beyond the oppositions of inside-outside, spiritual-material. It belongs to a realm in which these and all other polarities are transcended. When a man for a timeless moment discovers his own Center, which, *pace* the moralists, occurs like a lightning flash with a blind indifference to humanly "spiritual" values — in a cathedral, on a mountainside, in a lamp-lit street, at a gaming-table — he discovers in that same instant the Center of all things, since he has momentarily entered a world in which the Center is everywhere.

What would be incredible if it were not for recent archaeological evidence to support it is that despite his cramped horizons archaic man had a not ignoble glimpse of this mystery, and clung to it as his living truth. Nineteenth-century archaeology, of course, had a label, brilliant but dismissive, for this miraculous insight of primitive man. It was called *participation mystique,* was ascribed to a lack of ego-development, and unfavorably contrasted with the precise, ego-conscious, objective thought-processes of later times. Such judg-

ments fail to recognize that the Western mode of thinking and the archaic mode of thinking are themselves a
pair of opposites, and that in placing the whole meaning of his life on what is sacred and timeless archaic
man was holding a life-attitude as valid and substantial
in its basic assumptions as our own. He undervalued
and misunderstood the mechanisms of Nature and lived
symbolically and timelessly; we undervalue and de-
grade the symbol and are obsessed by time and the
mechanics of life. There is not much room for conde-
scension either way.

The one solid advantage we have over primitive man
in this respect is that while he could by no possible
means have grasped even the basic elements of our control of the environment, we can, if we will, incorporate
his sensitivities to the inner world with our own objective certainties. Primitive man has something to tell us,
and in the purely symbolic language of our dreams he
speaks to us still. We should have the courtesy to listen.
For in what the dreaming mind is trying to say may
well be concealed the key to that unwritten fourth act.
And when it is written — who knows? Not every play
ends at the fourth act . . .

PART

THREE

"What an abyss of uncertainty, whenever the mind feels that some part of it has strayed beyond its own borders; when it, the seeker, is at the same time the dark region through which it must go seeking, where all its equipment will avail it nothing. Seek? More than that: create. It is face to face with something which does not so far exist, to which it alone can give reality and substance, which it alone can bring into the light of day."

Marcel Proust — *Swann's Way*

7

PSYCHE UNBOUND

THE FIRST TWO parts of this book have presented a brief series of pictures of the human animal in its current surroundings. Taken as a whole they constitute a point of view. So the world and man appear, seen translucently. But this is only half the story, and perhaps the less important half. As well as man's imaginative responses to the world around him, there remain to be considered his responses to the world within.

The idea of an inner world that is as "genuine" as the external world has only recently gained general acceptance. For many centuries popular imagination regarded the individual human mind as something essentially outward-looking. All events took place externally to the observing mind, all mystery was contained in the phenomena of Nature. Heaven was up in the sky, hell beneath the earth. The mind was regarded as an ultimate, indivisible datum, in roughly the same sense as was the atom in the realm of physics.

Suddenly, within the memory of many now living, physics "discovered" that the indivisible atom was, in fact, a micro-universe with suns and satellites whirling in a zone as relatively huge and empty as interplanetary space. And at the same time (in accordance with the mysterious synchronicity that connects the inner with the outer life) two pioneers of psychological research, Freud and Jung, almost simultaneously opened a long-locked door in the human mind, to reveal the illimitable world of the so-called Unconscious.

Modern man's imaginative responses to this new world have hardly begun. Interest is certainly awakening, but it has by no means dawned upon us yet that this world of darkness, primeval parent of light and life, has an autonomous existence as valid as that New World which confronted the bold spirits of the Renaissance. Its exploration — with which the rest of this book is concerned — could be the specific achievement of the new Elizabethan age.

*

Today we live in an atmosphere which is pervaded by a growing and extremely uncomfortable conviction that something is about to burst. By the great majority this possibility is referred to the external world, where indeed it may very well occur. The big bang may be a multimegaton H-bomb, or some space experiment which calls down upon us a brief, annihilating gesture of cosmic irritation.

But it is also possible that our external anxieties may be projections of an approaching explosion *within ourselves*. Man may be about to burst from his psychological swaddling clothes — an event as crucial and as perilous as any that could occur in the external world. Something of the sort is already happening. Psyche, the immortal butterfly, is struggling within her cocoon. Spiritually as well as physically man begins suddenly to feel the world he lives in is too small for him, suddenly to realize the intolerable crampedness of the human situation. With the blind urgency of an embryo that has reached its term man strains to escape, to burst through to an unimaginable Beyond, making unconsciously, as he does so, some noble, some foolish, some dangerous, some ludicrous movements.

It is not, of course, by chance that this inner impulse towards liberation is paralleled by outer impulses of the same nature. It is no accident, for instance, that the wind of change, rising soon to hurricane force, is blowing through the Dark Continent of Africa. What more vivid symbol could there be of the awakening of dark and urgent forces in the human soul? Nor is that other impulse accidental, which is carrying man at last beyond the seemingly insurmountable barrier of space. The world's attention is held by these more showy outer impulses; but beneath the surface of daily life the other, inner, impulse is equally active. The plain fact is that in both directions man is getting too big for his boots. And of these two, the inner impulse is incomparably the more revolutionary, the more fateful.

"As above, so below." The outer and inner worlds are aspects of a unity. Therefore one may soberly believe there can be no large discrepancy in date between man's deliberate penetration of outer space and his conscious penetration of the multidimensional barrier to the inner world, where time and death are conquered.

These may be dangerous notions to entertain. To suggest that mankind is on the verge of a crucial psychic mutation, a breakthrough to an enhanced personality that can grasp without flinching the formidable values of the inner world, while retaining its intellectual grip on externalities — is to sail extremely close to the wind. Go a little further and you are apt to find yourself sitting among a small band of fellow fanatics on a mountaintop, waiting for the Apocalypse. Go only a little further still, and you may find yourself harmlessly weaving baskets in the Occupational Therapy Department of a mental hospital. It is necessary to keep one's head. On the other hand, one can be too careful. All new insights wear at first an air of lunacy to the Establishment. And luckily Establishments are no longer in their formidable heyday, as, for example, in the time of the first Shogun of Japan, who authorized his nobility to cut down on the spot any commoner who was "behaving in a manner other than expected." Nonconformity among the unprivileged is now appreciably safer, at least in this country; and as Professor Price of the Wykeham Chair of Logic at Oxford refreshingly remarked, "One should not be too strongly deterred by the fear of talking nonsense . . . if the Logical Positivists had been alive in the early part of the seventeenth century, physics would never have got itself started." In any case what I suggest is in one sense nothing new. It may be the oldest human impulse in the world.

There is strong archaeological evidence to show that
with the birth of human consciousness there was born,
like a twin, the impulse to transcend it.

*

Perhaps at this stage the most sensible thing to do
is to gather the indications — faint and tentative as
they are, mistaken as many of them will inevitably be
found to be — of a concern with this impulse towards a
different level of Being. To the attentive eye and ear
these indications are found in a wide scatter of human
movements, ideas, writings. But one needs to be attentive. As Simone Weil has said: "Every order which
transcends another can only be introduced into the
older order in the form of something infinitely small."
    Where, then, in the contemporary scene are to be
found these "infinitely small" indications? First and obviously there is psychiatry. It is evident that with the
advent of Freud and Jung the study of the psyche became essentially concerned with the impulse to penetrate the inner world, and so to facilitate the addition of
a new dimension to human consciousness. And it is unnecessary to demonstrate this impulse by quotations
from their works, since it informs all that they and their
followers have written and done; preeminently the
work of Jung. Indeed, it might seem that the massive
impact of organized psychiatry on the modern world re-
moved it entirely from the category of "the infinitely
small."
    There is, however, a distinction to be made. Psychi-

atry, as its name implies, is concerned with healing, and, therefore, with the manipulation of the inner in the service of the outer world. The majority of both doctors and public summon the unfathomable powers of the psyche only to serve some immediate therapeutic end. This is natural and legitimate. But there is nevertheless something infinitely disheartening in the spectacle — as of tigers jumping through circus hoops. For the timeless images of the unconscious are not ancillary to waking life. *They are its Ground.* To treat them otherwise is fatally to mistreat them, and to lose a path that leads, more directly perhaps than any other, to the enlargement of human consciousness.

In philosophy, as might be expected, these faint and early indications we are looking for are more clearly grasped. Nietzsche, for instance, whose fate incidentally underlines the dangers of this kind of speculation, was possessed by one transcendent idea. He was rude enough to kick over the chessboard on which so many fascinating philosophic games had been played through the centuries, and to proclaim that the primary human need is not that someone should think up yet another philosophy, but that "man must surpass himself" — that is, must reach a new level of Being. Since Pythagoras no Western philosopher till Nietzsche had put this in the forefront of his program.

Nietzsche's aspiration was passionate but vague. In Bergson the indication is more precisely defined. In our context his essential intuition is that the brain is to be regarded as "an organ of limitation." This brilliant concept suddenly, like the invention of the microscope, opens a door for man on a vast new world waiting to be explored. The brain, Bergson believes, limits man's conscious awareness of the exterior world to what is practically useful. It is the organ of *attention à la vie*, and, as such, enormously valuable. But, in fact, man unconsciously perceives far more than he realizes. And it is only when his brain barrier is working inefficiently and his *attention à la vie* wanders, that certain of these other perceptions slip through — like refugees from a too well-ordered state. Now these "refugees" are precious. They come from a different level of consciousness, a level not normally experienced.

Yet one may not reproach the human brain for its ruthless censorship of such perceptions. Consciousness has quite enough of a job mediating, like a harassed traffic policeman, between the hostile environment and the precarious spark of individual life which it guards — without being simultaneously distracted by data arriving from beyond space and time. This may, in fact, be the secret of the incalculable strength of the "common-sense" attitude: "common sense" could be described as the *ad hoc* weapon forged by man to preserve himself on the physical level. Busy life simply cannot afford the time to listen too raptly to the faint voices hailing him from far beyond the boundaries of his own demanding world . . But these are the very voices to which we must now set ourselves to listen.

❀

One man who has listened with an exceptionally perceptive ear is the existentialist philosopher, Karl Jaspers. In his book *Truth and Symbol* he shows, with elegance and precision, that the symbol, rightly considered, is a key to release us from the three-dimensional prison in which we live, an aerial enabling us to tune in to a whole bright world of meaning that would otherwise slip soundlessly and invisibly past. "The symbol," says Karl Jaspers, "catches what would otherwise stream out of us and be lost in the void. The symbol shows what, without it, would remain completely hidden from us . . . Only he who recognizes the symbols becomes man."

This, of course, is Symbolism with a difference. We are not being invited to march again under the fly-blown banner of the 1890 Symbolists, who confused symbols with signs and sentimentalized both. Karl Jaspers agrees with Jung, and with that remarkable theological historian Eliade, in looking on the symbol as the rediscovered growing-point of human awareness. Jung connects it with the archetypal depths of the psyche, Eliade relates it to archaic man and the dawn of religious consciousness, Jaspers declares that "to make the language of the symbols clear, is the highest achievement of philosophical thinking."

To look at life symbolically in this sense is to direct attention, not wearily away from this world, but on to the crucial intersection of this world with eternity, to the junction of the profane with the sacred, to the ever-recreating level of hierophanies. This is so, because a true symbol is Janus-faced: one face directed towards the concrete, everyday aspect of Being, the other towards a level of Being which man has not yet reached. A symbol, therefore, constitutes in itself a kind of *rite d'entrée*. To see everything as a symbol is the first step towards a state which lies beyond accepted human consciousness. To see everything as a symbol is an expression of the longing of human consciousness to transcend its limitations and to exist simultaneously on the plane of the concrete and of the Spirit.

Apart from the philosophers, other indications of this penetrative impulse can be found in many fields. In science, for instance, there is the statement of Hermann Weyl, a distinguished contemporary mathematician, that "the world is being made by modern science to appear more and more as an open one . . . pointing beyond itself." There are also the provocative experiments of E.S.P. To many established scientists, of course, E.S.P. forms a three-letter word more offensive by far than any four-letter word they have ever heard; but their fury may be no more than a measure of their dismay to find the axiomatic walls of their privileged playground tumbling down. E.S.P. is, indeed, a somewhat crude attempt at the unbinding of Psyche; and there is no need in this context to examine the validity of its observations, impressive as some of these are. But it is surely incontestable that what E.S.P. calls for is a broadening of consciousness to include phenomena which lie outside the range of generally accepted mental powers.

In mathematics, J. W. Dunne in his *Experiment with Time* made another notable attempt at a breakthrough. Dunne was a gifted mathematician, and had his psychological insight been on a comparable level — had he known, for instance, the real meaning of a symbol, had he realized that dreams are not merely ingenious rearrangements of conscious material — his work might have been a decisive contribution towards opening the door to the inner world.

For the rest, scattered through the contemporary scene are, or recently have been, a multitude of others the meaning of whose lives is summed up in the single supreme effort to open that door. It has been charmingly said of them that they "have come into the world on no other errand." The list of them could be almost endless: theologians "with a difference," like Mircea Eliade; explorers of the two worlds like Laurens Van der Post; Simone Weil, that uniquely tortured spiritual genius; time-obsessed writers like Proust and T. S. Eliot; painters of the invisible such as Paul Klee and Chagall; unclassifiable men like Ouspensky, Maurice Nicol, Alan Watts . . . all these pioneer spirits, with numberless others, peering through, pressing against, knocking on — *the door* . . .

In one sense, of course, there is nothing new in this. For, as Jung has said, "there are and always have been individuals who cannot help but see that the world and its experiences are in the nature of a symbol"; and who know, in consequence, that man's chief need is to break through his three-dimensional limitations and reach "his

own transubjective reality." In small groups, or in isolated figures, this often secret aim has always existed; it
is older than Christian or Persian mysticism, older than
alchemy, or that strange flower of Thibetan mysticism,
the *Bardo Thodöl,* older than Orphism; coeval only
with man himself.

But what is perhaps new is the simultaneous lighting
up all over the world of innumerable points of activity
in this kind, the convergence of so many widely differing disciplines and fields of inquiry on the same unlikely
goal. Though, indeed, there is also a sense in which not
even this is really new, since all discoveries are at the
deepest level rediscoveries; and there was a time, before
the first of the iron-bound, man-made Moral Systems
was set up, when men everywhere saw the whole of
their limited world as a continuous sacral experience;
and devised techniques, such as the initiation rites of
archaic societies, to lay hold on it. The destruction of
those primitive values, the de-sacralizing of the world
of archaic man, which went step by step with the development of that arrogant delusion, the sense of moral
rectitude, is for some minds the greatest of all human
catastrophes. By that desecration the real meaning of
living, and of dying, was lost; and nothing we have
learned or gained since then can ever recompense us for
that most bitter forfeit, over which the human heart
still secretly grieves.

The question arises, is this an irremediable grief? Is
this the price, not to be redeemed, which has had to be
paid for the development of the ego and the liberation

of consciousness? One voice, and a formidable one, since it is Erich Neumann's, says "Yes." In his book *The Origins and History of Consciousness,* Neumann writes as follows: "The very things which the child has in common with the man of genius, the creative artist, and the primitive, and which constitute the magic and charm of his existence, must be sacrificed . . . These developments are indispensable for ego formation and the separation of the conscious and unconscious systems . . ." And a few pages later — "The values of the collective, of the Fathers, and of Law . . . must be acceptable as the supreme values in order to make possible Social Adaptation" (Capital "S," of course, capital "A"). Neumann then lists specifically, among the natural riches of the spirit that man must necessarily renounce in the interests of Ego Formation and Social Adaptation — "the world of myth and legend, of magic and fairy tale."

The world of myth and legend, of magic and fairy tale! This lost golden world lying outside Space and Time where there live on those warm and fugitive aspects of beauty and of truth on which the modern world has turned its back; this lovely Cinderella-sister of life, relegated now to the less "enlightened" nurseries, to the interpretations of bored schoolmasters, even to "The Stars Foretell" columns and comic strip sections of the daily papers, where nevertheless the ancient and indestructible images contrive dimly to reappear; this golden world, the missing key to which has impoverished the human spirit progressively for the last three hundred years — has had to be renounced, we are told, in the interests of Full Social Adaptation. It is surely the bleakest pronouncement on the human situation that it is possible to conceive. Man has made his choice. The door is closed. And it is useless to knock on it.

But other voices are to be heard with a different answer; and in particular, two. Professor Eliade, the brilliant and scholarly historian of primitive religion, sees "those very things" which the primitive has in common with the child and the creative artist as still recoverable. "Man's desire," says Eliade, "to free himself from his limitations, which he feels to be a kind of degradation, and to regain spontaneity and freedom — the desire expressed at all cultural levels from the primitive to the present day — must be ranked among the specific marks of man." In Eliade's view, then, the door is not, nor ever can be, completely closed. He even makes suggestions on how to open it wider, and what may be found on the further side. "By the simple fact," he says in his book *Images and Symbols*, "that, at the heart of his being, modern man rediscovers the cosmic rhythms — the alternations of day and night, for instance, or of winter and summer — he comes to a more complete knowledge of his own destiny and significance . . . All these things still exist in modern man, it is only necessary to reactivate them and bring them to the level of consciousness. By regaining awareness of . . . the archaic symbolism, modern man will obtain a new existential dimension, a new, authentic, and major mode of being, totally unknown to the present day." Elsewhere he says it succinctly in a single phrase: "*We must reawaken the images.*" This is also the intention of this book.

The other voice is that of the writer and explorer, Laurens Van der Post, whose loving and intuitive interpretation of the life and beliefs of the African Bushman, particularly in his book *The Heart of the Hunter*, is one of the major contributions of our time towards the enlargement of human consciousness. *The Heart of the Hunter* can, in fact, be described as an entirely successful attempt to "reawaken the images."

It is not that either of these men, and those who think with them, are romanticizing archaic man, or falling afresh for the long-discredited image of Rousseau's Noble Savage. Primitive life, we well know, was in many ways harsh and meager, and primitive man was not, on the conscious level, a philosopher. The miracle and the mystery is precisely this: that he answered questions which he was not capable of even formulating — and his answers have never been bettered.

*

Where did primitive man's stories come from? Many solutions have been offered, but all, or nearly all, are tainted with a monstrous complacency. It is, in fact, a question to which Western man, wrapped in a warm sense of superiority to the primitive, has ascribed a merely minor importance, whereas it is perhaps the most penetrating question of our day. The delicate accuracy and stubborn strength, the startling objectivity and many-layered meaningfulness of such age-old tales as *The Stories of the Beginning* recorded by Mircea Eliade, or of fairy tales like *The Sleeping Princess,* or of the animal stories that Laurens Van der Post's Bushmen told each other in the overarching and luminous dark of an African night: these subtle constructions, so far beyond the apparent range of their simple narrators — where did they come from? In whose brain were these perfectly articulated works of art conceived? For assuredly at the time of their creation no individual human mind existed capable of consciously constructing insights into human aims and ends so accurate that modern psychology and theology are only now beginning to overtake them. Until we find the solution of this mystery, we should surely approach with humility and gentleness the symbolic insights of archaic man. For if once we learned again to speak his dawn-fresh language, we might speak it better than he, or at least speak it with a fuller consciousness. But we must first condescend to learn it.

Even if this is agreed, the question then arises where and how to relearn this language, this attitude to life born of an equal valuation of the visible and the invisible, this secret of seeing the world not as a series of problems but as a network of mysteries? An historian of primitive cultures may begin to decipher its alphabet and grammar, an explorer may actually hear tantalizing fragments of it spoken by living voices round a forest camp fire. But these are exceptional opportunities. By good fortune there is another approach, which is open to all. Within every human being there is to be found an inspired but largely neglected master of this lost language of symbols: the dreaming mind.

It is, after all, no new idea that the dreaming mind can be equated with a crucial mutation of consciousness. In the *Bardo Thodöl* it is said that in the Fifth Stage of the world's development, a stage not yet actualized, "Ether" will dawn in the consciousness of man. This is the kind of statement from which contemporary educated minds turn away in immediate distaste. The word "Ether" used in such a context evokes memories of dusty and discredited systems of thought about the structure of the universe, or even less acceptably, recalls the woolly abstractions of Theosophy. But this is mere semantic prejudice. The psychical attributes of "Ether" as conceived and defined by the Lamas are, in modern terms, precisely those of the Deep Unconscious. They believed, in fact, that what we call the Unconscious is a "transcendental" consciousness higher than normal consciousness, and as yet undeveloped; and that it will become the active consciousness of the next stage of the world's development, which they estimated would occur in the twentieth century. This is at least an intriguing anticipation, across the intervening centuries, of the increasing attention now paid to dreams and the unconscious.

Contemporary interest in these matters is still largely in the hands of the scientists and doctors. Popular imagination remains unawakened. But treated as it may one day be, not as a therapeutic technique but as a numinous experience, the dreaming mind may prove to be an instrument of incalculable power pointing in a totally new direction — a magic casement opening on the foam of an uncharted sea, a space-machine cruising through the night above a strange new world, a Geiger counter recording radiations from an unknown source. Experienced truly, it may be capable of translating man to a new level of consciousness, a level where the general union of opposites begins to be possible, and the particular quarrel, peculiar to our Western culture, of science and religion may at last be stilled.

That there is such a quarrel, no one but the wishful-minded would deny. The production of a list of leading scientists who go regularly to church, and of eminent divines who think a proton is somehow more "spiritual" than the leg of a chair, does nothing to heal the deep division modern man feels within himself. Yet he also knows that it need not, it ought not, to exist. For the scientific impulse and the religious impulse — the search for fact and the search for value — are the two prime and vital movements of the human spirit. They are the coordinates of existence at the human level, the systole and diastole in the heart of being, the masculine and feminine aspects of spiritual life. Granted exactly equal validity, pursued with exactly equal sincerity, the search for fact and the search for value lead to the threshold of the world of meaning which is at once their origin and their goal. To pursue either exclusively, however far, however passionately, is to live on a lower dimensional level than the truly human. It is also to miss another of the paths that can lead to a transformation of consciousness.

This, then, is the existential predicament of contemporary man. There is no escape from the Nietzschean melodrama: Man must, indeed, surpass himself or die. He must take the dangerous step of submitting to a breakthrough from the unconscious that will enormously enlarge the conscious field without destroying its existing contents. Undeniably it is a dangerous step: irruptions from the deep unconscious can easily overthrow the precarious autonomy of the conscious mind. For this very reason men normally keep locked and barred the door to the unconscious — just as they lock up criminals and psychotics, who are the manifestations in social life of the lawless impulses of the unconscious. It is, in fact, another pointer to the crucial period we live in, another symbol of the imminent unbinding of Psyche, that we are now starting to unlock the doors of prisons and mental hospitals. Men are unlocking more than they know.

But perilous as it is, this step must be taken, and is, I believe, in process of being taken in spite of our conscious intentions to the contrary, because of man's absolute need for an increase of consciousness to meet his emergent destiny.

The trouble is, we have strayed into the second half of the twentieth century still equipped in the main with nineteenth-century ways of thought. The keynote of nineteenth-century scientific thinking is the unconscious deification of the Evolutionary Process: that is to say, the evaluation of this Process as standing outside all polarities, instead of as being merely one aspect of a pair of opposites — the other aspect being "the Timeless Now." This compels the nineteenth-century type of thinker to look for the ultimate answers, the union of opposites, within the Evolutionary Process — where it will never be found. Many still look in this unrewarding direction. What is needed, and within our reach, is an enlargement of human awareness that can carry man effortlessly past this outmoded problem. Paradoxically, the only way forward is an apparently enormous step backward. Without relinquishing his social achievements (such as they are), his new psychological insights, and his staggering technical triumphs, man must nevertheless go back to his horn book, and learn again the lost alphabet of living. To survive in any meaningful way he must reawaken the pristine power to see every object and every event translucently — that is, not only as a vividly concrete reality but also as a semipermeable membrane, through which another order of experience begins to become manifest; and to give exactly equal validity to these two aspects of Reality's Janus-face.

Man was once brave enough to do this after a very limited fashion. When it has recovered this specifically human virtue, the modern world, with its infinitely larger horizons, its infinitely greater knowledge and skills, can then — and not till then — move forward into regions of the human spirit which man of the archaic societies could never have imagined. But first of all, contemporary man must swallow his pride and turn to his only authentic teachers in this matter: the primitive, the child, the nature-mystic, and, perhaps above all, to that numinous guardian of our symbolic life, the Dreaming Mind.

8

THE FOREST OF
INTERLOCKING OPPOSITES

THE EMBRYO of our species, as is well known, develops in two almost symmetrical halves, joined at the back along the spine, and stitched together rather hastily and at the last moment in front. In several places the seam still shows in the adult human being, and in two the stitches occasionally fail to hold at all, and a cleft palate or a similar but sadder deformity results. Even the machinery for thinking is split into two almost separated cerebral hemispheres. Man, in common with most highly developed forms of life, is in literal fact divided within himself. It is therefore not surprising that throughout his biologically brief history two opposing types of force have struggled for possession of his mind, and that his first aim and final longing has been to find a symbol rich enough to harmonize and contain them.

It could be said, therefore, that there is no contemporary crisis peculiar to modern man. From his first appearance on earth man was faced with the riddle of the opposites and with the urge to find an answer. He was born, very uncomfortably, on the horns of this dilemma. Yet it remains the concern of contemporary man, because it is a problem which needs to be restated and re-attempted in each successive age. Though we are always trying to do so, we cannot make use of the answers found by our forefathers until we have translated them into the idiom of our own time, into language which is meaningful for us — and foreign to any other age. To search for the best contemporary formulation, while recognizing its conditional status, is not only worth doing; it is a necessity for a certain kind of man. But only for a certain kind. What I am trying to say contains no hint of a Universal Message.

The contemporary formulation here advanced is based on the long-established concept of the Classic-Romantic polarity. But before going further it may be well to consider more closely the meaning of the term. In the violent ferment of our time this particular concept is vital for orientation, and it is becoming blurred — because it includes and confuses two very different meanings. At first sight it appears that the modern world is overwhelmingly Romantic. Age-old barriers of space and time are now being continually broken through. On the psychological level, venerable moral attitudes, pillars of the nineteenth-century social structure, are falling like ninepins, to the delight of some natures and the consternation of others. Even the sectarian churches, grim defenders of tradition, have been swept along by the winds of change towards syntheses and acceptances which would have been unthinkable a generation ago. Today's world is the world of the Romantic. The Classic is in retreat or on the defensive everywhere.

But there is more complexity in the concept than can be covered by the simple distinction between those who must live within a "framework" and those who must break out of it. Many people will spend their whole lives happily and unquestioningly within one kind of framework, for example, religious orthodoxy, while desperately concerned with bursting out of another kind, say, the social or economic. They want, in fact, to remain classically undisturbed about religious ultimates, while becoming romantically rich and important.

It is necessary, therefore, to specify the framework. Where this framework consists of scientific boundaries, moral and social taboos, economic and political stabilities, and the like, the iconoclastic and Romantic upsurge of our time is plain for all to see. But there is another kind, curiously hard to define, where the Romantic is hard pressed and fighting for his life. The framework here involved is the existing level of consciousness. Contained within it are those who are content to live permanently on this level, and regard it as the only one to be taken seriously by a rational human being; who look on life as something to be endlessly experienced, analyzed, and discussed, but at this level only, and who are impatient and contemptuous (and unconsciously scared) of any other approach; it includes those who consider a successful appeal to logic as in the last resort final and irrefutable: all these are Classics in the sense I mean, though they may be among the leading scientific, religious or political pioneers of the contemporary world. For clarity's sake they should perhaps be called "Neo-Classics." In this context "Neo-Romantics" are those who are possessed by a tormenting conviction that life on the accepted level of consciousness, fascinating and rewarding as it undeniably can be, is simply not enough. To them such self-limitation is as mysterious as that of certain species of ants who, born with wings, bite them off after one short nuptial flight and deliberately opt for a crawling existence. This kind of Romantic feels claustrophobic in the world as presented by his five senses and their technological extensions, and seeks tirelessly for the combination that will unlock the secret door. Even the current dazzling manipulations of the material world, by his "Neo-Classic" counterpart, are to him no genuine burst-through — merely delightful and ingenious exercises within the prison yard.

But how delightful and how ingenious they are! It would seem at first sight to be a singularly unromantic spirit that did not respond to these virile adventures in contemporary thought and deed; and it is natural for many to see in the scientist and technologist the outstanding Romantic and Faustian figures of our day.

Nevertheless, for all their boundary-breaking and limit-passing, contemporary science and technology remain manipulations of the existing level of human consciousness. Undeniably brilliant manipulations; it is certainly a miraculous impact on life that man, a relative newcomer to the earth, has made with his ten soft, clawless fingers, his buzzing brain-box, and the pitiful little octaves of color, sound, touch, taste and smell to which he was originally confined by his curiously limited sense organs. And in this direction he is getting smarter all the time.

But he has had to pay a price for his spectacular successes. And the price is this: he has had to confine himself to just those few stimuli, of the incalculable millions streaming out of total Reality, which are germane to his purpose of controlling the environment; and to teach his consciousness to ignore all others. In addition to the limitations of his sensory apparatus, he has thus imposed further and arbitrary limitations on himself — not from willfulness, but from a perfectly natural instinct to ensure his own immediate survival in this dangerous world. If the brain, as Bergson has suggested, is essentially an organ of limitation to enable man to give full attention to what is necessary for survival, it follows that it is possible for a human being in a period of relative personal security to give heed to those stimuli which hitherto have been ignored. The Neo-Romantic, in my sense, is passionately concerned to do this. The Neo-Classic is passionately convinced that it is a waste of time.

❋

The opposition remains and must be accepted. This is not easy. It is, for instance, disconcerting for me to realize, which I can do only with continuous effort, that half the world feels no need whatever to "escape from time," has no sense of being imprisoned in a three-dimensional prison, is, in fact, perfectly content with

Reality as defined and limited by the five senses, extended, of course, by all the resources of modern technology; and wishes for nothing better than to go on exploring the exciting possibilities contained within this ample framework. To the other half of the world — my half — such an attitude is as inconceivable as for an embryo to be content to live and die within the womb.

The other side, of course, will not accept this simile, and tells me my trouble is that I cannot face up to Reality with its tragic implications, and try to escape into some Never-Never Land of my own imagining.

The devil of it is, *he may be right*. There are as many of him as of me; perhaps in the contemporary world, far more. I should hate to risk a vote on it. In the last resort I have only a passionate conviction to sustain me, and he has an opposite conviction as passionate as my own. But at least I will not let him get away with this story that I "can't face up to Reality." By putting it in this way he begs the question. The whole point is that his Reality is different from mine. If his Reality is the more basic, then I am, in his sense of the word, "an escapist"; if mine is, then he is spending his life in a locked room without bothering to look for the key.

Fortunately, this impasse is a false dilemma. To see these matters in terms of one half of the world as against the other half is an oversimplification. The dichotomy is there, but it is an *inner* division, existing within each individual in varying proportions. To label a man one or other, though convenient for certain purposes, is grossly to oversimplify his inner balances and complexities. It is perhaps not even a question of whether either impulse within a man is nearer to Reality. Neither can ever, or should ever, be acclaimed "the winner." Although in many individuals one side or the other does plainly win, nevertheless within such an individual, however one sided or polemical he may be, there lives on in the shadows the opposite standpoint, sometimes coming to the surface in the most curious disguises, sometimes revealing itself only by a vague but persistent sense of spiritual malaise. The less a man is aware of this shadow-side the less complete a human being he appears — and is. And this is true not only of this particular opposition, but of the whole dark forest of interlocking opposites in which human life wanders like a lonely child.

❈

That the human mind operating at its customary level is lost, whichever way it turns, in a forest of tangled and interlocking opposites is a truism. Apart from those simple souls who believe that their own religious or political dogma is irrefutable, and that those who disagree are either stupid or secretly malevolent, the majority of men pride themselves on their broad-mindedness, and are aware that the converse of any possible opinion can be sincerely and validly held. But to know this is one thing; simultaneously to feel it is quite another. The mind needs practice to operate in such a way. There are no schools for it, and the difficulties of self-training are severe; you travel on a razor-edge, with abysses of the obvious on either side.

Suppose a man were to take up, one by one, the attitudes of which he is intellectually and emotionally most certain; suppose he were to regard each attitude as one of a pair of opposites (as, in fact, it must be); and then to examine its polar opposite with a determination to extract and honor the positive values in that opposite: would he be training himself in this way? Or would he actually be doing nothing more than echoing the cliché that "one should always look at both sides of a question"? There is something extraordinarily irritating about people who are always saying in a deprecating tone — "The trouble with me is I can't help seeing both sides of a question." This enables them to congratulate themselves on never being able to make up their minds. These are the vast company of the uncommitted, led by the nose through all human history by the passionately committed few. These are the floating voters, the "Don't Knows" of psychic life, ever open to the wiles of the propagandist, to the convictions of the enthusiast, to the bees buzzing in the fanatic's bonnet.

Nevertheless there have been many to extol the capacity to stay uncommitted. An early Zen Buddhist poem declares — "If you want the truth to stand clear before you, never be *for* or *against*. The struggle between *for* and *against* is the mind's worst disease." And in one of his letters John Keats defined as an attribute of genius "the ability to remain in uncertainty and doubt, without any irritable reaching out after fact and reason." Two questions thus arise: is it possible to be utterly committed to remaining uncommitted? And, if possible, is it admirable?

In that terrifying book and play *The Deputy*, Pope Pius XII, as portrayed in it, was entirely committed to remaining uncommitted — *about Auschwitz*. And what a sorry figure he cuts! For the world now is absolutely certain that its attitude of total condemnation is in this case the right and only possible one.

What is it that we are faced with in the grisly phenomenon of Auschwitz? One hesitates to write anything about Auschwitz. To theorize at all about this giant evil seems deplorable. And yet any contemporary attitude to life which does not take Auschwitz into account is self-condemned.

Auschwitz is the revelation of the undiluted evil lurking in the depths of ordinary, even "respectable," men and women. It extends immeasurably, in a downward direction, our consciousness of the range of ordinary human nature. Gazing appalled into this sickening pit, it is immensely hard to remember that even here the law of polarity must be applied. Its polar opposite, then, can only be the unguessed heights of awareness and compassion to which ordinary human nature can also rise. The one cannot have existed, as it manifestly did, unless the other exists in equal measure. Out of Auschwitz, therefore, regarded as one of a pair of ineluctable opposites, could come a recognition that human nature is, potentially, infinitely "lower" than we had feared, and infinitely "higher" than we had hoped. A terrifying range exists in every human being. It follows that even the humblest individual should be approached with the same caution that an engineer shows towards a million-volt generator, which can light a city,

or cause a holocaust . . . *We should be far more care-*
ful of each other.

One can be as certain of the goodness of one experience as of the evil of another. Perhaps the purest good
that can be humanly experienced is that grace-given
moment of illumination that comes, unexpected and
unsought, maybe once or twice in a lifetime. This
strange event is something which happens to many,
though they seldom speak of it. It is tempting not to
choose this experience for present discussion, to regard
it as outside the concept of polarity — which in a sense
it is, in so far as it appears to lie outside ordinary concepts bounded by space and time. On the other hand, it
is an experience which enters and affects human consciousness; and all things perceivable by human consciousness are of necessity one of a pair of opposites,
since the mind is so constructed that one pole without
its counter-pole is not only meaningless but unimaginable. In theological terms such an experience is a
theophany — an intersection of Time and the Timeless.
It therefore contains an aspect which belongs to the
world of polarities, as well as an aspect which lies outside it.

What is the essence of this experience? To try to put
it into words is manifest folly. But at least one can say
it has an intense immediacy and vividness; every object
holds a sudden blinding significance; "the doors of perception are cleansed and everything appears, as it is, infinite." And with it comes a feeling of complete release
from the bounds of the everyday, from morality how-

ever lofty, from all human goals and aspirations however spiritual. It is *ganz andere,* altogether "other."

Dare one say that even this must not be lifted up beyond the realm of the opposites? If so, then there must
be an equal and opposite pole to this state of fullness
and significance and bright immediacy. It would be a
state of darkness, despair and utter emptiness.

There is such a state. The existentialism of Sartre not
only reveals it, but if fully entered into can lead a man
partially to experience it. The intolerable "Dread"
which he so brilliantly lays bare, the dread of finding
oneself poised on the edge of absolute Nothingness, is
the exact polar opposite of the experience of "illumination."

But in these matters the professional philosopher is
an unconvincing witness. Only personal evidence is acceptable. Two patients of mine have suffered this annihilating, all-cancelling experience. Two cases in twenty-
five years suggests a high degree of rarity, but as with
the illuminative experience I believe it is something of
which the subject is very reluctant to speak.

One of these cases was a Surrey cowman, an illiterate
farmhand, who came to me many years ago, hesitantly,
and said — "It isn't that I'm *ill,* doctor, but I get the
queerest, damnedest feeling sometimes, for no cause at
all. Last time was in the middle of Guildford Cattle
Market. Suddenly the notion came over me that all this
— the animals, the farmers and their dogs, the smells,
the noise, the sunshine — was just silly, empty, made
no sense. My life, and everyone's life, somehow went

blank. There wasn't no point in going on . . . It
didn't seem 'ardly right, doctor, to feel that way, so I
thought I'd pop in and see you. Mind you, it doesn't
last long — in a few minutes I'm meself again . . . I
suppose it's nothing, really."

The other patient was a woman in her middle forties,
friendly, vivacious and attractive, but with a curious almost imperceptible detachment running like a dark ice-
cold river through the depths of her personality. She
was a widow, and had married her husband not for love
but for perfectly clear reasons of security which she had
lucidly explained to him beforehand and which he had,
rather surprisingly, accepted.

Searching for the source of her detachment, I learned
that she had what she called "attacks of gloom" from
time to time. They would last from an hour or two to
half a day, and she feared them and would try, sometimes successfully, to distract herself with housework or
shopping or conversation. In an "attack" it would become steadily and remorselessly clear to her that life
was void and meaningless, that (to use her own words)
"the whole world with its swarms of living creatures
was like a great lump of putrefying meat, crawling with
maggots, fit only for some cosmic dustbin." She said —
"My whole life is an attempt to escape from this recurrent horror. When it is in the ascendant my only wish is
to die."

These two experiences, I suggest, are at the opposite
pole to the state of what is called "illumination" — for
want of a better name. I am not unaware that both of

them, especially the second, fall into the category known to psychiatric medicine as Recurrent Depression. Having thus characterized such experiences as pathological, psychiatry is free to concentrate on their treatment, and absolved from considering their tremendous implications. But can we be so sure that there is nothing beyond the pathological in these chilling and nihilistic visions? By the principle of "honoring the opposites" we may regard them as valid glimpses of one aspect of Reality, not merely as distortions of a sick mind.

What would follow from this? Could it be that the state of illumination, momentarily experienced by many, lived in by the mystic, *is not an ultimate* — as it so convincingly appears to be — but one pole only of a total experience? An ultimate experience of this kind, unimaginable at our present level of awareness, would include and transcend both the state of illumination with its brilliant immediacy and overflowing significance and the annihilating abyss of the Void. Such an experience demands nothing less than an increase in the range of human consciousness.

The foul historical fact of Auschwitz, the timeless moment of illumination . . . such overwhelming glimpses of darkness and light serve only to reveal our dilemma and to expose the terrifying nature of that primeval forest of opposites in which almost the whole human race, like pygmies in an African jungle, has lived and died, groping among the gigantic tangled roots and lianas of good and evil. To dream of complete escape is an illusion, the dear fantasy of salvationists. But it is possible that <u>an expansion of human consciousness could provide a compass,</u> could give man the greatest gift of sublunary existence — a sense of direction within the dark forest.

*

Archimedes once said that if he could reach a point completely outside the world's influences, he could construct a system of levers to move the whole earth to a new position. What is needed to lift man to a new level of consciousness is an Archimedean Point lying outside and independent of the world of which we are normally aware.

This might seem an impossible requirement but for the fact that time and again in the history of human consciousness such a demand has been made — and met. The discovery of the uses of fire by primitive man was such an answer. As Mircea Eliade has shown, the emergence of the smith or metallurgist accelerated as by miracle certain processes of nature, and resulted in this Promethean figure being venerated for centuries as a magician. The victory of the heliocentric over the geocentric view of the universe was another such answer. The unguessed world revealed by Depth Psychology was a third. From time to time man has found a point lying outside the range of his previously accepted consciousness by which his whole attitude to life has been altered.

Where to find, for our own generation, this Archime-

dean Point? At first sight it might seem that a sufficiently intelligent astronaut, traveling at such speed as
to be practically liberated from the limitations of space
and time, might be literally in such a position. To imagine some speculative scientist of the caliber of an Einstein packed into a space capsule with instructions to
enlighten the human race from a new angle is an engaging thought, but lacks practicality. For on his return he
would find the world several thousands of years older,
and his report, however illuminating, would be somewhat outdated. But another possibility exists.

There is in all men, irrespective of age, race, or intellectual power, a function, curiously neglected except
for immediate and therapeutic purposes, which is
largely independent of human limitations of time and
space, and of human structural necessities of thought. I
refer to the *Dreaming Mind*. Within this peculiar function, I suggest, there may be concealed the means by
which once more the whole world of human consciousness can be levered into a new position. It is at least
worth investigation. For without some such assistance
from "outside," contemporary consciousness is plainly
on its way towards an unmanageable explosion of ideas,
and a fatal loss of the sense of direction.

9

WORLD

OF SHADOWS

WHAT is "dreaming"? Is it a shadow-play, meaningless and fragmentary? Or a variant of the fortuneteller's crystal? Or a delicate diagnostic convenience for the doctors? Through the centuries dreaming has been looked upon in all three of these ways, now one, now another coming into fashion or falling into disuse. Our own generation has added a fourth, a strictly scientific and physiological approach. And beyond all these, stranger than any of them, lies a fifth possibility, now beginning to emerge for the first time in human history.

There are, and have always been, those who dismiss dreams as a chaos of unrelated details; sturdy, common-sensible folk, holding what could be called the Stuff-and-Nonsense Theory of Dreams. Yet it can hardly be other than unwise to turn away with contempt from any phenomenon big enough and compelling enough to engage the attention of countless generations of human beings. For quite apart from specialists and cranks, ordinary men and women have always been enthralled by dreams and their possible meanings. Dreams are a human preoccupation that is as old as man himself. Natu-

rally so; since they reveal to him glimpses of a whole
world of being that might else have remained for ever
unknown.

The second attitude to the dreaming mind is to consult it, as one consults a clairvoyant, for hints of what
the future holds in store. This would seem silly
enough; and often is. But again it ministers to an unas-
suageable longing of the human heart. Man is an inquis-
itive creature, and like a ragged urchin outside the Big
Top circus, simply cannot resist trying to lift a corner of
the tantalizing curtain of Time. He can, of course,
make little sense of it; but no matter; to see anything at
all is a big thrill.

And by what crazy and fantastic tricks man has tried
to gain that forbidden glimpse! Indeed, Oneiromancy,
or divination of the future by dreams, begins to appear
the height of rationality compared to most of his strate-
gems; compared, for instance, to Ichthyomancy, divination by the entrails of fishes, or Crithomancy, which,
believe it or not, is divination by the dough of cakes, or
Coscinomancy, by a balanced sieve, or Electryomancy,
by a hen picking up grains . . . Admittedly these
methods are somewhat outmoded. On the other hand,
Necromancy, or divination by communing with the
dead, is still with us in the thriving form of Spiritualism;
while at this very hour there are young ladies anxiously
awaiting the results of Myomancy, or divination by
mice. As for the ancient art of Skiomancy, which
means divination by shadows, it is perhaps enough to
say that the correct name for an X-ray plate is a skia-

gram. For all our sophistication we are still trying for a small boy's sneak view.

In the light of these highly peculiar activities, dream-divination seems reasonable enough; and, in fact, there is now some impressive support for the scientific use of dreams in relation to future events. Dunne's remarkable books on the subject, for example, have aroused worldwide interest; and the strictly controlled investigations of the Extra-Sensory Perception researchers have provided, among many other things, startling evidence of the dreaming mind's capacity to "see ahead." The claims of E.S.P., incidentally, have aroused such solid resistance from orthodox scientists as to raise the possibility that they are of real importance.

The third approach to dreams, the therapeutic approach, has had a curiously *regional* history. In the Far East, and among primitive peoples everywhere, the value of dreams for individual and social therapy has been recognized and employed for at least five thousand years, and perhaps far longer. But in the Western world few things are more subject to the whims of fashion than medical opinion; and in these areas the therapeutic status of dreams has sharply fluctuated through the centuries. At the moment, owing to its involvement with current psychological theory, it is enjoying something of an intellectual vogue. After many centuries of medical neglect, dreams as valuable curative agents were thrust suddenly upon the Western world's attention by the publication in 1900 of Freud's epoch-making book *The Interpretation of Dreams*. Given some measure of scientific respectability by the impact of this work, the secret perennial human interest in dreams surged into the open. Jung produced his profoundly different approach to the dream-process, and Adler came forward with a third hypothesis. Following these three giants a host of minor dream interpreters of varying skill and validity sprang like dragon's teeth from the ground, constituting almost overnight a new and powerful profession.

In one sense there was nothing new in this. More than two thousand years ago Aesculapius, legendary Greek physician and "patron saint" of medicine to this day, used dreams both for diagnosis and treatment. Nearer to our own time, Sir Thomas Browne, wise physician of Norwich in the seventeenth century, had a high opinion of the dreaming mind, and declared in his charmingly florid style — "We are somewhat more than ourselves in sleep, and the Slumber of the Body seems to be but the waking of the Soul." Or as the medieval Richard Rolle more briefly and beautifully put it — "I sleep, and my heart wakes."

It seems, therefore, that in one or another of these three modes theories about the meaning and utility of dreams have been a time-honored human concern. But the fourth mode of approach to dreams — the scientific study of their physiological mechanisms — is of very recent origin. In fact, it is only in the last ten years that it has really got under way at all. But now, like the rest of the sciences, it is advancing with vertiginous speed, and fascinating objective facts about the dream-process are emerging almost daily.

Perhaps the most outstanding contemporary researcher in this particular field is Professor Kleitman of Chicago University. Kleitman noticed a short while ago that when a person is asleep there are movements of the eyes under the closed lids at certain regular intervals during the night. It occurred to him that these eye movements might be made because the sleeper is watching, as at a play, the actions of a dream. By waking the sleeper during these periods of eye movements, he found that at such times the sleeper was, in fact, always dreaming, and could invariably remember something of his dream. If the sleeper were waked when his eyes were not moving his sleep appeared to have been dreamless. By these means (checked and confirmed by the demonstration of specific E.E.G. waves which correlated with the eye movements) it has been established that dreams occur to everyone in an unchanging pattern of four to six dreams a night, at regular intervals.

This was interesting enough. But there was more to follow. It was found that if a sleeper were regularly waked at the beginning of each dream-period, in a few nights the dream-deprived person became intensely irritable and forgetful during the day, whereas if he were wakened the same number of times, but during non-dreaming periods, this did not occur. It would seem, therefore, that to preserve our psychological health dreams are actually a necessity. Confirming this is the further experimental fact that if a person who has been deprived of dreaming-periods for some nights is then allowed to sleep undisturbed, he dreams about twice as long as usual until he has made up his lost dream-time.

Some of Kleitman's findings have been disputed. But for our present purposes, the relevant conclusion arising from these physiological investigations is that for some reason, still unexplained, *we need to dream.*

*

With so many theories and facts about dreams and the dreaming mind, it might be thought that modern man was reasonably equipped with information on the subject, and that this peculiar nocturnal activity was receiving all, and perhaps more than, the attention it deserved. There are indeed a number of distinguished scientists, including certain psychiatrists, who are at no pains to conceal that this is their opinion. But the odd fact is that the most important question about the dream-process has never yet been asked, far less answered.

This question is concerned with the nature of the dreaming mind itself — not with what it *does,* but what it *is;* a mystery which both the doctors and the clairvoyants, in their haste to extract from dreams something practical and useful, have largely neglected.

The dreaming mind, I suggest, in addition to all its other functions, is an instrument of liberation, capable of breaking up the conventional patterns of human perception, and releasing new forms of awareness. I invite you to regard the dreaming mind as a *file* smuggled into the space-time cell where man lies captive; a cell whose walls and ceiling are our five senses, and whose warders are the inflexible concepts of logic. With the help of this file man might be able — provided always he could evade the vigilance of the Authorities — to saw through the bars of his prison and escape . . . But into what terrifying, what unimaginable world?

Not, certainly, into a world of tranquillity, not into any traditional heaven-haven. The dreaming mind leads — not into Paradise, but into paradox . . . into a world that is fluid and ambiguous and dangerous, a phantasmal world of symbols whose meaning is at once concealed and conveyed by a dazzling and bewildering interplay of opposites . . . And man is afraid of it. The panic reaction of suddenly liberated prisoners swells here to nightmare size. In the last resort man has not dared to use his own escape route. He shudders away from freedom.

Here, then, is one of the unattempted soul-adventures facing modern man. I have no wish to exaggerate its importance. It is only one among many such adventures. But for some minds there could be an incomparable excitement in suddenly recognizing the dreaming mind as an organ of liberation, as an Archimedean point by which man might one day lever his consciousness into a new orbit. This is the fifth possibility of dream interpretation, now at last rising near enough to the conscious level to allow at least two questions about it to be formulated. I will venture to ask them.

Who, or what, is the Dreamer within us? And to whom is the Dreamer talking?

Such questions are admittedly naïve. It will occur at once to many that I am committing the heresy of personification. I am making a graven image of the unimaginable. And in this specific field Jung has declared, "We must not ascribe the functioning of the dream . . . to any 'subject' with a conscious will." This, however, is a statement with which we can all be in agreement. It would indeed be a fallacy to suppose that our dreams are constructed logically and with rational aims in view by any part of the individual conscious mind. Dreams *happen* to us; and what Jung calls "a dark impulse" from far beyond the reach of conscious striving is the final arbiter of the dream pattern. Agreed. And there, for Jung as a declared empiricist, the matter rests. But I suggest that there can be no final prohibition against inquiry into the nature of this "dark impulse." Such an inquiry is nothing less than an attempt to conceptualize something that has not yet arrived at the conscious level; and for this attempt a certain license, a certain *naïveté* of imagery, must be allowed.

Moreover, it is historically justifiable. Many of the forward movements of human consciousness have used some form of personification or analogy as a scaffolding. Pythagoras, for example, held that all numbers had geometrical shapes. Kepler's discoveries in astronomy were motivated by his lifelong belief that there existed a music of the spheres. They may have been mistaken; but they certainly started something. The world would have suffered infinite loss without the advances in consciousness built up by these men within the protection of their faulty imagery. For all their inadequacies we *need* these temporary supports for our new constructions. When the building is completed the scaffolding can be discarded.

Unrepentantly, therefore, I propose to pursue the personification of this "dark impulse" as an image, the crude image of the Dreamer; in the hope of establishing in men's minds the shadowy outline of a hitherto unrecognized power.

Who, or what, is the Dreamer within us? The question has a numinous feel. We know at once that it is supremely worth asking — and supremely unanswerable. It is unanswerable, perhaps, because the terms employed are ordinary everyday terms that seem to invite an ordinary everyday answer, and on this level no possible answer fits. We lack the categories. We cannot even guess whether the Dreamer is a personality or a force. In some unknown but convincing way we recognize it is both, and neither. In other words, we find ourselves struggling to express something for which the means of communication are lacking, or at least grossly inadequate.

This sounds like the classical difficulty of the mystic. Am I then saying that dreams are mystical experiences? To say "No" to this is to throw away perhaps the nearest analogy there is to the spellbinding power of the dream when taken as a pure experience, not a means to an end. On the other hand, to say "Yes" would be to give an immediate sense of relief to a great many people. "Ah, mysticism," they would say, closing their minds like closing a book, "that's not for me." It is strange that the majority of men are in such haste to dissociate themselves from the "taint" of mysticism that they have never even paused to observe that it has two fundamentally different forms. One is God-mysticism, contemning the world and longing impatiently for union with the Absolute; a form of mysticism that is, in the last resort, in love with death. (This kind is, incidentally, the inspiration of all tragic poetry and drama, and is the reason why such tales, to the bewilderment of simple minds, must always end in death.) The second is Nature-mysticism, which looks at all creation with a delighted wonder, and at all human beings, from mighty saints to monstrous sinners, with a kind of surprised recognition; a mysticism that is, in fact, in love with life.

But in any case, is it not time that we achieved more range and plasticity in our concepts? Must experience be pushed for ever into either a little box labeled "Mysticism or a little box labeled "Empiricism"? Now, when E.S.P., for instance, is nibbling impudently at the edges of orthodox Science, and Science itself is staring incredulously at its own rationally "impossible" conclusions — now is surely the time to reexamine the modes of human experiencing.

This is why the concept of the Dreamer is among the most fascinating and relevant of the mysteries facing contemporary man. It is nothing less than an invitation to transcend our normal and habitual level of consciousness, to develop a long-latent function, to enter a *terra incognita* of which, paradoxically, we are free-born citizens. As Dante was led through realms beyond the human range by the ghost of Vergil, so the Dreamer can lead us, through the labyrinthine corridors of sleep, to a realm of being where the human mind blooms phantasmally in new and brilliant and unimagined forms of life. Sleeping could be the archaic *rite d'entrée* to this realm — and the Dreamer could be our ghostly guide.

The identity of the Dreamer . . . who is as close to us as our own unspoken thoughts, who is concerned with our individual destiny while ranging infinitely beyond it, who is a tireless if often terrifying and incomprehensible Teacher . . . The Dreamer who sees with eyeless eyes, who hears with earless ears, who wakes when the senses sleep . . . Can we draw nearer to this mystery within ourselves?

✻

Let us consider what we know of the characteristics of the Dreamer. I mean by this quite simply *what he is like* — as when you say of someone you have never met, "But tell me, what is he like?"

Well, I should say that the keyword is — *disconcerting*. The Dreamer is extraordinarily disconcerting to waking thought-processes, in particular to our cherished laws of logic, including that venerable pair, the Law of Contradiction, and the Law of the Excluded Middle — acceptance of which has always been regarded as essential to rational discussion. To put it less technically, the Dreamer constantly and effortlessly performs the rationally inconceivable feat of being both the experiencing subject and the observed object at the same moment and to the same degree. We have all dreamed that — "I am standing in a street, but at the same time I am watching myself standing in the street" — both experiences being equally valid, vivid and immediate, so that it would be false to give either priority; or that "I met a man who was certainly my friend John Smith and yet certainly not John Smith" — this rational absurdity being nevertheless contained in a single precise image.

All very disconcerting and confusing to the waking mind. But this is nothing. Like the mysterious Juggler of the Tarot Pack, the Dreamer is continually doing the apparently impossible, capsizing our solemn ultimates of birth and death, manipulating space and time with a breathtaking impudence, riding roughshod across all our most treasured and assured convictions. With the Dreamer you never know where you are. At one moment he chills by an inhuman cruelty, at another uplifts with a sheer grandeur of spiritual vision; he irritates us by trivialities, silences us with an unreachable wisdom, charms us by his subltety and wit, and often enough disgusts us with his coarse and bestial fantasies. In fact, he behaves with the strangeness, the power, the fascination and the unpredictability of *a being from another world* . . . Which, perhaps, he is. The hypothesis has been advanced before. Wundt, one of the pioneers of modern psychology, has written: "This unconscious mind is for us like an unknown being, who creates and produces for us, and finally throws the ripe fruit in our lap."

The possibility of other worlds close to and interwoven with our own is, after all, no longer a mere frolic of the imagination. Denys Wilkinson, Professor of Nuclear Physics at Oxford University, had this to say in a recent broadcast: "Perhaps there do indeed exist universes interpenetrating with ours; perhaps of a high complexity; perhaps containing their own forms of awareness; constructed out of other particles and other interactions than those we know now, but awaiting discovery through some common but elusive interaction that we have yet to spot. It is not the physicist's job," the Professor added, "to make this sort of speculation, but today, when we are so much less sure of the natural world than we were two decades ago, he can at least license it."

Is it not possible that the Dreamer, this mysterious Guest who lodges uninvited in the psyche of every man — and, for all we know, of every living thing — may be one of the "common but elusive" factors which link us to other and higher-dimensional forms of existence? . . . Is it not possible?

*

The second question, or rather the second half of the same question — *to whom is the Dreamer talking?* — leads us into still more peculiar paths of thought. It gives one the same baffled, slightly disquieting feeling that I used to create deliberately as a child — no doubt as many children do — by gazing at myself in a mirror until a moment came when I could not decide whether

I was looking at my reflection or my reflection was looking at me. My sense of identity, my "I"-ness, came out
from its unknown hiding place and hovered between
me and my reflection in a way that was at once frightening and fascinating. It was, I suppose, a kind of childish
evocation of the *I-Thou* mystery. Perhaps Chouang-
Chou put himself in the same state some two thousand
years ago, on waking up from his famous dream that he
was a butterfly, and asking himself whether he was in
reality a man who had dreamed he was a butterfly, or a
butterfly now dreaming that it was a man.

But to return: here is the dreaming mind night upon
night, like Scheherazade, spinning its lovely, meaningful yet perplexing tales — for *someone*, surely? Do "I"
dream my dreams? And if so, am I merely chattering to
myself as children do? Jung, as we have already seen,
says No: that "we" do not dream our dreams, but that
dreams happen to us in the same way that experiences
in everyday life happen to us. The African Bushman,
still cocooned in his Stone Age wisdom, goes farther.
Of human life as a whole he says surprisingly — "There
is a dreamer dreaming us."

If Stone Age man and this great modern are right, the
Dreamer may be some *supra-personal mode of experiencing,* and the dream process, when attended to by
the conscious mind, may be a unique form of colloquy
between the personal and the supra-personal. On this
hypothesis the Dreamer is talking to the conscious
mind, the Ego. It is trying to awaken the Ego to those
factors in the total situation which lie outside the Ego's

range, and which the Ego could never arrive at by its own efforts, however far the conscious mind *at its existing level* were developed.

This last admission could be the crucial act of humility demanded of the conscious mind if it is to pass beyond its present frontiers — and the conscious mind has almost always rejected it. That is to say, the educated and "influential" conscious mentality. Among the simple and illiterate this attitude of humility towards the factors that lie outside consciousness is natural and habitual. They, in fact, are the inarticulate but faithful guardians of the door that opens out of the prison of the time-obsessed conscious mind towards the Timeless. Unluckily the feebleness of their conscious powers leads them to mishandle this priceless opportunity and so to make easy butts and fools of themselves. Nevertheless, without their stubborn resistance the door might long ago have finally closed, to man's immense impoverishment.

But not all educated minds have rejected the Dreamer's power to solve intellectually insoluble problems. There are men of outstanding genius who have deliberately and successfully sought its aid, and others of equal caliber who have gratefully acknowledged its unexpected assistance. Poincaré, the French mathematician, himself recorded that when faced with a problem which defeated his most determined conscious efforts, he would go to sleep in the hope, frequently justified, that the dreaming mind would find the solution. James Brindley, the great engineer, when confronted with an unusually difficult question used to go to bed till it was solved. Kekulé, Professor of Chemistry in Ghent, whose major discovery has been called "the most brilliant piece of prediction in the whole range of organic chemistry," was given the vital clue to this discovery by a vision of circling atoms which appeared to him in a dream. In describing this occurrence to a scientific congress, he ended with the words — *"Let us learn to dream, gentlemen."* These random examples are drawn from Arthur Koestler's remarkable book *The Act of Creation,* in which he records, in strictly attested detail, many similar illustrations of the value — if not indeed the necessity — of coopting the Dreamer when attempting to solve the apparently insoluble. Koestler himself believes that "the essence of discovery is the unlikely marriage of previously unrelated things . . . and the ultimate matchmaker is the Unconscious." The acknowledgments of such men cannot, I suggest, be lightly disregarded.

Accepted or not, however, it is a strange and bewildering thing, this concept of one part of our mind talking to another. *What is the terrain on which this ghostly colloquy takes place?* Is there a third Person in whom this happens? Could it be that the basis of mental life is not the Cartesian duality, nor the unitive goal of the mystics, but a Trinity? Jung asserts that there is a third entity, and calls this entity the Self.

To the Western mind, however emancipated it may now believe itself to be, the concept of a trinity remains a deep and living and ineradicable symbol. Quite apart from Christian significance, we are bounded by Time's trinity of past, present and future, and the world we live in is three-dimensional. This concept is now enriched in a new sense from the field of modern physics where, according to Professor Matthews of London University, the view is gaining ground that "the fundamental pattern of matter is itself a triangle, representing just three basic particles." At a philosophic level, Professor Price of Oxford University considers that a more adequate theory than Cartesian duality would be to divide human nature into three parts, body, mind, and the fundamental "I" — a term which he equates with the Atman of the Hindu. It was also Goethe's belief that man is a threefold being. Attempts have even been made to express total reality itself by means of the image of two *triangles,* superimposed to form a six-pointed star. To go farther back, Nicholas of Cusa in the fifteenth century, and St. Austine a thousand years before him, both regarded the basic nature of the universe as a "triunity." Farther back still, archeologists tell us that for the primitive the Center of the World was any place where the three cosmic zones — Sky-world, Earth-world and Under-world — intersected. And to move for a moment altogether outside Western culture, the Tao is a threefold way . . . It is perhaps possible that in the symbol of a trinity we are near the heart of the matter — near the heart of many matters.

In pursuance of this idea I will venture to make a tentative analogy between the dream-process and that concept of the Trinity held by orthodox Christianity. Anal-

ogy, I well know, is anathema to the strictly logical
thinker. But certain ideas have no other means of
reaching expression. And since we have their own written evidence that Kepler, Newton, Pasteur — and in
our own day, Einstein and Fleming — all reached their
chief discoveries by the use of analogy, there seems little need to be defensive about it. In any case, no claim
is being made for the factual truth of what I am sug-
gesting. It is no more than the scaffolding for a building
that others may one day raise. As Heinrich Zimmer has
said, a meaningful idea "can never be anything other
than an arrow aimed at reality, the intangible reality
which transcends the sphere of the intellect and of
speech."

In my analogy, then, the psyche appears as a mirror-
image of the Christian Trinity; the Self emerges as an
aspect of the Father, the conscious mind as an aspect of
the Son, and the Dreamer — an aspect of the Holy
Ghost.

The Dreamer as an aspect of the Holy Ghost, the
Comforter, the Paraclete within the individual . . . is
this merely and ignorantly blasphemous? It could be
so — but it could be otherwise.

For the Dreamer, I suggest, is the source not only of
dreams, but of symbol, myth, and fairy tale; he is the
ruler of a twilight kingdom which lies between the temporal and the Timeless, or in theological terms, between
man and God. The Dreamer is he who tells us golden
stories, coming from afar, that are the only true salve
and comfort of our existential condition; and who

brings to us in the night, as his final gift, intimations of the possibility of other forms of awareness — coexistent with our conscious life, close, close to it, interpenetrating — which perhaps need only a fractional turning of the head to be seen and known.

MOOD SWING

The Climate of Despair

ALL SENTIENT creatures live and move against a background of despair. Coexistent with consciousness is an awareness of being in the grip of elemental forces unconcerned with life. Growing intelligence merely gives greater variety, civilization different names, to these annihilating powers. We pursue geology, only to learn in what an infinitesimal fragment of time is contained the whole human story; or astronomy, to find our universe to be no more than a dust speck dancing in a momentary sunbeam. By the light of this gray truth happiness is no better than a brief forgetting, wisdom a fleeting mastery, of despair.

This is the truth from which the beautiful sick philosophies derive, the sad and lovely visions of Ecclesiastes, of Khayyam, of Santayana; the strength of whose appeal lies in their subtle compensations. At the cost of abandoning hope, of becoming acclimatized to despair, such philosophies offer equality of justice, at last, to both heart and head; giving at the same time a poignant

and autumnal beauty to the world scene, and a calm
assurance of rational superiority over the mass of hope-
deluded men.

A considerable achievement: for undeniably, confronted by the subtle web of forces from which, fly-
entangled, life struggles to be free, most of the meliorist
philosophies begin to wear a rather sorry look: Idealism
"grows pale and spectre-thin and dies," the silly progressive grin is wiped off the Humanist face, the cla-
mant theories of a Nietzsche or a Whitman sound like a
nervous whistling in the dark; and even the creeds and
consecrated rituals of the great religions are seen to be
no stronger than the little dams that beavers build . . .

The Climate of Delight

Delight is a secret. And the secret is this: to grow quiet
and listen; to stop thinking, stop moving, almost to stop
breathing; to create an inner stillness in which, like
mice in a deserted house, capacities and awarenesses
too wayward and too fugitive for everyday use may delicately emerge. Oh, welcome them home! For these
are the long-lost children of the human mind. Give
them close and loving attention, for they are weakened
by centuries of neglect. In return they will open your
eyes to a new world within the known world, they will
take your hand, as children do, and bring you where life
is always nascent, day always dawning. Suddenly and
miraculously, as you walk home in the dark, you are
aware of the insubstantial shimmering essence that lies
within appearances; the air is filled with expectancy,

alive with meaning; the stranger, gliding by in the lamp-
lit street, carries silently past you in the night the whole
mystery of his life . . .

Delight springs from this awareness of the *translucent* quality in all things, whereby beauty as well as ugliness, joy as well as pain, men as well as women, life as
well as death — the grinding clash of opposites between whose iron teeth all systems of philosophy are
crushed at last to pulp — are seen to be symbols; in the
true meaning of a symbol, whose Janus-face contains at
once that which exists in time and space, and that
which transcends it.

Delight has a glancing, dancing, penetrative quality,
the quality of Sophia the Consort of God, as when she
sings —

From the beginning I was with Him, forming all things:
And was delighted every day, playing before Him at all times:
Playing in the world; and my delights were to be with the
children of men.

Playing in the world! This is what Wisdom does.
And this is what they miss, those sad, resigned ones.
And what they also miss — the thinkers cast in the
mold of a Paul, a Marx, a Freud: the will-driven, over-
masculinized betrayers of life.

Delight is a mystery. And the mystery is this: to
plunge boldly into the brilliance and immediacy of living, at the same time as utterly surrendering to that
which lies beyond space and time; to see life translucently . . .